Reading Like a Girl

Reading Like a Girl

Narrative Intimacy
in Contemporary American
Young Adult Literature

Sara K. Day

University Press of Mississippi / Jackson

Children's Literature Association Series

www.upress.state.ms.us

The University Press of Mississippi is a member
of the Association of American University Presses.

Some material in chapters 1 and 3 first appeared in "Narrative Inti-
macy and the Question of Control in the *Twilight* Saga," in *Genre,
Reception, and Adaptation in the* Twilight *Saga* (2012), edited by
Anne Morey. It is reprinted by permission from Ashgate Press.

First printing 2013
∞
Library of Congress Cataloging-in-Publication Data

Day, Sara K.
  Reading like a girl : narrative intimacy in contemporary American young adult literature / Sara K. Day.
    pages cm. — (Children's literature association series)
  Includes bibliographical references and index.
  ISBN 978-1-61703-811-2 (hardback) — ISBN 978-1-61703-812-9
(ebook) (print) 1. American fiction—21st century—History and criticism. 2. Intimacy (Psychology) in literature.
3. Young adult literature, American—History and criticism.
4. Teenage girls—Books and reading—United States. 5. Adolescence in literature. 6. Girls in literature. I. Title.
  PS374.I57D39 2013
  813'.60992837—dc23   2012045553

British Library Cataloging-in-Publication Data available

For Jeremy,

who inspires me,

and for Lucy,

who inspired this

Contents

Acknowledgments

This project, which began at Texas A&M University, would not have been possible without the generous, patient guidance of my mentor, Claudia Nelson, and of Lynne Vallone, Mary Ann O'Farrell, and John Lenihan. I am grateful to each of you for your insights, advice, and support. I am grateful as well to the Texas A&M Department of English and the Melbern G. Glasscock Center for Humanities Research, both of which provided me with research fellowships. I am also indebted to the always helpful and efficient librarians at Texas A&M University and Southern Arkansas University.

Sarah Peters, Sonya Sawyer Fritz, Emily Hoeflinger, and Emily Janda Monteiro read and commented on countless drafts; their hard work and friendship proved invaluable at every step of the writing process. I am also grateful to the other members of my various writing groups, my colleagues at Southern Arkansas University, and the two readers who provided comments during the editorial process. Thank you all for your willingness to read first and finished drafts, to offer constructive feedback, and to remind me so often of the joys of scholarly community.

This work has always been inspired and informed by the love and support of my family, particularly my parents and my sister; my friends, especially Jacquelyn Brown, Jennifer Haley-Brown, Tracy MacLawhorn, Christopher Zieger, and Anna Hall-Zieger; and my husband, Jeremy.

Reading Like a Girl

Chapter 1

"She Is a Creature Designed for Reading"
Narrative Intimacy and the Adolescent Woman Reader

I n a review of Meg Cabot's *The Princess Diaries* posted on Amazon .com, teenage reader Claire says, "When I read the book, I feel like my friend is telling me a story." Reviewer Ashton identifies so strongly with Jessica Darling, the narrator of Megan McCafferty's *Sloppy Firsts*, that she declares, "Me and her are practically related." And Khy says of the narrator of E. Lockhart's *The Treasure Map of Boys*, "I didn't realize how much I missed Ruby Oliver until I started reading this third book in the series." These comments, which cast fictional characters as peers, relatives, and especially friends, provide insight into a desire on the part of many adolescent women readers to identify so strongly with characters that the line between fictional story and real reading experience can be blurred or disregarded entirely. In turn, the authors of many contemporary American novels for and about adolescent women actively encourage this blurring of boundaries by constructing what I term "narrative intimacy"—in other words, by constructing narrator-reader relationships that reflect, model, and reimagine intimate interpersonal relationships through the disclosure of information and the experience of the story as a space that the narrator invites the reader to share.

Generally speaking, narrative intimacy is established through constructions of the narrator and reader that reflect and emphasize the creation of an emotional bond based on trust and disclosure. As I discuss in more detail later in this chapter, this construction employs a first-person narrator who self-consciously discloses information and who implicitly or explicitly signals an awareness and expectation of a reader, either through direct address (which may identify the specific audience to whom the story is being related) or through a more general construction of the narrator's tale as disclosure, confession, or other interpersonal discourse. These constructions are highlighted by the content of the texts, particularly the narrators' experiences with friends, objects of romantic affection, and others; the narrators' stories frequently reveal a desire to share personal, private feelings, questions, and struggles as well as a hesitation to share them with other characters within the fictional world of the novel. The basic construction of storyteller and listener, then, must be shaped by concerns about privacy, secrecy, and trust, which in turn allow for an understanding of the narrative relationship as distinctly personalized and intimate.

While these qualities and, by extension, narrative intimacy can be found across literary genres, times, and cultures, it is particularly relevant and prevalent in contemporary American young adult literature, which has come to be associated with revelatory first-person narration.[1] Furthermore, the thoughts, knowledge, and emotions disclosed by the narrators of adolescent fiction frequently reflect the various personal bonds adolescents explore as part of their transition into adulthood. Although many of these relationships—particularly those between friends and romantic partners—play an important and generally positive role in adolescent development, the prevalence of narrative intimacy in contemporary American literature for adolescent women reflects a concern with the threats posed by these interpersonal connections while suggesting a more general understanding of the reading experience as a type of interpersonal relationship. Ultimately, I argue that narrative intimacy in novels written for and about adolescent women highlights and reinforces often contradictory cultural expectations regarding young women's involvement in interpersonal relationships.

Intimacy and the questions that frequently surround it—what it is, how it can be achieved and maintained, what role it should play in our lives—have long been of concern to philosophers, theologians, psychologists, sociologists, and, in the past few decades, talk show hosts. Generally, discussions of intimacy have been concerned with the associated feelings of love and affection that mark intimate relationships, particularly in terms of the sense of closeness that is assumed to accompany these feelings. In the prologue to her work *Literary Folkloristics and the Personal Narrative*, Sandra Dolby Stahl writes, "One gets to know someone else by sharing experience; *intimacy* is our word for the exciting sensation that comes with our perception of someone else in our personal world. We 'know' others and assume they 'know' us when we believe they have shared a similar perception of a mutual experience" (x, emphasis in original). Stahl's assertion demonstrates the degree to which the idea of "knowing" and being "known" is tied to the sharing of experiences, thoughts, feelings, and so on. Furthermore, intimacy is assumed to rely upon at least some degree of disclosure, as what we have not immediately shared with another person in the form of a mutual experience can only be shared through confession or reminiscence.

More generally, as Stahl's description of intimacy as an "exciting sensation" suggests, this process of sharing, through mutual experience or disclosure, is generally regarded as a positive one; indeed, conversations surrounding intimacy have emphasized its benefits for both individuals and the relationships they share. Psychologists Valerian J. Derlega and Alan L. Chaikan, for example, rather effusively encourage people to seek "the joy of knowing another human being on a deep, intimate level, and of being known in return" because, they claim, "accomplishing this can add meaning and zest to life" (142).[2] At the same time, growing concerns about the nature and development of intimacy have been prevalent in American society since the mid-1970s, when psychologists and sociologists performed a series of studies regarding pervasive feelings of loneliness and isolation. The findings of these studies—which trace the problems to increased mobilization, decreased time spent in communities, and the emphasis that American culture places on individual achievement—led to an ongoing conversation that has introduced concepts such as "fear of intimacy." This increased public interest in private thoughts and feelings highlights both the cultural importance of intimacy and the degree to which culture dictates the boundaries of intimacy.

For all of its emotional and psychological benefits, intimacy also necessarily involves elements of vulnerability and danger, as one must determine whether or not it is "safe" to share certain information or feelings with others. As Derlega and Chaikan note, "In general, intimate disclosure indicates that the discloser trusts his listener. The former has made himself vulnerable by revealing information that could possibly be used to hurt him by an indiscreet listener. In addition, the discloser has left himself open to ridicule or rejection" (4). Intimacy thus requires both a willingness to open oneself to the possibility of betrayal and an understanding that the information, feelings, or experiences shared with another may be used as weapons. While some spaces within which intimate information may be revealed are specifically marked as "safe"—confession to a priest or therapist will remain confidential, for example—the real concerns surrounding the safety of intimacy typically lie with those relationships that must be based upon disclosure but within which information cannot be guaranteed to remain a secret, such as close friendships and committed romantic relationships. To some degree, furthermore, intimacy represents a risk because, as Dan P. McAdams notes, "When we feel no intimacy, we are lonely. But when we experience intimacy with someone else, we risk even greater loneliness should that someone and we part" (11). By engaging in an intimate relationship, then, we must acknowledge the dangers inherent in the possibility of losing that intimacy. Cultural critic Lauren Berlant goes so far as to assert that intimacy can never be divorced from this threat; she writes, "[Intimacy's] potential failure to stabilize closeness always haunts its persistent activity, making the very attachments deemed to buttress 'a life' seem in a constant state of latent vulnerability" (2).

For the purposes of this discussion, I focus on certain elements of what makes up the larger concept of intimacy in contemporary American culture. Specifically, my concern lies with the process of disclosure as a means of creating and maintaining intimate ties, which is particularly pertinent in this discussion because narrative intimacy relies on a narrator's willingness and ability to disclose to the reader thoughts, feelings, and experiences. Because I call upon novels as shared spaces within which fictional narrators and real readers can be said to experience a story together, I am also concerned with other types of sharing, such as sharing physical space (as in sexual intimacy) or sharing experiences (a common aspect of friendships and romantic relationships alike). In turn, I consider the process of learning how and when to conceal information—even within apparently intimate relationships—as messages regarding disclosure are necessarily tied up with those regarding discretion. The relationship between disclosure and discretion also signals the prevalence of other contradictions associated with intimacy; as Berlant writes, "Contradictory desires mark the intimacy of daily life: people want to be both overwhelmed and omnipotent, caring and aggressive, known and incognito" (5). These "contradictory desires" color intimacy throughout American culture, but, as I discuss in more detail later, adolescent women in particular face conflicting expectations and demands.

In *Sharing Intimacy: What We Reveal to Others and Why*, Derlega and Chaikan explore the social and psychological concerns surrounding self-disclosure and its role in intimacy, particularly questions such as, "Should we reveal our thoughts, our feelings, or our past to another person? How intimate should our disclosure be?" (1). To some degree, our answers to these questions are determined by our personalities, the attitudes we develop about intimacy during our childhoods, and the relationship we have or wish to have with a potential recipient of our disclosure. In general, there is a reciprocal relationship between the closeness of a relationship and the level of disclosure allowed—the closer we feel to someone, the more willing we will be to share our thoughts and feelings with him or her, and vice versa. However, studies have found that Americans have become increasingly likely to make surprisingly personal disclosures to acquaintances or strangers, particularly during times of stress or fear.[3] Researchers suggest that in some cases, people will more willingly disclose secret thoughts or feelings to strangers whom they may never see again rather than to closer friends or family members precisely because the risk of rejection or betrayal is somewhat allayed by the lack of an ongoing relationship. Indeed, this concept is the basic foundation for group therapy and organizations such as Alcoholics Anonymous.

That people are frequently willing to make personal information available to an audience of strangers reflects the degree to which the construction of intimacy in contemporary American culture has expanded to include the possibility of a public element. As Berlant remarks, intimacy

> involves an aspiration for a narrative about something shared, a story about both oneself and others that will turn out in a particular way. Usually, this story is set within zones of familiarity and comfort: friendship, the couple, and the family form, animated by expressive and emancipating kinds of love. Yet the inwardness of the intimate is met by a corresponding publicness. (1)

As guests of talk show hosts such as Oprah Winfrey, Dr. Phil McGraw, and even Jerry Springer have repeatedly demonstrated, a desire to make public information that might ordinarily have been considered private marks a larger cultural impulse toward the publicness that Berlant identifies. In the past decade, the increasingly public nature of intimacy, particularly as it relates to young people, has also been demonstrated by the growing importance of online social networking sites such as MySpace and Facebook, where members can post information about their lives and carry on public conversations with friends.[4] This "corresponding publicness" of the ostensibly private nature of intimacy influences my understanding of narrative intimacy because, as I discuss later in this chapter, the desire to offer intimate information to an audience of strangers shapes the disclosure made by narrators of adolescent literature for and about adolescent women.

The experience of intimacy, as well as the contradictions and struggles that often accompany it, plays a role in every stage of life; during adolescence, however, both the types and degrees of intimacy sought change as people grow out of childhood attachments and begin to consider the lifelong commitments associated with adult relationships. In the most general sense, adolescence has been defined as the period between childhood and adulthood; over the past fifty years, however, the length of time and degree of importance associated with adolescence have both grown significantly. Today, a life stage that was once so short as to be almost nonexistent has stretched to more than a decade, as young people postpone or reject the milestones—choosing a career, getting married, running a household of one's own—that have traditionally signaled entrance into adulthood. As adolescence has come to occupy a longer period of time, it has also become more central to American culture, particularly in ongoing conversations about adolescent behaviors (or, perhaps more accurately, *mis*behaviors). Particularly in the years since World War II, concerns about teen drug use, sexual activity, and violence have played a prominent role in portrayals of and discussions about adolescents, leading to a more general understanding of adolescence in America as a time fraught with insecurity and instability, anger and alienation.

As the twentieth century neared its end, a specific focus on adolescent women began to emerge.[5] In 1994, Mary Pipher's *Reviving Ophelia: Saving the Selves of Adolescent Girls* brought adolescent women and their problems into the spotlight. Drawing from her experiences as a psychotherapist, Pipher focuses on the challenges that cause young women such as her patients to become isolated, angry, and sometimes self-destructive, asserting that "adolescence has always been hard, but it's harder now because of cultural changes" (28). At the same time, the rise of Girl Power—which emphasized sexuality and empowerment—offered the possibility of "a 'new girl': assertive, dynamic, and unbound from the constraints of passive femininity" (Gonick 2). Ultimately, while both constructions of adolescent womanhood seemed to offer new perspectives, neither Girl Power nor

Reviving Ophelia freed young women from the confusing social expectations they faced. On the contrary, as Marnina Gonick asserts, "in rearticulating femininity as comprising both powerful ambitions for autonomy and vulnerability so extreme as to threaten extinction, Girl Power and *Reviving Ophelia* bespeak the two central and interrelated contradictions of the time" (19).

The publication of *Reviving Ophelia* inspired a flurry of studies, articles, books, and debates regarding young women's social and personal development; parents who wished to help their daughters manage the perils of adolescence turned to Pipher's work, as well as to texts such as Barbara Mackoff's *Growing a Girl: Seven Strategies for Raising a Strong, Spirited Daughter* (1996) and Cheryl Dellasega's *Surviving Ophelia: Mothers Share Their Wisdom in Navigating the Tumultuous Teenage Years* (2002), for advice and guidance. The concerns these works expressed soon led to corresponding publications for adolescent women themselves. One of these books, Sara Shandler's *Ophelia Speaks: Adolescent Girls Write About Their Search for Self* (1998), directly refers to Pipher's work,[6] while *Deal with It! A Whole New Approach to Your Body, Brain and Life as a Gurl* (1999) by Esther Drill, Heather McDonald, and Rebecca Odes alludes to Girl Power. Like books for parents, these texts frequently allude to adolescence as a stage that must be survived; works such as Julia Devillers's *GirlWise: How to Be Confident, Capable, Cool, and in Control* (2002) and Jill Zimmerman Rutledge's *Dealing with the Stuff That Makes Life Tough: The 10 Things That Stress Teen Girls Out and How to Cope with Them* (2003) implicitly construct adolescent womanhood as a period that challenges young women's sense of self, presents them with obstacles that cause "stress," and requires strategies that will protect and maintain confidence.

The conversations regarding adolescent women that continue to preoccupy scholars and society alike reflect an ongoing concern about young women's physical, emotional, and developmental well-being that in turn reveals problematic expectations of the transition from girlhood into womanhood. To some degree, the role of the adolescent woman in American society continues to be defined by cultural expectations of adult women; in other words, the roles of wife and mother for which young women are encouraged to prepare are closely tied to larger concerns about intimacy as a primarily female pursuit. Rubenstein and Shaver call women "the undisputed intimacy specialists in our society" because they have historically been raised to nurture and care, whereas men have tended to experience intimacy in adulthood only "with the guidance—and usually at the

insistence—of women" (24). For girls making the progression into adulthood, then, "the capacity to care for others and to receive care from them
becomes a part of rather than antithetical to self-definition" (Gilligan 151).
As a result, an emphasis on the development of interpersonal relationships, particularly those of a romantic nature, continues to be prevalent in
literature and other popular culture media produced for and about adolescent women. At the same time, the vulnerability required of intimacy
leads to certain threats strongly associated with cultural representations
of what Judith L. Fischer, Joyce Munsch, and Shannon M. Greene call "the
dark side of intimacy"—namely, "the phenomenon of the adolescent broken heart, the consequences of betrayal by a best friend, and so forth [that]
are all possible contributors to upset and distress in adolescents' lives"
(120). As young women navigate their relationships, they internalize not
only the value of disclosure in establishing intimacy but also the pressure
to learn and use discretion in their dealings with others. Indeed, adolescent womanhood is marked by a growing understanding of what should
not be expressed or shared.

It is important to note that here and in this study as a whole, I am primarily concerned with the concept of the adolescent woman as white,
middle class, and heterosexual, a "norm" about which and to whom much
popular culture is presented: books, films, television, and other media,
as well as most psychological, sociological, and anthropological studies
about American adolescence, tend to focus on this specific group. I by
no means wish to privilege the experience of young women who belong
to these categories, assume that all women who fit this model have iden-
tical experiences of intimacy, or dismiss the experiences of adolescent
women of other ethnicities, classes, or sexual identification; likewise, I
do not mean to suggest that adolescent men do not encounter problematic models of intimacy in culture and in literature. Instead, I rely on this
paradigm because of its greater prevalence and the degree to which it has
shaped and continues to shape concepts about adolescent womanhood
in contemporary American culture, particularly in terms of interpersonal
relationships and intimacy. The emphasis on this norm that has been
demonstrated since the mid-1990s in the popularity of Britney Spears and
Miley Cyrus, *Gilmore Girls* and *Gossip Girl*, *Clueless* and *Mean Girls*, has
resulted in a more general, implicit insistence upon the prevalence of this
model in the lives of the young women who make up the primary audience
for such pop culture products.

As a result of these assumptions of whiteness, wealth, and heteronormativity, in turn, this version of adolescent womanhood has cultivated an expectation that young women may focus almost exclusively on the development and maintenance of interpersonal relationships without facing the challenges that confront young people whose race, class, and/or sexuality sets them outside of this narrow definition. Largely free from the oppression, rejection, and other trials that mark many young people's experiences, the adolescent women presented in popular culture generally concern themselves with the friendships and romances that are understood to be the foundations of social acceptance and markers of maturation into adulthood. Obviously, as works such as Sapphire's *Push* and its recent film adaptation *Precious* demonstrate, the representations of intimacy and the emphasis on "normal" social interactions that accompany most representations of adolescent womanhood do not accurately reflect all lived experiences of intimacy; in turn, works such as *Push* challenge the construction of narrative intimacy as I discuss it here. Teenaged Precious, the poverty-stricken African-American narrator of *Push*, does not seek the same type of narrator-reader relationship as the wealthier white narrators discussed in this project, and for good reason—because she has been the object of verbal, physical, and sexual abuse at her parents' hands, her experiences of intimacy are almost exclusively informed by pain, exploitation, and rejection; her interpersonal relationships have served to isolate and limit her rather than to provide a foundation upon which healthy adult relationships can be built. Likewise, queer narrators often understand intimacy in general, and the necessity of narrative intimacy in particular, differently than the heterosexual narrators discussed in this project. For example, as Holland, the narrator of Julie Ann Peters's *Keeping You a Secret*, illustrates, the specific challenges that accompany her first homosexual relationship and her decision to come out to her friends and family are met by emotional dangers and threats of rejection that are much larger in scope than those detailed by most heterosexual narrators.

Again, by focusing on works that represent the "norms" of adolescent womanhood, I by no means wish to reject or deny the importance of literature about young women outside of the norm; indeed, I believe that the possibilities such texts present for further discussion of narrative intimacy help to illuminate the problematic nature of narrative intimacy as I consider it here, in its most prevalent forms. By focusing on novels about white, middle-class, and heterosexual women, I hope to demonstrate that narrative intimacy in popular works for adolescent women perpetuates an understanding of intimacy for all readers that problematically informs young women's understandings of intimacy by clearly establishing representations that do not allow for lived experiences outside of the "norm" presented in literature, film, and other pop culture forms. In other words, the lived experiences of people of color, lesbian/bisexual/transexual/questioning teens, or working-class readers are not represented by the majority of texts that address what it means to be adolescent and female.

As the discussions of intimacy by Stahl and Berlant make clear, the development of intimate relationships depends heavily upon the establishment of a story or narrative. In order to more fully develop the concept of narrative intimacy and its specific applicability to the contemporary American young adult novels discussed here, I turn to narrative theory, drawing particular points from Mikhail Bakhtin, Wayne C. Booth, and Wolfgang Iser, among others, as well as from the more recent theories of Richard Walsh, Robyn Warhol, and Andrea Schwenke Wyile.[7] In "Narrative Theory, 1966–2006: A Narrative," his contribution to the fortieth anniversary edition of Robert Scholes and Robert Kellogg's *The Nature of Narrative* (1966), James Phelan distinguishes between three branches of narrative theory: narrative as formal system, narrative as ideological act, and narrative as rhetoric. While the distinctions and definitions provided by the other models[8] are often helpful, for the purposes of this discussion, I am primarily concerned with the model of narrative as rhetoric, which has grown from works such as Wayne C. Booth's *The Rhetoric of Fiction*, first published in 1961. As Phelan explains, this approach

> conceives of narrative as a purposive act of communication about characters and events: somebody telling somebody else on some occasion and for some purpose(s) that something happened. Given the emphasis on communicative action, the approach pays special attention to the relations among tellers, audiences, and the something that happened. (297)

Because, as Phelan notes, rhetorical approaches to narrative theory "put special emphasis on the reader's share in the production of meaning even as they retain a strong interest in the textual signals that guide the reader's role and acknowledge the author as the constructive agent of the text" (297), this model provides a helpful perspective from which to consider the construction of narrative intimacy. Specifically, the idea that authors, characters, and readers each have a "share" in the creation of meaning has important implications for my discussion of narrative intimacy, as it highlights the necessary connections between these rhetorical positions. In works that develop narrative intimacy, I argue, the "purpose" or "occasion" for telling is, primarily, the act of telling in and of itself as a means of establishing trust and creating implicit emotional bonds between these figures, particularly narrator and reader.

In order to explore the rhetorical situation involved in narrative intimacy, I first wish to identify the roles involved in fictional narratives and their relationships with each other in the larger context of narrative theory. Since Seymour Chatman introduced the following diagram in 1978, it has often been employed to illustrate the relationship between author and reader, as well as the positions that exist between the two:

Real author → [Implied Author → Narrator → Narratee → Implied Reader] → Real reader

By establishing not only the six distinct roles involved in the composition of a fictional narrative but also positioning them in relationship to each other, Chatman's diagram offers a helpful visual representation of many of the concepts discussed here (151). In particular, this diagram adds nuance to the more generalized discussion of narrative as rhetoric, as it draws attention to the ways in which the roles of author, narrator, and reader are all shaped by their positioning in either the real world or a fictional space.

One of the most important points illustrated by Chatman's design is the interconnected roles of real author, implied author, and narrator, particularly the manner in which the relationships between these roles help to shape the various levels of storytelling in a work of fiction. Essentially, the real author is the person who "holds the pen," while the implied author relays the real author's message. Frequently, the purpose of the implied author is to shape the narrative in such a way as to suggest the real author's priorities and ideals; in some cases, the implied author and narrator stand in cooperation with each other in this effort, but many authors employ the implied author in order to contradict or question the narrator. As Chatman explains, "Unlike the narrator, the implied author can *tell* us nothing. He, or better, *it* has no voice, no direct means of communicating. It instructs us silently, through the design of the whole, with all the voices, by all the means it has chosen us to learn" (148). The narrator, then, occupies a space that is necessarily defined by the ability to *tell*—in other words, the narrator is the voice that tells the story, presenting both the events and, in many cases, the thoughts and feelings experienced by the characters within a text.

While, as Booth explains at length, narrators may occupy any number of points of view, varying greatly in terms of their relationships with the action and characters within a story, for the purposes of this discussion I focus on a specific subset of narrators—namely, first-person narrators who are the main characters of the stories they narrate, who act as their own subjects, and who focus on the presentation of their own thoughts, feelings, and experiences. Narrative intimacy requires this type of first-person narration precisely because it allows for insights into the choices regarding the type and degree of disclosure that must be made by the narrator regarding the reader. In third-person narration, we may gain access to intimate details about a character; however, those details are not being made available to us by the character but by a narrator who exists outside of the character. In order to discuss narrative intimacy, then, I will be focusing on novels in which the narrator is a character who speaks for and about herself, offering at her own discretion the details that may allow for an intimate relationship between her and the reader.[9]

The narrator is typically defined not only by the information that she provides—her name, her age, her location, and so on—but also the means by which she makes that information available. In turn, an awareness and understanding of audience, particularly the assumptions the narrator makes regarding the audience's possible attitudes, beliefs, and opinions, necessarily shapes the narrator's storytelling. In order to tell a story—to become a sender—a narrator must participate in this process of communication, which requires at least some awareness of the audience who will receive the story. Mikhail Bakhtin articulates the most basic relationship between narrative senders and receivers in his concept of addressivity, which holds that "every word is directed towards an *answer* and cannot escape the profound influence of the answering word that it anticipates" (280, emphasis in original). Susan Sniader Lanser also offers the concept of "narrative self-consciousness," which relies upon the narrator's explicitly drawing attention to the act of storytelling; according to Lanser, it is only in first-person modes "that there is even the opportunity for the narrator to reveal an awareness of the communicative activity in which s/he is involved" (176). Lanser's concept of narrative self-consciousness plays a particularly important role in the potential development of narrative intimacy as it marks an awareness of audience as part of a larger communicative process. Indeed, several of the narrators discussed in this work—particularly Ruby Oliver in Chapter 2 and each of the fictional diarists in Chapter 5—rely heavily on narrative self-consciousness as they invite their readers to share the space of the story with them.

Just as the roles of real author, implied author, and narrator variously shape the telling of a story, the interconnected roles of narratee, implied reader, and real reader determine how a story is received. In fictional narratives, the narratee is the most immediate receiver of the communication sent by the narrator; however, it is important to note the potential overlap between narratee, implied reader, and real reader, which in turn helps to shape and define the narrator-reader relationship at the center of narrative intimacy. The narratee, as defined by Gerald Prince, most frequently plays the role of a mediator between the narrator and the reader; although the narratee may be aligned with a character within the text (and thus named and described by the narrator), the narratee is often indicated only by the manner of the narrator's telling a story (225).[10] The implied reader, as set forth by Booth and Iser, among others, is established and defined by the narrative as the "ideal" audience to whom the narrator may direct his or her tale. Specifically, the implied reader is defined by the text and the narrator by means of the specific expectations that the narrator assigns to the reader, as well as the values, desires, and so on that the narrator assumes the reader to have. As Iser writes, "The concept of the implied reader is therefore a textual structure anticipating the presence of a recipient, without necessarily defining him: this concept prestructures the role to be assumed by each recipient" (145); the "recipient," or real reader, thus enters a text through the constructed role of the implied reader. In turn, the real reader, like the real author, exists outside of the text—just as the real author holds the pen, the real reader holds the book. The real reader may, but will not necessarily, adopt the role of implied reader as a means of engaging with a text.

Because the roles of narratee, implied reader, and real reader so frequently overlap, I wish to clarify this point: when I use the term "reader" throughout this discussion, I am referring most immediately to the construction of the reader set forth by a text, with a particular interest in the ways this construction invites the real reader to, at least temporarily, occupy the fictional space of the story. In focusing on this version of reader, I do not wish to discount the importance of the real reader; instead, I wish to focus on the manner in which the reading experiences of real readers are informed by, if not wholly created by, the expectations set forth by a narrative. By adopting this treatment of readers, I share with

Warhol an interest in what she calls "the susceptible reader"—the concept that readers are prone to the emotional responses constructed by popular cultural forms of narrative at least in part because cultural models have developed the expectation of those responses. In *Having a Good Cry: Effeminate Feelings and Pop-Culture Forms,* Warhol focuses on the physical signs of emotion that accompany susceptible readers' experiences of reading texts and films designed to evoke specific responses. While my discussion is more broadly concerned with emotional experiences that are not generally associated with signs such as tears, I find persuasive and useful her assertion that "if we think about the reader's tears as, in part, a consequence of the text's technical arrangement of the reader's consciously or subconsciously feeling that the miserable or triumphant sufferer is 'just like me,' however, audiences' participation in sentimentalism becomes more positively performative, less revealing of some presumed hidden truth about the readers' 'real feelings'" (45–46). In other words, the meaning of emotional responses in both Warhol's view and my own is more indicative of the success of narrative techniques than of individual readers' actual experiences of specific feelings.

Furthermore, in focusing on this construction rather than the individualized real reader who has typically been of interest to narrative and reception theorists, I borrow Molly Abel Travis's understanding of readers as "both constructed and constructing in that they read as part of interpretive communities and are involved in collective cultural imagining and reimagining" (6). The reader at the heart of this discussion, then, is a construction that is shaped and guided by both the general cultural expectations that readers will be susceptible to the emotional machinations of popular culture forms—crying in response to "tearjerkers," for example, or laughing at romantic comedies—and by the specific techniques at play in individual works of fiction such as those presented in this discussion. As this is not an ethnographic study, furthermore, my discussion will rely almost exclusively on the techniques employed by the narratives in question rather than on the specific responses of actual readers; only in the conclusion, which concerns the role of new media in reimaging narrative intimacy, do I draw on real readers' expressions of their emotional attachment to works of fiction.

Narrative intimacy, then, both relies on and complicates the narrative roles laid out by Chatman; as his diagram illustrates, the real author and real reader are inherently separate from the positions available within the fictional space of the text. While that necessary distinction informs much of our understanding of literature and rhetoric, my concept of narrative intimacy depends on the efforts of authors, narrators, and readers to navigate the boundaries between real and fictional worlds in ways that insist upon the possibility of impossible relationships that cross the real/fictional divide. Essentially, just as the author and the narrator exist in separate spheres (one real, one fictional), the narrator and the reader are necessarily separated by their ontological statuses. One of the determining features of narrative intimacy, I mean to suggest, is that the author actively constructs the narrator with an eye toward minimizing the reader's awareness of that difference, allowing for the (at least temporary) possibility that the narrator's fictional status may be ignored or set aside in favor of the implicit relationship within which narrative intimacy may function. In turn, the construction of fictional narrator directly shapes the role of the constructed reader, which allows for—and in fact depends upon—the possibility that the real reader will accept the fictional narrator's expectations and attempts at intimacy in a way that mimics real-world interactions.

Questions of breaching the metaphorical boundaries between fictional and real worlds have long been of interest to narrative theorists. Scholes and Kellogg articulate one possible understanding of reading as a boundary-crossing activity, saying, "Meaning, in a work of narrative art, is a function of the relationship between two worlds: the fictional world created by the author, and the 'real' world, the apprehendable universe" (82). More recently, Walsh has advanced a theory of fictionality that echoes Scholes and Kellogg's assertion; he writes, "Fictionality is neither a boundary between worlds, nor a frame dissociating the author with the discourse, but a contextual assumption by the reader, prompted by the manifest information that the authorial discourse is offered as fiction" (36). For Walsh, the value of fiction lies in the possibility of vicarious experience: "What we understand, feel, and value may be ultimately grounded in the abstract and the general, but it is not in general terms that we experience understanding, feeling, or valuing it. Fiction enables us to go through that process, for the sake of the experience" (51).

To a large degree, the possibility of experiencing through fiction depends upon the potential for a relationship between the narrator and reader that involves a sense of identification. Scholes and Kellogg offer this consideration of identification:

> The highly individualized character draws the reader into a very intimate connection with the fictional world and makes that world assume something

like the solidity of reality. By awakening complex correspondences between the psyches of character and reader, such characterization provides a rich and intense "experience" for the reader—an experience which may not only move him but also exercise his perception and sensibility, ultimately assisting him to perceive and comprehend the world of reality more sharply and sensitively. (103)

While Scholes and Kellogg emphasize the role that the narrator plays in alerting the reader to potential new understandings and knowledge, Iser privileges the role of the reader in this process, noting that "The reader discovers the meaning of the text . . . he discovers a new reality through fiction which, at least in part, is different from the world he himself is used to; and he discovers the deficiencies inherent in prevalent norms and in his own restricted behaviors" (xiii). As these comments suggest, both the telling and the reading of a story may be understood as creating a space that is meant to be shared for the more general purposes of the reader's not only gaining knowledge but also vicariously experiencing emotions. The distinctions made by Walsh, Scholes and Kellogg, and Iser have important implications for this discussion, as the "process," the "experience," and the "correspondences" they note all play important roles in establishing the foundation of what I call narrative intimacy; in particular, they allow for the possibility of adolescent women readers "experiencing" the realities of young adulthood vicariously through the narrators' stories.

While the construction of the narrator necessarily informs the reader's experience of the text, however, the reader's responses cannot be enacted through reciprocal expressions of thoughts and feelings. In *Fictional Points of View*, Peter Lamarque argues that "reading fiction requires active involvement: readers 'fill out' characters, draw implications, form hypotheses, and make judgments. Fiction can provide not only the occasion for this involvement but also a content and subject matter to which readers might otherwise have no access" (19). At the same time, Lamarque is careful to define the limitations of readers' engagement with fictional texts and their characters. When discussing readers' emotional responses to fictional characters, he says, "They [the fictional characters] seem to be able to induce in us sorrow, fear, contempt, delight, embarrassment. But we have no comeback for them. We cannot thank them, congratulate or frighten them, or help, advise, rescue or warn them. A logical gap exists between them and us" (Lamarque 114–15). In many ways, narrative intimacy acts as an attempt to bridge this "logical gap," particularly on the part of the narrator who offers disclosure. At the same time and conversely, this logical gap is actually necessary to the development of narrative intimacy in novels of adolescent literature.

These insights regarding the process and goals of narration provide a helpful foundation for consideration of the more specific impact of first-person narrators who are, to use terms presented by Warhol and Schwenke Wyile, engaging and immediate. Notably, one of the primary efforts of an engaging narrator, according to Warhol, is to minimize or erase the distinctions between narratee and reader—in other words, "such a narrator addresses a 'you' that is intended to evoke recognition and identification in the person who holds the book and reads, even if the 'you' in the text resembles that person only slightly or not at all" ("Toward" 811). Schwenke Wyile expands upon the concept of engaging narration by incorporating the concept of immediacy; specifically, she argues that works featuring what she calls immediate narrators—who are concerned with recent or still-occurring events—are the most engaging. The concept of immediacy plays an important role in narrative intimacy, as it further encourages readers to seek and understand similarities between themselves and the narrator in question.

Immediacy depends on a minimal degree of difference between what Dorrit Cohn calls the narrating and the experiencing selves. In *Transparent Minds: Narrative Modes for Presenting Consciousness in Fiction*, Cohn uses these terms to distinguish between narrator and protagonist in first-person narration. Because the narrator is at a temporal remove from the experiences he or she narrates, the narrative self is necessarily distinct from the experiencing self being described, even if the pronoun "I" marks the two as being in a "relationship that imitates the temporal continuity of real beings, an existential relationship that differs substantially from the purely fictional relationship that binds a narrator to his protagonist in third-person fiction" (Cohn 144). In some cases, the narrating self explicitly discusses the amount of time that has passed between the past experience and the present narration; in others, the temporal distance is implied by, for example, differences in language or the narrating self's passing judgment on the actions of the experiencing self.[11] Although such differences can result in what Cohn calls "dissonant self-narration" (145), particularly when the narrating self is markedly different in personality, values, and so on from the experiencing self, it is important to note the possibility of "consonant narration," which features an "unobtrusive narrator who identifies with his earlier incarnation, renouncing all manner of cognitive privilege" (155). Thus, present-tense narration, which is employed in many novels discussed here, frequently allows for the impression that there is no distinction between the experiencing and narrating selves. Notably, the works I discuss that are written in past tense also generally minimize the potential for narrative dissonance, either explicitly (by noting that only a short amount of time has passed between experience and narration) or implicitly (through the similarities in voice shared by the narrating and experiencing selves, for example, or by the absence of narrative judgment).

In addition to her emphasis on immediacy, Schwenke Wyile also emphasizes the ways in which "active engaging narration provides a number of reminders to immersion prone readers that they are reading, while also serving as an invitation to actively consider the relationship between their reading and their experience of the world" (Schwenke Wyile 119). Such immediate and engaging narration, according to Schwenke Wyile, allows for the establishment of identification between narrator and reader as "the narrator seeks to reconstruct the events being related in a way that engages readers, a way that invites them to consider themselves in, or close to, the position of the protagonist" (116). Warhol also suggests that the tendency of engaging narrators to be employed by women authors reflects a gendered desire to extend the feelings evoked by a novel into real-world actions on the part of the reader; it is worth noting that all of the novels discussed in this study were written by women.

This imagined proximity between protagonist and reader is crucial to the development of narrative intimacy. Lanser uses the term "affinity" to characterize the ability of readers to identify with narrators, noting, "Affinity with a character thus depends to some extent on the degree to which that character is 'subjectified'—made into a subject, given an active human consciousness. The more subjective information we have about a character, as a rule, the greater our access to that persona and the more powerful the affinity" (206). In the development of narrative intimacy, because the narrator is self-consciously disclosing not only experiences but also thoughts and feelings, the reader is given access to a great amount of subjective information, allowing in turn for a stronger "affinity" and a greater sense of intimacy between narrator and reader. Iser likewise discusses the potential for a connection between these positions in his consideration of "identification." He writes, "What is normally meant by 'identification' is the establishment of affinities between oneself and someone outside oneself—a familiar ground on which we are able to experience the unfamiliar" (291). Furthermore, he argues, when readers relate to a text, the understood boundaries between subject and object may seem to diminish or disappear entirely.

If Lanser and Iser are correct about the importance of identification and affinity in blurring the boundaries between fiction and reality, then these concepts provide a helpful context within which to consider the constructions of narrators and readers that allow for the development of narrative intimacy. Specifically, adolescent women narrators such as those I discuss frequently signal their understanding of the reader as being, like the narrator, an adolescent woman. To some degree, this assumption is marked by occasional direct address that calls upon the reader's ability to relate to the narrator's thoughts as well as other gestures of awareness. For example, the narrator of Natasha Friend's *Perfect* offers the reader (at times questionable) advice, while other narrators both ask and respond to questions as though they are engaging in a conversation with the reader.

Although the possibility of identification does, for some critics, signal potential successes within fictional works and their relationships to readers, it is important to recognize that other critics have questioned the contemporary emphasis on relatability in the reading process. In *Power, Voice and Subjectivity in Literature for Young Readers*, Maria Nikolajeva discusses what she calls the "identification fallacy," primarily in response to the tendency of teachers and other adults to encourage young readers' attempts to "identify" with characters in fictional texts. Arguing that questions such as "What character do you relate to most?" create the expectation that readers should seek parallels between themselves and fictional characters, Nikolajeva considers the manner in which such an emphasis on identification may result in habitually uncritical reading; in contrast, she asserts the importance of "the readers' ability to liberate themselves from the protagonists' subjectivity in order to evaluate them properly" (185). While I agree with Nikolajeva's arguments regarding both the causes and the effects of the identification fallacy, I also wish to underline the manner in which many novels themselves—particularly those discussed in this project—work to create feelings of identification among certain readers. Indeed, Nikolajeva's claims regarding the dangers of such identification for young readers are well taken: although many texts discussed here present models of intimacy that could or perhaps should be interrogated, resisted, or rejected outright by critical readers, the sense of identification that makes narrative intimacy possible discourages the sort of distance from the character that Nikolajeva figures as necessary for such judgments. As I argue in subsequent chapters, many narrators seek identification and affinity precisely to avoid the possibility of judgment or rejection on the part of the reader.

While readers of all ages may seek this identification and affinity, furthermore, adolescent readers in particular have explicitly identified these aspects as important to their reading experiences. In his *Becoming a Reader: The Experience of Fiction from Childhood to Adulthood*, J. A. Appleyard notes that "from what adolescents say it does seem that one reason they read . . . is to imagine real lives to help them understand the possibilities of their own lives" (104). Appleyard gestures towards the concept that adolescents view the characters within these novels as guides, which in turn provides insight into the more didactic purposes that reading serves in the lives of young people. Robyn McCallum, whose *Ideologies of Identity in Adolescent Fiction: The Dialogic Construction of Subjectivity* specifically addresses questions of narrative in young adult literature, asserts that "the genre of children's and adolescent literature is a particular kind of discursive practice which is culturally situated and which constructs an implied audience position inscribed with the values and assumptions of the culture in which it is produced and received" (9). If we accept McCallum's assertion regarding the role culture plays in shaping the implied adolescent reader, then the implications for narrative intimacy are evident: the cultural expectations and demands associated with young people, particularly young women, shape the ways that readers approach and understand the messages within literature. Narrative intimacy in literature about friendships, romance, and other subjects that relate to interpersonal relationships, then, provides a specific model of these relationships, particularly the role of disclosure and intimacy within them, to which young people are implicitly instructed to attend.

Though I have primarily been concerned with narrative theory, it is important to note that the related field of reception theory also has implications in the understanding of narrative intimacy. To some degree, the focus on the reader's response to literature aligns neatly with the concepts put forth by Scholes and Kellogg and Iser in their discussions of the creation of meaning. On its most basic level, reception theory holds that readers are responsible for the creation of meaning in a text. In turn, readers' responses to literature may help them understand not only a text but also their own lives and experiences. Travis describes reading as "compulsive, reiterative role-playing in which individuals attempt to find themselves by going outside the self, engaging in literary performance in the hope of fully and finally identifying the self through self-differentiation" (6). In other words, the process of seeking and finding affinity with characters through the act of reading contributes not only to the creation of meaning within the text but to a larger sense of understanding about one's own identity.

In *Having a Good Cry*, Warhol argues, "We should think of narrative structures as devices that work through readers' bodily feelings to produce and reproduce the physical fact of gendered subjectivity" (24). Her suggestion that emotional reactions such as crying have been dismissed because they are effeminate seems to me to provide important insights into the treatments and expectations of adolescent women as narrators and as readers. Though the texts I discuss in this study do not all attempt to cause a tearful reaction (indeed, many seek to draw a reader's laughter rather than tears, though some may seek to do both), they do, by constructing the reader as an adolescent woman whose ability to relate to and identify with the story at hand is crucial to the larger project of developing an intimate relationship, play into Warhol's consideration of gendered subjectivity and narrative and reception theories. Many of the techniques that Warhol identifies as common to "sentimental" nineteenth-century texts, furthermore, readily apply to the contemporary American fiction for adolescent women, particularly in terms of cultivating expected responses through specific types of language, the focus on one character's consciousness, and the manner in which readers are encouraged to identify with the successes and defeats of that central character.

In considering this point, I wish to draw attention to the emotional responses to literature that typically mark cultural representations of adolescent women readers. The degree to which adolescent women as a market and audience have been understood as particularly receptive to literature in emotional (rather than intellectual or analytical) terms allows for the examination of narrative intimacy in particularly pronounced terms. In "What Girls Want," Caitlin Flanagan suggests that the adolescent woman understands literature in a unique way:

> She is a creature designed for reading . . . because she is a creature whose most elemental psychological needs—to be undisturbed while she works out the big questions of her life, to be hidden from view while still in plain sight, to enter profoundly into the emotional lives of others—are met precisely by the act of reading.

While this description gestures towards a need for escapism, it also indicates that seeking a place "to be hidden from view while still in plain sight" is part of a larger process of learning and understanding that occupies many young women.[12]

As I have suggested, contemporary American cultural demands of young women, which perpetuate contradictory messages about the role of intimacy during adolescence, inform my discussion of literature written for and about this specific group. Specifically, my consideration of the novels discussed in this study draws on the expectations and demands of late twentieth- and early twenty-first-century American culture, which help to shape the treatment of intimacy both in the interpersonal relationships between fictional characters and in the implied relationship between narrator and reader. For the purposes of this project, I examine literature for and about adolescent women published between 1994 and the present; these dates were chosen to correspond with the cultural shifts that accompanied Pipher's *Reviving Ophelia* and the ongoing conversation about adolescent women's emotional health. Although the novels I discuss are by no means the only examples of narrative intimacy in contemporary literature for adolescent women, they do provide a helpful overview of the specific concerns about narrative intimacy that I explore throughout the study while gesturing toward the larger tendency of texts for this group to employ such strategies.[13]

Furthermore, in order to place the fictional texts in a broader context, this study also considers the role of other popular media, particularly nonfiction (often in the form of self-help books), in shaping cultural expectations about adolescent womanhood, interpersonal relationships, and intimacy. Many self-help books employ direct address to the reader and encourage readers to identify with the young people whose anecdotes often support the claims made by the author. Films and TV shows, likewise, often allow for the possibility of narrative intimacy by employing voiceovers and other techniques that allow the main character to communicate thoughts and feelings to the viewer without revealing them to other characters within the fictional space of the story. For example, the teenaged title character of the late 1990s TV show *Felicity* recorded her most intimate thoughts on audiotapes to send to an unseen friend named "Sally." The content of these tapes acted as voiceover narration for each episode, positioning the viewer as Sally and granting more access to Felicity's experiences than the characters surrounding her. The 2010 movie *Easy A*, in which main character Olive speaks directly to the camera as a means of telling the viewer her story, likewise positions the viewer as a more intimate recipient of the narrator's thoughts and feelings than those around her, from whom she actively conceals her true thoughts, feelings, and experiences. This latter example is particularly pertinent to this discussion because its interest in the problematic expectations that surround young women's experiences of intimacy—specifically, the double standard that surrounds adolescent women's engagement with sex—demonstrates the larger cultural significance and prevalence of narrative intimacy as it pertains to adolescent women.

The chapters that follow examine prevalent types and locations of narrative intimacy as it relates to literature for adolescent women. In the second chapter, "'Opening Myself Like a Book to the Spine': Disclosure and Discretion in the Construction of Friendship," I examine texts that offer models of friendships and provide insight into the cultural construction of adolescent women's platonic interpersonal relationships. While the narrators' reflections on such relationships ostensibly allow for a consideration of closeness, familiarity, and relatability, they also frequently demonstrate some resistance to or limitations of intimacy. Novels such as Sarah Dessen's *Keeping the Moon* and Natasha Friend's *Perfect* model the ways in which the development and maintenance of friendships allow adolescent women narrators to develop their own sense of identity while demonstrating the occasional difficulties in sharing personal feelings, thoughts, and experiences with others. Other novels, such as Siobhan Vivian's *A Little Friendly Advice*, take a slightly different approach, portraying friendships in which problems like peer pressure challenge and can potentially cause damage to adolescent women. In both cases, the construction of the reader as a participant in an interpersonal relationship with the narrator allows authors to demonstrate the benefits and challenges of intimacy while working within a social construction of adolescent women's friendship, particularly the expectation that young women should engage in relationships that allow shared feelings and experiences.

The third chapter, "'He Couldn't Get Close Enough': The Exploration and Relegation of Desire," expands on the basic model of narrator-reader relationships as friendships as it considers the exploration of sexual desire. In novels about romantic relationships, readers are frequently figured as voyeuristic confidantes and partners in desire, often privy to more information than the narrator reveals even to the object of her affection. Novels that depict adolescent women's involvement in romantic relationships often rely upon an understanding of young women as refraining from full self-disclosure, sometimes while engaging in physical intimacy. Works such as Kristen Tracy's *Lost It* and Stephenie Meyer's *Twilight* saga feature adolescent women narrators who explicitly distinguish between the feelings and information they willingly disclose to the reader and those that must be kept from their romantic partners. In novels that portray teen romance and sexual relationships, then, the model of intimacy paradoxically depends upon readers' accepting the narrators' disclosures while acknowledging the ways in which the narrators maintain secrecy from those characters with whom they ostensibly share their most intimate experiences.

While the second and third chapters are concerned with both the potential benefits and the implicit dangers related to interpersonal relationships, the fourth chapter shifts to consider the specific impact threats such as abuse and assault may have on young women's understandings of intimacy. In "'She Doesn't Say a Word': Violations and Reclamations of Intimacy," I discuss texts in which rape and other violations of interpersonal space reveal the potential dangers and threats of intimacy. In many young adult novels that deal with topics such as sexual assault and abuse, the treatment of narrative intimacy shifts to reflect the ways in which a violation of intimacy may lead adolescent women to eschew or avoid other types of intimacy. The victims of abuse or assault in novels such as Deb Caletti's *Honey, Baby, Sweetheart* and Laurie Halse Anderson's *Speak* thus frequently reject the possibility of intimacy by refusing to speak to those around them about their experiences while simultaneously (and perhaps contradictorily) revealing the cause of their silence to the reader. In turn, using a process that I argue can be understood as a sort of reverse bibliotherapy, the narrator casts the reader as a therapist, relying upon a construction of the narrator-reader relationship as a confidential, nonjudgmental space within which to rehearse the disclosure that eventually leads to the possibility of healing and a reclaimed understanding of intimacy.

Each of the first three chapters focuses on interpersonal relationships as crucial, if sometimes dangerous, elements of adolescence. In contrast to novels defined by the type of disclosure, the texts discussed in the fifth chapter, "'What if Someone Reads It?': Concealment and Revelation in Diary Fiction," have been selected because they allow for the consideration of one specific location of disclosure—specifically, the diary. Novels such as Meg Cabot's *The Princess Diaries* and Megan McCafferty's *Sloppy Firsts* use diary entries as they chronicle the events that lead the narrators' decision to withhold information even from their closest friends. The content of the diaries—which require readers to assume the roles of friend, partner in desire, and therapist (at times simultaneously)—draws attention to the ways in which fictional diarists simultaneously assert a desire for privacy and signal an expectation of a reader as the narrator self-consciously discloses thoughts and feelings. In diary novels, I assert, the reader's increased awareness of the limitations of the narrator-reader relationship provides insights into larger cultural expectations about the degree to which young women should share their thoughts, feelings, and experiences with others, and to what degree young women are encouraged to keep some things to themselves.

Ultimately, I investigate the inward-directed intimacy of the reading experience, in which the constructed reader is encouraged to temporarily engage in a perceived relationship with a fictional character; the concluding chapter, "'Let Me Know What You Think': Fan Fiction and the Reimagining of Narrative Intimacy," considers the ways in which narrative intimacy allows for an outward-directed reconsideration of the reading experience. In order to explore the ways in which some fans attempt to extend their reading experiences beyond the fictional spaces of novels, I investigate the ways in which the popularity of fan fiction based on novels for and about adolescent women reveals a desire on the part of some readers to reimagine their roles within the construction of narrative intimacy. By crafting stories that are based on the characters and situations of popular literature, I suggest, many fan fiction writers may be attempting to gain power over the narrative situation—and over their understandings and experiences of intimacy more generally—by moving from role of constructed reader to constructing author.

This chapter has primarily been concerned with examining *how* narrative intimacy comes to be developed in contemporary literature for adolescent women; I wish now to briefly address *why* narrators and readers occupy roles that allow for the implicit understanding of intimate relationships between these two roles. As the following chapters will demonstrate, narrators often construct an understanding of the reader that depends upon the logical gap identified by Lamarque. Even as narrators indicate their need for a reader through the type and content of their disclosure, their concerns about privacy, secrecy, and the potential for betrayal at the hands of friends or romantic partners signal that it is the reader's being situated outside of the text that makes the narrator's disclosure possible. In other words, both narrator and reader must be able to recognize the impossibility of their relationship in order to fully engage in it. Because the reader exists outside of the text, the narrator may make confessions and reveal secrets without fears of the negative responses or violations that characters within the texts may pose. For the reader, in turn, engaging in such a relationship with the narrator allows for the possibility of enjoying disclosure without facing the pressure of having to reciprocate with disclosure of one's own secret thoughts and feelings. The reader may experience intimacy without risk, just as the narrator seeks to do. Ultimately, then, novels that employ narrative intimacy suggest that the only "safe" space within which to fully explore the possibilities of intimacy is the impossible narrator-reader relationship. As the novels discussed here illustrate, this paradox reflects the larger cultural contradictions that surround young women as they navigate their relationships and attempt to determine what they should share, how much they should share, and with whom they should share it.

Chapter 2

"Opening Myself Like a Book to the Spine"
Disclosure and Discretion in Constructions of Friendship

I n *Queen Bees and Wannabes: Helping Your Daughter Survive Cliques, Gossip, Boyfriends, and Other Realities of Adolescence*, a study of adolescent womanhood published in 2002 and marketed to parents of teenage girls, Rosalind Wiseman asserts,

> Your daughter's friendships with other girls are a double-edged sword—they're key to surviving adolescence, yet they can be the biggest threat to her survival as well. The friendships with girls in her clique are a template for many relationships she'll have as an adult. Many girls will make it through their teen years precisely because they have the support and care of a few good friends. . . . On the other hand girls can be each other's worst enemies. (3)

This construction of friendships as a "double-edged sword" reflects a larger cultural tendency to understand the relationships between adolescent women as either crucial or detrimental to their psychological, emotional, and social "survival." By framing girls' friendships as little less than a question of life or death, works such as Wiseman's advance the belief in contemporary American culture that such friendships are necessary for, and simultaneously rife with dangers to, adolescent women's development of identity. In this chapter, I consider how such contradictory messages about friendship are represented in fiction for adolescent women, both in the portrayals of intimate peer relationships and in the construction of narrator-reader relationships.

Although this discussion is concerned primarily with fictional representations of adolescent women's friendships, it is important to note the degree to which this subject has been examined in other media, such as television, film, and particularly nonfiction works for both parents and young women themselves. In the post–*Reviving Ophelia* era, these portrayals have frequently embodied the "double-edged sword" model that Wiseman discusses. Television shows have highlighted the on-again, off-again friendships of girl characters, from Kelly and Brenda on the original *Beverly Hills 90210* in the mid-1990s to Blair and Serena on the current television show *Gossip Girl* (based on a popular series of young adult novels by the same name). Reality shows have likewise capitalized on such portrayals of friendships: the falling-out between *Simple Life* costars and one-time best friends Paris Hilton and Nicole Ritchie made headlines on tabloids and entertainment magazines for months, as did the fighting between *Laguna Beach*'s Lauren Conrad and Kristin Cavallari. Movies such as *Mean Girls*[1] and *Jawbreakers* have also promoted models of adolescent women's friendships as fraught with the danger of betrayal and rejection. The recent popularization of the term "frenemies"—which refers to relationships in which the pretense of friendship is paired with passive aggressive attempts to hurt one another's feelings—further illustrates the degree to which this understanding of friendships between young women has colored cultural representations of this form of intimacy and its potential threats.[2]

The degree to which young women's friendships have served as the subject of nonfiction and self-help literature also demonstrates the prevalence of the "double-edged sword" model. To return to the example of *Queen Bees and Wannabes*, the discussion of adolescent friendships undertaken by Wiseman emphasizes not only the "life or death" construction but also the lifelong significance of these youthful relationships. Because these friendships act as a "template" for the friendships and romantic relationships that may develop during adulthood, Wiseman argues, "girls' reactions to the ups and downs of these friendships are as intense as they'll later feel in intimate relationships" (3). However, while Wiseman sings the praises of adolescent friendships throughout her introductory chapter, the majority of *Queen Bees and Wannabes* is dedicated to a more thorough investigation of the ways in which these peer relationships can be potentially harmful to growth and development. Wiseman spends one chapter identifying and defining the primary roles girls may hold in their social groups or cliques; with the exception of the roles labeled "the floater" (a girl who moves freely between different groups rather than aligning herself with just one) and the self-explanatory "the target," each of these categories depends upon young women's active or passive attempts to claim social power at the expense of others. Whether a young woman is "the queen bee," dictating social interactions among her peers, or "the torn bystander," unable to speak out against the mistreatment of others for fear of becoming a target herself, Wiseman warns parents to consider carefully how their daughter's peer interactions may be damaging to herself or those around her.

Queen Bees and Wannabes is not unique in its celebration and condemnation of teenage girls' friendships. Many other post-*Reviving Ophelia* works explicitly frame friendship and social hierarchies in terms of survival; the title of Charlene C. Giannetti's *Cliques: Eight Steps to Help Your Child Survive the Social Jungle* (2001), for example, not only employs the word "survive" but also equates the interactions of young people with those of wild animals. Other works, such as Natalie Madorsky Elman's *The Unwritten Rules of Friendship: Simple Strategies to Help Your Child Make Friends* (2003), more implicitly create the impression that young women must approach their social interactions as something of a war zone, one that requires them to strategize and build courage. These and many other works aimed at an adult audience of scholars and concerned parents are matched by a number of nonfiction and self-help books written for adolescent women themselves. Like the books aimed at their parents, these works frequently emphasize the importance of having good friends while acknowledging the potential landmines girls might encounter. For example, in the first few paragraphs of her book *Best Buds: A Girl's Guide to Friendship* (2000), Victoria F. Shaw writes, "Everybody needs friends, but in the teen and preteen years, you really need them. . . . You want to hang out with people your own age who share your interests and can understand what you're going through. Your buds help you feel safe and secure as you make your way toward adulthood" (5). Many authors also link friendship to self-esteem, as Carole Weston does in *Girltalk: All the Stuff Your Sister Never Told You* (1997) when she comments, "[A] friend who likes you teaches you to like yourself. Friends exchange the gift of self-confidence" (57–58).

These self-help books also frequently emphasize the importance of intimacy, often framing it as a result of shared interests, activities, and experiences, as well as the importance of both trusting and being trustworthy. Several of the texts I discuss here encourage their readers to make friends with people who are involved in the same activities or seem to enjoy the same types of entertainment, claiming that sharing a common interest is fundamental to developing a lasting friendship. Shaw, for example, explains that you may have found a good friend when "you like to do a lot of the same stuff and talk about the same things" (13). More importantly, though, these books emphasize the importance of being able to tell and keep secrets. In *The Girls' Guide to Friends: Straight Talk on Making Close Pals, Creating Lasting Ties, and Being an All-Around Great Friend* (2002), Julie Taylor writes, "There are no other people in the world like your pals, your buds, your compadres. They're the ones who stick by you through thick and thin, the ones you can tell anything to without worrying that they'll laugh at you or think you're weird" (11). Taylor also claims that a girl's best friend should be one of the most important people in her world because she can "share clothes, makeup, and secrets"—apparently in that order (85).

Because it claims to be written from the point of view of an adolescent girl, *Camy Baker's Love You Like a Sister: 30 Cool Rules for Making and Being a Better Best Friend* (1998) provides a particularly interesting example of nonfiction books about friendship.[3] In a series of brief chapters punctuated with dozens of exclamation points and smiley face emoticons, the titular narrator describes how friendships should be made and maintained. Many of Baker's rules are fairly basic: "Have fun!" she instructs readers. "The most magical moments in life are the really small moments. The moments when no one else is looking. The moments with a great friend when you're just being silly and enjoying each other's company" (132–33). However, Baker also insists upon the necessity of sharing thoughts, feelings, and secrets, a point she emphasizes by sharing—in the form of interviews, emails, letters, or other forms of personal communication—the thoughts, feelings, and occasionally secrets of her own friends, using these as evidence to validate her claims of expertise in the area of friendships.

At the same time, many of these books counter their positive discussions of adolescent women's friendships by including chapters regarding more negative topics: how to handle a fight with a friend, how to "break up" with a friend, and how to deal with being bullied or ignored. For example, Clea Hantman's *30 Days to Finding and Keeping Sassy Sidekicks and BFFs: A Friendship Field Guide* (2009) features an entire section on "How to Overcome the Hard Times: The Obstacles," which includes a chapter titled, "Friendship Is *Not* a Competitive Sport," while L. L. Owen's *Frenemies: Dealing with Friend Drama* focuses exclusively on the problems that are assumed to plague adolescent women's friendships. Like Wiseman, then, these authors draw attention to the potential "dark side" of intimate friendships by alerting adolescent women and their parents to the dangers of losing friendships.

Notably, books for both parents and adolescent women employ many of the techniques of narrative intimacy. Wiseman's introductory chapter directly addresses parents and defines the implied relationship between narrator and reader: "I'm reaching out to you, as parents, educators, and role models, to show you what I think girls are up against as they struggle to become healthy young women who will make our communities better" (17). Likewise, in *Girltalk*, Weston's direct address to the teenage reader is paired with letters and her responses to them, demonstrating her desire to share her thoughts and hear theirs in return. And Taylor not only employs direct address but also makes promises: "You'll never find anyone more supportive, more loving, more loyal, or more *awesome* than your best friend. Promise" (92, emphasis in original). In each of these cases, the use of narrative intimacy acts as a means of creating an implicit bond based on trust, one of the crucial aspects of friendships; in other words, Wiseman, Weston, and Taylor actively develop a narrator-reader relationship that reflects the claims they make about how friendships should function.

It should be noted that many of the claims that such nonfiction works make about the role of friendship in adolescent women's lives reflect the major findings in psychological and sociological studies concerning friendships among young women during adolescence. In particular, psychological studies have repeatedly found that "positive experiences of friendship and peer relations contribute considerably to cognitive, social, and moral development as well as to psychological adjustment and socioemotional health" (Brown, Way, and Duff 206).[4] More generally, studies have shown that during adolescence, friendships may shift from relationships based on shared activities to connections based on shared feelings and beliefs; thus, these relationships tend to become more intimate as young people move from childhood into adolescence (McNelles and Connolly 144).

Furthermore, while adolescent boys' friendships often remain centered on activities (such as sports), adolescent girls' friendships depend more heavily on conversation, gossip, and other opportunities for disclosure. At the same time, the types of "indirect aggression"—gossip, betrayals of trust, and so on—frequently associated with breakdowns of young women's friendships are tied to acts of disclosure, as the vulnerability required by intimate friendships makes possible the type of "mean girl" behavior noted by Wiseman and widely incorporated into cultural portrayals of adolescent women's friendships.[5]

The contradictory models of friendship presented by the nonfiction works I've discussed are frequently matched by similar representations in works of fiction; in particular, the degree to which conflicts regarding disclosure and discretion (or a lack thereof) color these texts reinforces the "double-edged sword" concept as the dominant cultural understanding of adolescent women's friendships. Indeed, questions surrounding disclosure are central to constructions of friendship and, in turn, narrative intimacy in novels such as those discussed in this chapter. Generally speaking, a narrator who understands the reader as occupying the role of friend uses the space of the story in order to make disclosure, often with a degree of immediacy and completeness that suggests an inherent trust in the recipient. Frequently, the narrator self-consciously draws attention to assumed similarities between herself and the reader, actively constructing the reader as an adolescent woman whose ability to identify with the narrator is understood as crucial to the development of their implicit relationship. In turn, the narrator not only models the role of disclosure by offering detailed accounts of her thoughts, feelings, and experiences, but also calls attention to the importance of discretion by highlighting the pieces of information made available to the reader that are withheld from the friends within the text. Likewise, the narrator may position herself as a listener in order to model the reader's role; by acting as a recipient of information herself, the narrator provides an example of how she hopes the reader will respond. Paradoxically, however, the narrator relies on the reader rather than other characters within the text precisely because the reader is prevented from responding by the logical gap between the fictional world and the real that Lamarque describes.

As a result of this paradox, the narrator's relationship with other fictional characters within the novel also works to inform the construction of the reader and narrative intimacy more generally. In their focus on how young women's friendships begin, grow, and change, novels such as those discussed here emphasize the role of intimacy in these relationships largely by asking readers to recognize where it is lacking or absent. Whether the narrator in question is struggling to make friends, questioning the nature of her friendships, or mourning the end of a friendship, her disclosure to the reader almost without exception exceeds that made to any character within the novel itself. In other words, as the narrator shares with the reader her experiences of and feelings about friendship, narrative intimacy becomes a lens through which to recognize flaws in the narrator's relationships with her (fictional) friends—flaws that almost always return to questions of disclosure and discretion.

The novels discussed in this chapter thus provide helpful insights into questions of intimacy through their representations of the relationships between adolescent women as well as their construction of relationships between narrator and reader that mimic, reflect, or complicate understandings of intimate friendships. Sarah Dessen's *Keeping the Moon* and Natasha Friend's *Perfect* both follow their narrators as they seek and explore intimate friendships; Stephanie Hemphill's *Things Left Unsaid* and Siobhan Vivian's *A Little Friendly Advice* follow their narrators' struggles to determine appropriate levels of disclosure within established friendships; and Lizabeth Zindel's *The Secret Rites of Social Butterflies* and E. Lockhart's *Ruby Oliver* series consider the downfall and destruction of once ostensibly intimate friendships. Although these novels approach their representations of friendships in a variety of ways, each offers a view of the often fundamental role that these relationships play in the experiences of adolescent women. More importantly, each of these novels constructs the role of the reader as friend, even as the construction of this role may draw attention to or deny constructions of disclosure within friendships as difficult or dangerous.

Dessen's 1998 novel, *Keeping the Moon,* follows fifteen-year-old Colie Sparks, daughter of a famous fitness guru, who is sent to spend the summer with her eccentric aunt in Colby, North Carolina. Because she is used to identifying herself as what Wiseman would call a "target" and has generally been isolated from her peers as a result, Colie anticipates that her summer vacation will be equally lonely and boring. However, soon after she arrives, Colie accidentally lands a job at the Last Chance Bar and Grill, working with two young women, Morgan and Isabel, with whom she gradually develops her first real friendships. More importantly, she learns that sharing her thoughts, feelings, and experiences with those around her may be difficult, but that such disclosure allows for the possibility of closer relationships and a greater sense of security. Because it follows the development of Colie's first friendships, furthermore, *Keeping the Moon* offers a fairly basic model of narrative intimacy, aligning the relationships that Colie pursues within the novel with the implied relationship that she develops with the reader.

For most of Colie's childhood and early adolescence, she had been overweight and shy, problems that were exacerbated by the fact that she and her single mother moved frequently. However, even after losing almost fifty pounds and living in the same city for a few years, Colie remains an outcast saddled with a false reputation as a slut. When she meets Morgan and Isabel, therefore, Colie initially seeks only to protect herself from further torment; rather than speaking openly to either of them, she actively avoids conversations and generally remains silent. Her early interactions with them in fact only strengthen Colie's resolve to remain isolated, as she prefers being ignored to being mocked. For example, when Isabel insults Colie's lip ring, Colie simply walks away; to the reader, she explains, "Over the years I had perfected removing myself from situations. It was kind of like automatic pilot; I just shut down and retreated, my brain clicking off before anything that hurt could sink in" (26). Even as Morgan and Isabel make friendly gestures towards her, Colie tends to accept their kindness somewhat stiffly, not always understanding how to reciprocate.

Over time, however, Colie begins to consider the possibility of becoming more open to friendships with her coworkers as she closely observes the interactions between Morgan and Isabel, who provide Colie with a model of an intimate, mostly functional friendship. Friends since childhood, Morgan and Isabel work and live together; they anticipate each other's words and behaviors, and they frequently depend on each other for reassurance and guidance. Because they live next door to her aunt, Colie is able to watch them at night, as they sit on their front porch listening to music and talking late into the night. "I was amazed that they always had so much to talk about," Colie says. "From the second they saw each other, there was constant laughing and sarcasm and commentary, something connecting them that pulled taut or fell limp with each thought spoken" (74). This assessment of Morgan and Isabel's friendship demonstrates Colie's own growing understanding of how friendships can operate; Dessen reminds us that because Colie herself has never had a best friend, she has never had access to the kind of communication and comfort that friendships such as Morgan and Isabel's allow, and she struggles to comprehend the fluidity and ease of their relationship.

Colie also learns, however, that even relationships as strong as the one she sees between Morgan and Isabel may face certain challenges. For example, despite the fact that she relies on her as a roommate, coworker, and confidante, Morgan describes the often blunt Isabel as being "friendship impaired" (31). The two also frequently fight over Morgan's relationship with her fiancé, Mark, whom Isabel distrusts. After one fight, Morgan asks Colie if she has a best friend, to which Colie replies, "I don't have any friends" (140). Although this admission temporarily silences Morgan, she eventually says, "Sometimes they're more trouble than they're worth" (140). Colie, who has seen Morgan and Isabel fight and forgive each other several times already, understands that Morgan is simply expressing her frustrations about Isabel rather than truly suggesting that she does not value the friendship. At the same time, this exchange represents a shift in the relationship between Morgan and Colie, who has come to recognize that friendships require some degree of disclosure and trust. By confessing to Morgan that she has no friends, Colie has in fact allowed more fully for the possibility of developing a friendship with Morgan.

Even as she slowly opens herself to Morgan, Colie remains somewhat hesitant to extend any such disclosure to Isabel. Their tense, silence-filled relationship takes a sudden turn, however, following the appearance at the Last Chance of a vacationing classmate of Colie's. When Caroline Dawes, who has been tormenting Colie for years, announces that Colie "is like, the biggest *loser*" and "the biggest slut in our school," Colie initially believes that Isabel will use these comments against her (81). Instead, after hearing Caroline's insults, Isabel invites Colie to spend the afternoon with her, offering Colie advice about her appearance and observing that "the world . . . is chock full of bitchy girls" (84). Although Colie tentatively accepts these gestures of friendship, she remains hesitant about revealing herself to Isabel, believing that the beautiful, strong-willed woman will not be able to understand Colie's struggles. It is not until Colie discovers that Isabel herself was a pudgy, unhappy girl only a few years earlier that she can fully understand and accept Isabel's friendship. While she and Isabel never speak explicitly about their struggles with their appearance and feelings of being excluded, Colie learns that Isabel's often tough-minded advice reflects a genuine awareness of Colie's experience. In contrast to her relationship with Morgan, who both offers and expects disclosures of feelings and thoughts, Colie comes to see that her connection with Isabel can be founded on mutual understanding of each other without necessarily engaging in explicit disclosure.

Colie's growing willingness to create and nurture friendships with Morgan and Isabel also allows Dessen to examine the ways in which those friendships differ from each other. For example, Colie quickly recognizes Morgan's tendency to be overly emotional and notes that Morgan seems to find it easy to reveal her thoughts and feelings to Colie. Although Colie shares neither Morgan's optimism nor her ease in trusting others, she admires these qualities and allows Morgan's behaviors to guide her in some ways. However, she also notes that Morgan's readiness to trust her deceitful fiancé leaves her vulnerable to a great deal of unhappiness when she discovers his infidelity. On the other hand, Isabel does not reveal herself to anyone the way she does to Morgan, and she remains cynical about romance. She and Colie are in fact alike in many ways, and once Colie notes those similarities, she is able to accept Isabel's advice about respecting herself. At the same time, Colie also reflects on Isabel's being "friendship impaired," noting that her unwillingness to engage in disclosure with anyone but Morgan results in difficulties in developing other relationships. Interestingly, then, while Dessen crafts the relationship between Morgan and Isabel in order to provide insight into intimate friendships based on disclosure and trust, Colie's own experiences of friendship with Morgan and Isabel provide some warnings about both being too open or too closed. Colie is thus able to seek the appropriate degree and occasion for disclosure by examining Morgan and Isabel in their relationships with each other and with her.

Dessen actively constructs each of these friendships, which differ in their reliance on explicit disclosure but all depend on some degree of shared experience, as models for both Colie and the reader. As Colie comes to a better understanding about how to develop peer relationships by observing and then becoming friends with Morgan and Isabel, the reader is likewise offered lessons about friendship and intimacy from which to learn. Furthermore, the relationship Dessen establishes between the narrator and the reader follows a gradual progression similar to Colie's developing relationships with her new friends: at the beginning of the novel, Colie's narration attempts to maintain some amount of distance, but she slowly becomes more willing to reveal the events that cause her to be so cautious about peer relationships and eventually establishes a connection with the reader based on full disclosure. By aligning the reader with Colie's new friends in this way, Dessen highlights her message regarding intimacy in friendships that allows the reader to reflect on Colie's being willing to share her story.

The novel opens with a direct address to the reader that draws attention to Colie's role as storyteller: "My name is Nicole Sparks. Welcome to the first day of the worst summer of my life" (1). Although Colie immediately engages the reader's attention and awareness of herself as the recipient of the story, the sarcastic, negative tone suggests an intentional aloofness. The implicit distance that this moment creates is underscored a few pages later by the reader's discovery that "Nicole's" mother and aunt actually call her "Colie." In other words, although Colie's narration immediately addresses the reader, it also represents an attempt (much like those she makes with other characters within the novel) to limit the exchange of information. This moment of simultaneously revealing and concealing herself is inherently contradictory, especially because the very act of acknowledging the reader draws attention to the ways in which Colie is sharing some things with the reader while highlighting the ways in which Colie refrains from sharing others. Furthermore, the present-tense voice used in these opening lines signals that, even though she tells the majority of her story in past tense, this narrating Colie is not significantly temporally different from the experiencing self she narrates.

Once she establishes Colie's attempts to create and maintain a distance from those around her, Dessen begins to use that sense of being separate or apart as a means of highlighting an experience shared between Colie and the reader. For example, Colie develops a habit of sitting on her roof and watching Morgan and Isabel in secret, physically apart but emotionally developing a secret wish to share in the girls' conversations and laughter. This desire becomes particularly clear one night when she disappears into the restaurant's kitchen while Morgan and Isabel have a fight. As their disagreement turns into a celebration, Colie says,

> I stood there, listening with Morgan while Isabel told her the whole story. . . .
> They'd both forgotten I was even there. As Isabel acted out her date, both
> of them laughing, I stayed in the kitchen, out of sight, and pretended she
> was telling me, too. And that, for once, I was part of this hidden language of
> laughter and silliness and girls that was, somehow, friendship. (71)

By not only listening to but imagining herself a part of Morgan and Isabel's conversation, Colie experiences something like intimacy at a remove; she has been made privy, along with the reader, to a conversation that does not involve her, yet her awareness of that conversation allows her to reveal a desire to be part of "that hidden language" of friendship. At the same time, her description of this particular moment of eavesdropping allows Dessen to align Colie's experience of witnessing with the act of reading, which necessarily enables readers to observe events while remaining distinctly removed from them. At the beginning of the novel, then, Colie seems to explore the possibility of developing a friendship with the reader based on their mutual exclusion from other people's relationships, creating an expectation of a susceptible reader who understands and will relate to experiences of loneliness or isolation.

However, even once Dessen establishes this shared experience as the basis for a possible relationship between Colie and the reader, for much of the novel Colie hesitates to reveal to the reader all of the circumstances surrounding her lack of confidence and her fear of establishing new relationships. Eventually, she confesses that she received the nickname "Hole in One" after a country club party, during which she and a young man who had recently moved to their neighborhood spent much of the evening talking on the golf course. When (to borrow Wiseman's term) "queen bee" Caroline Dawes and her friends discovered them, however, they openly derided Colie as a slut; rather than correcting Caroline or defending Colie, the young man walked away. Based on this experience, Colie concluded that disclosure leaves one vulnerable to pain rather than to intimacy, leading her to isolate herself until her summer in Colby. Having confessed this experience to the reader, Colie reinforces her growing willingness to make such disclosures. Notably, she does not share this story with Morgan and Isabel, which signals that the intimacy between the reader and Colie is specific to their relationship, modeled after but not shared with Morgan and Isabel.

Late in the novel, Dessen frames the sameness between Colie and the reader specifically in terms of the reading process. When Colie struggles with whether or not to be more open with Morgan and Isabel, she explains to the reader that "there was something that stopped me, that prevented me from opening myself like a book to the spine, leaving the pages exposed" (141). Colie here reveals her willingness to lay herself open to the reader, explicitly demonstrating her understanding of the relationship between herself and the reader as an intimate one based on a degree of disclosure and trust. At the same time, Dessen's active reinforcement of the reader's position as distinct from that of the characters within the text allows her to construct an implicit message about friendships, suggesting that Colie's ability to reveal herself to the reader does not in fact leave her vulnerable to betrayal or ostracism precisely because the reader, as confidante, remains apart from the fictional world in which Colie operates. In other words, the "logical gap" between them makes possible this construction of the narrator-reader relationship as a friendship.

Generally speaking, *Keeping the Moon* offers a positive view of friendships based on common experiences and open disclosure of thoughts and feelings. Indeed, over the course of the novel, Colie's growing understanding of the value of openness in friendships allows her to freely express herself to those around her and to the reader. However, while Colie finds herself a member of a healthy group of friends at the end of the novel, the presence of Caroline Dawes and her group of "bitchy girls" also draws attention to the fact some peer groups may offer friendship but maintain negative undertones.[6] Although Dessen only briefly highlights the contrast between the real friendships that Colie establishes and the more problematic relationships between Caroline and her social group, the differences between types of friendships does allow her to draw attention to larger questions of adolescent women's friendships.

Although Isabelle Lee, the narrator of Friend's 2004 novel, *Perfect*, has a few friends, she expresses a sense of isolation similar to the feelings Colie expresses at the beginning of *Keeping the Moon*. And, like Colie, Isabelle comes to understand the role that friendship can play in healing from past trauma. Two years after her father's sudden death, Isabelle struggles with the loss of both a parent and the sense of security her former family life had afforded her. Now an eighth grader, she has begun to reclaim control over her life by binging and purging. When her younger sister catches her vomiting, Isabelle agrees to her mother's suggestion that she attend group therapy for girls with eating disorders. During the first meeting, she is shocked to see Ashley Barnum, whom Isabelle regards as junior high royalty. Because of their shared struggles with food, the two become close friends, binging and purging together. While their friendship initially depends on this self-destructive behavior, Friend emphasizes the ways in which disclosure and healthier shared activities help Isabelle and Ashley overcome their eating disorder; in turn, Isabelle uses the reader as a space within which to explore the possibilities of friendship in order to deal with her more specific fears and concerns regarding problems with her family and friends.

Early in the novel, Isabelle reports her lack of status in her school's social hierarchy; in her eyes, Ashley—who not only has many friends but is also the crush of most of the eighth-grade boys—is her exact opposite. Isabelle reveals a desire to develop a closer relationship with Ashley, looking for reasons to speak to her and interpreting each of their conversations as significant. For example, after the two girls have a brief conversation mocking their English teacher, Isabelle reflects, "As I was walking down the hall to my locker, it occurred to me that Ashley Barnum and I had just shared A Moment" (32). Later, when Ashley catches Isabelle's attention from across the room during group therapy, Isabelle thinks, "We were so bonded" (52). Because Isabelle believes Ashley to be special, she invests each of their interactions with a degree of importance that they do not necessarily warrant; indeed, in neither of these instances does either she or Ashley reveal anything about themselves or come to any deeper understanding of the other. However, simply being acknowledged by Ashley seems to Isabelle to be a step toward friendship.

As Isabelle pursues her friendship with Ashley, she acknowledges a willingness to abandon her old friends, Nola and Georgie. "It's weird," she notes: "We used to be really close, Nola, Georgie, and me. . . . We were always over at each other's houses, or going places with each other's families. After my dad died, though, it was different. Nobody knew how to act around me anymore, even my best friends" (81). In reaction to her friends' struggles to relate to her, Isabelle begins to cultivate a careful distance from Nola and Georgie. Although they sit together at lunch and talk on the phone every day—a ritual so well established that Isabelle can predict each stage of the conversation before it happens—Isabelle has carefully concealed from her friends her feelings about her father's death as well as her attempts to cope with those feelings by binging and purging.

While Isabelle keeps secrets from her old friends because she feels that Nola and Georgie will not be able to understand her feelings, her friendship with Ashley begins to develop precisely because the two share a secret. At first, their relationship revolves around their eating disorder; although they regularly binge and purge together, they both remain hesitant to reveal the deeper meanings and motivations behind their eating disorders. Indeed, in the beginning, their friendship has the potential to exacerbate each girl's self-destructive behavior rather than help her to overcome it. Over time, however, this shared activity allows both girls to feel more comfortable in disclosing their secrets to each other. After Isabelle finally summons the courage to confess her feelings about her father's death and her mother's depression, Ashley admits that she's having family problems of her own: her father is having an affair, and her parents are divorcing. Isabelle, then, is able to act as both sender and recipient of disclosure, providing models for the reader of both aspects of friendship.

Through this exchange of information, furthermore, Friend highlights the way in which the girls' attempts to share experiences have made a positive transition from a harmful shared behavior to a beneficial shared disclosure of feelings.

Through her friendship with Ashley, Isabelle gains insight both into her own troubles and into larger questions of intimacy. After having shared her story with Ashley, for example, Isabelle finally chooses to take part in discussion during group therapy and take her first steps toward recovery from her eating disorder. As she tells the girls in her group about the loss of her father, Isabelle reflects, "The words sounded so strange coming out of my mouth, like they belonged to somebody else. For a second I wanted to hide. But then I looked up at everyone and saw that they were looking right back at me, nodding. Getting it" (168–69). Isabelle's ability to disclose this information and accept the understanding of those around her represents, for her, an important step in her personal growth and healing process.[7] Over the course of the novel, then, Friend constructs the development of Isabelle's friendship with Ashley—which grows from nothing more than a secret habit to a relationship built upon mutual disclosure and trust—as an important element in Isabelle's identity development.

At the same time, Friend's construction of the reader mirrors the hesitations and desires for intimacy reflected in Isabelle's relationships with characters within the novel. Although Isabelle is fairly forthcoming about the facts of her father's death and her mother's inability to cope with the loss, she refrains from much personal disclosure on this subject for much of the book. Instead, she initially adopts a somewhat detached voice, directly addressing but not seeking an overly intimate relationship with the reader. When she first encounters Ashley in therapy, Isabelle tells the reader, "Here's what you need to know about Ashley Barnum to understand: First of all, the name. *Ashley Barnum.* Royalty, right? When Ashley Barnum walks down the hall at school, you know it" (12). More importantly, "she is the kind of person you wish you could be friends with, even though she doesn't know you exist" (13). Although these pieces of information are addressed to the reader, they reflect Isabelle's sense of distance from Ashley. Furthermore, because they construct an understanding of the reader as little more than a copy of Isabelle herself—assuming that the reader shares Isabelle's feelings of being an outsider and her desire to be friends with Ashley—these moments encourage the reader to feel an affinity with Isabelle. Notably, the shift from the past-tense narration Isabelle generally uses to the present-tense narration employed in her direct address to the reader allows Friend to draw attention to the immediacy of the telling, in turn emphasizing the engaging nature of the narration.

As Isabelle begins to develop her relationship with Ashley, her address to the reader changes, seeming at times to actively construct the reader as an outsider as Isabelle begins to feel like she may find a place to belong. For example, immediately before Ashley and Isabelle's first shared binge and purge session, Ashley asks if Isabelle is hungry, to which Isabelle replies, "I could eat." To the reader, she adds, "You have no earthly idea how much I could eat" (68). To some degree, this comment seems like nothing more than a sarcastic aside. However, it also casts the reader as an outsider in this situation, reflecting the closer bond between Ashley and Isabelle because of their shared eating disorder. Indeed, this moment reflects a trend throughout the novel in which Isabelle adopts a role similar to the role she believes Ashley has played in her own life. In other words, because Isabelle felt so gratified by Ashley's willingness to extend the possibility of friendship, she uses Ashley's behavior as a model for her own treatment of the reader, understanding herself at this point in the novel as being in a position either to exclude the reader as she herself was once excluded or to extend some sort of gestures of friendship as Ashley has done.

As a consequence of Isabelle's shifting understanding of her relationship with both Ashley and the reader, the ways in which she directly addresses the reader evolve over the course of the novel. Once she has begun to feel more secure in her friendship with Ashley, for example, Isabelle's disclosure to the reader frequently takes the form of advice. After an upsetting incident with her mother, Isabelle bikes to a local convenience store to binge and purge. She explains the process in detail: "I alternated handfuls of potato chips and HoHos with swallows of Diet Coke. The bubbles burned my nose and made my eyes water, but I didn't stop. It always feels better coming up than going down. You just have to get yourself to that point and then everything takes care of itself" (92). Following the example that Ashley has set by giving Isabelle "diet tips" (one of which leads to an ill-fated experiment with laxatives), Isabelle positions herself as a guide, offering the reader tips and assuming a position of authority over what is now treated as an activity she shares with both Ashley and the reader.[8]

More importantly, however, just as Isabelle recognizes the benefits of sharing through disclosure in her relationship with Ashley, she models that type of disclosure in her relationship with the reader, moving beyond the eating disorder to more fully explore her feelings and concerns in open address to the reader. In the novel's final pages, Isabelle has not only begun to take part in group discussions but has also had several successful individual meetings with the group leader; she has not binged or purged for almost thirty-six hours; and she and her sister have successfully arranged a Hanukkah celebration⁹ and persuaded their mother to grieve with them for their lost father. Isabelle reflects on the significance of this moment in her family's healing with a confidence that signals the degree of her own move towards better health: "You may think it's a crazy way to spend Christmas Eve, standing in the den with your mom and your sister, not hanging ornaments on a Christmas tree, but hanging pictures of your dead dad on the wall. You might think it's nuts, but it's not" (171). This direct address to the reader—and, more importantly, the implicit claim that she understands how the reader will react to this family moment—reflects both the now-established relationship and Isabelle's personal development into a more confident young woman.

Although Friend's novel certainly acknowledges the ways in which friendships built upon a shared unhealthy behavior can be threatening, her portrayal of Isabelle's growing awareness of her own identity within the context of her friendship with Ashley allows for a more positive representation of adolescent women's friendships. The positive impact of their intimate friendship is reflected in the development of the relationship between Isabelle and the reader, to whom she gradually reveals the full scope of her thoughts and emotions as she gains confidence; the reader becomes as much of a confidante—and thus as much a part of Isabelle's recovery and maturation—as Ashley does.

While both *Keeping the Moon* and *Perfect* ultimately offer positive views of friendship and the importance of intimacy, novels for adolescent women frequently explore the challenges and dangers of intimate friendships as well. In some cases, the recognition of a friendship's shortcomings allows for a break from negative or harmful relationships and a greater understanding of the benefits that healthy disclosure can bring. In *Things Left Unsaid*, her 2005 verse novel, Hemphill explores the narrator's growing understanding of her friendships and her own roles within those relationships as she struggles to develop her own identity. When Sarah Lewis, who has always been a good student and obedient daughter, develops a friendship with the moody, unpredictable Robin, her life changes completely. Sarah describes herself shutting down and shutting others out, defying and disappointing her parents, and filling her closet with black and gray clothing. As her friendship with Robin becomes central to her life, Sarah willingly distances herself from her friends Amanda and Gina. Robin's suicide attempt, then, leaves Sarah questioning not only how well she really knows Robin but also the degree to which that relationship has left Sarah isolated, vulnerable, and confused. As she struggles to regain a sense of control over her life, Sarah's evaluation of her past, present, and future friendships reveals her new understanding of the importance of intimacy.

When describing her best friends Amanda and Gina, Sarah reflects upon the qualities that once brought them together. Specifically, she recalls specific physical similarities that act as touchstones for her. When she first met Amanda in fifth grade, Sarah remembers, "I glanced down / at my purple flip flops, realized / she wore the same pair. Amanda giggled, / became my friend on the spot" (10). Likewise, Sarah uses a physical commonality between herself and Gina as evidence of their intimacy: "I know Gina like my face in the mirror, / We wear the same size shoe" (13). As they enter their junior year of high school, however, Sarah begins to feel frustrated with Amanda's immaturity and Gina's tendency to compete with Sarah for grades or boys. She thus enthusiastically pursues her new friendship with Robin despite Amanda's concerns and Gina's complaints, allowing the distance she has already noticed to grow; although she reflects upon the loss of the closeness that she used to feel with her old friends, she more actively desires the opportunity to redefine herself and sees Robin as her guide to new experiences and understanding.

When she first begins to spend time with Robin, Sarah initially adopts the same approach she has used to define her friendships with Gina and Amanda by seeking physical similarities between herself and her new friend. Eventually, she discovers that both she and Robin have a small scar in or near their mouths, in both cases the result of having bitten into an extension cord at eight months old (40). She says, "You don't find a friend / who had the same freak childhood accident / by chance. Robin and I are bonded by scar" (41). However, though Sarah imagines the scars as a sort of fated link between her and Robin, their placement near or in the girls' mouths also emphasize the ways in which Sarah's friendship with Robin becomes intricately tied to her understanding of her own ability to speak and express herself. She reports that she always thinks carefully before speaking when she's around Robin, frequently choosing not to say anything at all, "fearing that what I say will be stupid / or wrong or both" (91). Although she believes that Robin is now her best friend, Hemphill emphasizes Sarah's unwillingness or inability to speak openly to her in order to reveal that the friendship is in fact denying her the opportunity to develop an intimate bond with Robin.

More generally, Sarah finds herself depending on Robin not only for company at school and on the weekends, but also as a sort of guide, helping Sarah to shed her old "good girl" persona in order to develop a newer, more daring one. Over time, however, Sarah begins to understand Robin's instructions less as guidance and more as commands:

> I don't even choose the clothes I wear / to school anymore. The committee of Robin / casts her ballot, and the elected miniskirt / slides onto my hips. I am *always* / given advice and I am *always* taking it. (77)

In this moment, Sarah demonstrates her understanding of her role as recipient of disclosure; rather than hearing Robin's thoughts and feelings, Sarah has come to understand listening as little more than a synonym for obeying orders. Although Sarah initially welcomes Robin's interest in her, seeing it as a means of escaping her old friendships and her old, goody two-shoes self, Hemphill suggests that her new friendship has simply placed a new set of limitations on her sense of identity. While she no longer sees herself as the well-behaved honors student she was, she still lacks a sense of who she is, instead defining herself in terms of Robin's expectations.

After Robin's suicide attempt, Sarah finds herself lost and consumed with guilt, believing that she could have prevented her friend's desperate act. "I should have seen that she / gravitated toward black holes / and held back her coattails," she says. "But I misread the signs" (156). As a result of her feelings of confusion and guilt, Sarah begins to withdraw even more from those around her, especially when Gina voices Sarah's unspoken belief that she has been a bad friend. In the process, Hemphill highlights Sarah's growing awareness that her inability to speak to Robin may have been matched by Robin's own unwillingness or inability to speak to Sarah. When Sarah calls Robin in the rehabilitation center, those calls go unanswered; Sarah finds herself surrounded by silence, both in her own lack of a voice and the lack of her friends' voices around her.

In the second half of the novel, Hemphill draws parallels between Sarah's personal growth and her portrayal of Annie Sullivan in the school's production of *The Miracle Worker*, a play that emphasizes the development of relationships that allow for and depend on finding and maintaining lines of communication. At first, Sarah uses the role as a crutch: "Sometimes it feels easier to play / Annie than to walk through the school halls / in my own sneakers" (228). Although she no longer faces Robin's instructions and expectations, Sarah does not yet feel comfortable expressing herself; instead, she borrows Annie Sullivan's words and emotions. Over time, however, she finds confidence through this role, which allows her to explore her own struggles with open communication. She even finds the courage to confront Gina, saying, "I think our friendship / got lost somewhere. / And because we never really / talked about it, things sometimes / get weird between us" (236). This emphasis on Sarah's growing willingness to reveal her feelings and concerns to Amanda and Gina acts as an explicit acknowledgment of the importance of communication in friendships.

Ultimately, Sarah's struggles to understand herself and her relationships with those around her force her to recognize the importance of being able to express herself in her own terms. By renewing her friendships with Gina and Amanda, Sarah begins to understand how both she and the relationships benefit from her newfound willingness to reveal her thoughts and feelings. In the novel's final pages, she writes,

> I stopped hiding behind long sweater sleeves, / exposed myself to a few ultraviolet rays, / and let people see a little of the Sarah / behind makeup and wardrobe. / Not everyone loves what I can show them. / But a few oddballs, myself included, / are beginning to really like Sarah Lewis. (259)

Indeed, like Isabelle in *Perfect*, Sarah reveals a newfound confidence and a clearer sense of self through her strengthened friendships; furthermore, as both narrators must consider their new friendships within the context of earlier relationships, this shift in confidence plays an important role in modeling for the reader the idea that the types of relationships and the role disclosure will play in them change over time.

As Sarah's relationships with Gina, Amanda, and Robin demonstrate the ways in which friendships may either inhibit or encourage disclosure and the development of intimacy, Hemphill's construction of the relationship between Sarah and the reader likewise reflects that Sarah's frustrations with her inability to express herself out loud to her friends are paired with a constant, insistent degree of self-disclosure and desire for expression. For example, the novel opens with the words, "What you don't know is that / I have a sixth toe on my left foot" (1). The entire first poem, "Prologue," is in fact a list of information about Sarah, ending with the claim, "I am a piece of glass. I see you / stand behind me, and see clearly / when I stand alone" (2). This direct address and the content of the opening poem offer the first view of a contradiction that continues throughout the novel: Sarah claims to be concealing herself from the reader even as she actively reveals things about herself. Throughout the novel, Hemphill positions the reader both as witness to Sarah's struggles with her friends and as the confidante to whom Sarah feels able to express herself, offering insights into Sarah's complicated and often contradictory understanding of friendship and intimacy.

Although the "you" of this poem is never defined, Sarah seems to address not only the reader but also her parents, teachers, and friends, the people to whom she has always told "the truth, covered up under / a yellow rain slicker, diminished / by good deodorant, made palatable / with crimson lip gloss" (1–2). In some ways, then, Hemphill generally constructs the role of the reader as adjacent to but independent from the roles of any of the characters within the novel, aligning the reader with those figures from whom Sarah has repeatedly concealed herself—and, more importantly, from whom she continues to conceal herself over the course of the novel. Sarah's ability to confess to the reader that she has "covered [herself] up," however, acts as a signal that she has come to understand the importance of disclosure; indeed, because the reader occupies a position that forces an awareness of Sarah's desires both to hide herself from and to reveal herself to those around her, the reader effectively becomes Sarah's most significant friend.

However, on two occasions Sarah aligns the reader immediately with Robin. In the first case, in a poem entitled "What I Might Say if Robin Were Here," Sarah admits to her desire to be the kind of friend who actually takes part in the relationship, "not the doll of limited speech / who talks only when you pull her string" (245). With this temporary shift, Hemphill allows Sarah to direct her frustrations at the reader rather than the absent Robin. The shift occurs again in the final pages of the novel, when Sarah presents the reader with a letter to Robin (written in prose) entitled "Invitation." Rather than welcoming Robin to return to their old relationship, which Sarah now understands as harmful to both of them, Sarah tells Robin, "The species of friend we were is extinct to me" (261). By briefly redefining the application of the word "you," which refers to the reader in most other cases, Hemphill draws attention to the differences between Sarah's relationship with Robin and her relationship with the reader. Whereas Sarah has repeatedly expressed her concerns about being fully open with Robin, she has been able to reveal herself to the reader; only by conflating the reader and Robin can Sarah find herself comfortable in fully expressing herself regarding her frustrations, angers, and hopes regarding her relationship with Robin. The letter also provides insight into Sarah's motivations in relating her story to the reader. Moving beyond her previous understanding of intimacy, which was based on superficial phys- ical similarities rather than the sharing of feelings or experiences, Sarah reflects a new view of her relationships as dependent upon some degree of disclosure. Having learned, furthermore, about the dangers and struggles that may result from a friendship that stifles self-expression and disclo- sure, Sarah now seeks to explore a new "species of friend"; Hemphill, then, casts the reader in the role of a friend who not only allows Sarah to speak but also offers Sarah the opportunity to use that disclosure as a means of learning more about herself.

Unlike Sarah, who becomes aware of Robin's influence over her early in their friendship, Ruby, the narrator of Vivian's *A Little Friendly Advice* (2008), does not initially realize how much control her best friend, Beth, is able to exert over her. Indeed, they have been friends for much of their lives, and Ruby considers Beth the only person to whom she can speak openly about her thoughts and feelings. Ruby is therefore shocked to learn that Beth has not always been forthcoming with her; more to the point, Beth has concealed secrets from Ruby out of a misguided belief that she knows what is best for her friend. Over the course of the novel, as she struggles with the sudden reappearance of her absent father and confronts the possibility of her first romantic relationship, Ruby wonders to what degree her dependence on Beth as a confidante has limited her ability to make her own decisions and, in turn, reconsiders her already problematic understanding of intimacy. More importantly, unlike the novels discussed earlier in this chapter, *A Little Friendly Advice* frames the question of inti- macy not in order to reinforce the importance of disclosure, but rather to construct an understanding that even in close friendships, disclosure should be somewhat limited or restrained.

At the beginning of the novel, Ruby explains the very different relation- ships she shares with her friends Beth, Maria, and Katherine: she has been best friends with Beth since they were seven and close friends with Maria for about a year, but she has only known Katherine for a few weeks and feels conflicted about the new member of their small group. To some degree, Ruby's discomfort stems from the fact that Katherine does not hesitate to share her feelings with others; in fact, her inclusion in their group has resulted from her spontaneous confession to near-stranger Beth about her parents' separation. Despite the fact that Katherine's family dysfunction mirrors Ruby's own experience, Ruby reacts to the new friendship with suspicion, reporting, "I found it weird that Katherine would admit all that to a relative stranger" (8). In response to Katherine's tendency to say whatever she is thinking, Ruby becomes increasingly reticent around Katherine and resents it when Beth speaks about Ruby's problems in front of their new friend. Vivian constructs the tension between Katherine and Ruby in order to highlight the ways in which Ruby actively avoids self-disclosure and the possibility of intimacy with Katherine, even when it could offer the potential for healing.

Ruby's friendship with Maria is also marked by a lopsided degree of disclosure, again because of Ruby's reluctance to reveal information about herself. Even after her father's return, Ruby refuses to talk to Maria about it, noting, "I know Maria has a lot of questions about my family situation. Maybe it's weird that we've never really talked about it before, even though I consider her a close friend" (20). Throughout the novel, Vivian emphasizes the large gap between Maria's willingness to listen and Ruby's own unwillingness to speak to her. Indeed, at one point Ruby admits that "it's a wonder [Maria] still likes me. Our friendship is so one-sided" (175). While Ruby understands that her inability to share any secrets with Maria endangers their friendship, she also regards with some consternation Maria's tendency to talk about her thoughts and feelings, especially in terms of her romantic relationships. For example, when Ruby declines to share the details of her first kiss with a boy named Charlie, Maria complains, "You are so mean, Ruby. You never share anything with me!" Despite her awareness that Maria is right, Ruby excuses her behavior to herself, believing that "Maria shares that stuff easily because it happens so easily for her. I'm a different, difficult story altogether" (132). Just as she refuses to speak to Katherine about their family problems, Ruby avoids disclosing her experiences and concerns to Maria despite the possibility that doing so may help her to pursue her own romantic attachments. At the same time, Ruby's awareness of her friends' attitudes towards disclosure also provides insight into the value she places on listening. Because she has carefully attended to the thoughts and feelings her friends have revealed to her—even when they cause her discomfort—Ruby provides a model for the reader of listening as a fundamental aspect of friendship.

In fact, the only person with whom Ruby feels comfortable sharing her secrets is Beth, at least in part because Beth has shared so many experiences with Ruby. At the same time, even in conversations with her closest friend, Beth admits to a sort of reluctance about disclosing her thoughts and emotions. After her father's return, Ruby understandably struggles with feelings of anger and confusion, but she notes that

> part of me doesn't want to bother Beth about how I'm feeling. I mean, this is well-worn territory between us, and I doubt she could say something comforting to me that she hasn't already told me a million times before. The thing is, when friends ask you what's wrong, there's part of them that doesn't really want to know the answer. Especially if they've seen you upset before over the same thing, again and again and again. (68)

Here, Ruby reveals her concerns that she may be trespassing or abusing her friendship with Beth because she relies so heavily on her, suggesting that taking Beth into her confidence once again may be a "bother" rather than an expected part of friendship. More importantly, however, Vivian provides more insights into Ruby's struggles with interpersonal relationships; Ruby's belief that friends "[don't] really want to know" about her thoughts and feelings allows her to justify her own reluctance to be more open.

Throughout the novel, Ruby frames her friendship with Beth in terms of obligation, believing that she "owes" Beth for all the times that Ruby has burdened her with her troubles. As far as Ruby is concerned, Beth is her closest friend both because of all the things they have already shared and because of all the things Ruby is willing to share with her. As time passes, though, Ruby realizes that she may not actually understand the dynamics of her friendship with Beth. When Ruby finds a letter from her father that Beth has concealed from her, she is shocked not only by the note itself but also by Beth's decision to hide it. At first, Ruby believes that Beth is just waiting for the right moment to talk to her about the letter; however, Beth passes up several opportunities to talk to Ruby about the letter. Suspicious and confused about Beth's actions, Ruby says she "can't believe how easy Beth seems to lie to me, again and again and again. I wonder if it's something she's struggling with. Is it hard for her? If I were holding in a secret that big, I'd have it painted all over my face. It'd be really tough to keep it from her. Probably even impossible" (144). For the first time, Ruby begins to consider the effects of concealment not only in terms of what she conceals, but in terms of what is concealed *from* her. Furthermore, the realization that Beth does not share everything with her—which upends Ruby's understanding of their intimacy—leaves Ruby feeling hurt and vulnerable.

When Ruby finally, angrily confronts Beth about her secret, she is shocked to learn that this is only one of several pieces of information that

Beth has concealed from Ruby over the course of their friendship. Beth confesses that she discovered Ruby's mother having an affair, a fact that Ruby has never known and that completely alters her understanding of her parents' divorce, and explains that she kept this information from Ruby because she knew how much pain it would cause. Likewise, she has concealed the letter from Ruby's father because she believes that meeting with him would be a bad idea and she wanted to prevent Ruby from making an unwise decision. Because Beth knows so much about Ruby—in some ways, she knows more about Ruby's life than Ruby herself does—Beth is capable of truly hurting or endangering Ruby, attempting to dictate Ruby's actions and choices. Only after Beth confesses does Ruby fully appreciate the degree to which Beth's seemingly kind "advice" and her attempts to push Ruby into friendships with Maria and Katherine, as well as a romantic relationship with a boy that Beth has chosen but in whom Ruby has no interest, are acts of control rather than kindness. Through Ruby's new view of her friendship with Beth, Vivian illustrates the dangers of disclosing too much or too freely, even with someone who is considered a close friend; because Ruby has always understood that sharing her experiences and feelings with Beth is a necessary part of their friendship, she has never examined or questioned the ways in which Beth uses that information to limit Ruby's own choices. That Ruby begins narrating her story to the reader at a point in her life when she has come to question the role of disclosure in her closest friendship, in turn, signals her desire to find a safer confidante than Beth, a friend who can receive Ruby's disclosure without judgment or interference.

Ruby's struggle to navigate this shift in her relationship with Beth highlights Vivian's criticism of friendships that do not allow for or depend on mutual disclosure. For example, Ruby does not really benefit from her off-balance relationships with Maria and Katherine, who share with her without receiving such disclosure in return, until she becomes open to the possibility of being more open with them about her feelings. More importantly, however, Vivian emphasizes that the relationship on which Ruby has been most dependent and in which she has been the most emotionally available has likewise relied on one-way rather than mutual disclosure. In other words, although Ruby often expresses her willingness to share with Beth, all the reader sees of Beth is her willingness to conceal things from Ruby. Indeed, that Ruby has not had to play the role of listener for Beth despite her clear willingness to do so signals to the reader the imbalance of their relationship. Even if Beth's intentions are ultimately founded in her true affection and concern for Ruby, Vivian suggests, her actions illustrate the ways in which the uneven development of intimacy may render a friendship dangerous.

Throughout the novel, Vivian constructs the relationship between Ruby and the reader in order to emphasize the ways in which Ruby embodies contradictions about intimacy and friendship. From the beginning of the novel, Ruby acknowledges and emphasizes her struggles to be more open to friendships and disclosure. "It's certainly no secret that I've got some serious emotional baggage," Ruby admits to the reader. "Make that a complete set of luggage with wheels for easy transportation, zippered sections for compartmentalizing, and ballistic nylon for an impenetrable shell. . . . All my issues are packed nicely and neatly away" (33–34). However, while Ruby will not talk to Maria or Katherine about this "emotional baggage," she willingly unpacks it for the reader, revealing not only her thoughts and feelings about her present family situation but also including flashbacks that give the reader access to Ruby's personal history, which she has otherwise shared only with Beth. As the novel highlights the problematic assumptions that have dictated Ruby's relationship with Beth, however, Vivian allows Ruby to develop a friendship with the reader that, while similar in its degree of disclosure, relies upon the boundary between fiction and reality in order to figure the reader as an inherently safer confidante than Beth. By constructing an understanding of the reader as an ideal friend based almost exclusively on the fact that the reader cannot abuse or misapply the information Ruby discloses, the novel ultimately models a contradictory understanding of intimate friendships and the nature of mutual disclosure.

Like *A Little Friendly Advice*, Zindel's 2008 novel *The Secret Lives of Social Butterflies* examines the degree to which sharing intimate details may present the dangers of being manipulated, controlled, or even blackmailed by "friends." However, unlike the relationship between Ruby and Beth, which has been established and strengthened over time and which the reader is led to believe may be able to recover from the secrets that threatened it, the relationships that narrator Maggie Wishnick builds with her new friends Victoria, Sydney, and Lexi are based from the beginning on compulsory disclosure and the potential for betrayal or blackmail. Throughout the novel, Zindel critiques this type of "friendship," emphasizing the idea that intimacy achieved in this way may be particularly harmful to personal development; at the same time, she contradicts the novel's explicit messages about friendship as she constructs a relationship between Maggie and the reader that depends on mutual complicity in the sharing of other people's secrets.

When Maggie arrives at the exclusive new all-girls' preparatory school in New York City, she initially feels lonely and out of place. She struggles not only to make new friends but also to reconcile herself to changes caused by her parents' recent separation. However, after she meets Victoria—who, like Caroline in *Keeping the Moon*, is a fictional representation of Wiseman's "queen bee"—Maggie finds herself welcomed into a small, exclusive club called the Revelers. Although she initially feels gratified by her inclusion in this group, Maggie quickly discovers that Victoria and her friends expect a degree of disclosure with which Maggie feels uncomfortable. Maggie learns about the Wall, a secret document on which Victoria and her friends record the secrets that they collect about their classmates and teachers. At each meeting, each girl is expected to bring at least three "truths," which vary in degree from minor embarrassments to major scandals. When explaining the process to a hesitant Maggie, Victoria figures this disclosure as healthy: "'On this wall here,' Victoria [says], 'we can say it as we see it. No holding back—and not just about ourselves, about everyone at school, too'" (76). Victoria also frames this disclosure as a means of gaining a sense of security and comfort, arguing that sharing the information allows the girls to feel less alone in their fears and anxieties. At the same time, Zindel draws attention to the fact that the friends' rules deny Maggie the possibility of choosing her own comfortable level of disclosure; if she does not take part in the ritual to Victoria's satisfaction, she faces exclusion from the group. This understanding of disclosure therefore problematizes the friendships between Maggie, Victoria, Sydney, and Lexi, casting them as obligations rather than emotionally healthy and beneficial relationships.

The explicit connection Victoria sees between personal information and interpersonal relationships initially allows Maggie to feel more comfortable with taking part in the weekly ritual, and she begins to eavesdrop on and investigate the activities of those around her. In the process, Maggie offers a model of herself as listener that is distinct from that provided by other narrators discussed here. Whereas Ruby, for example, positions herself as a reader who willingly accepts disclosure from others as a necessary and generally healthy part of friendship, Maggie's version of listening relies on her either accepting Victoria's explanations and orders without question or positioning herself as an unknown (and not necessarily welcome) recipient of disclosure between others. For example, when she hides in a bathroom stall and overhears a conversation between two girls that provides her first "big" truth, Maggie provides a model of listening that effectively privileges eavesdropping and "stolen" information over willing disclosure in her friendships with the other Revelers.

When the Wall and all of the secrets that it contains are discovered during a party at Victoria's house, Maggie's fears are confirmed. While the members of the Revelers are each ostracized from the school community by classmates whose secrets have now been revealed to the entire school, they also face conflict within the group when Victoria places exclusive blame for the discovery on Maggie. Although Sydney stands by Maggie during the fallout, Maggie loses the tentative friendships she had begun to develop with people outside of the Revelers—particularly a young woman who had helped Maggie during the first days of school and who becomes the victim of Maggie's worst betrayal. Maggie's decision to betray the first friend she made at her new school in fact reflects Don E. Merten's finding that "socially ambitious girls were not only inclined to leave current friends for more popular girls but also often used a previous friend's secrets as 'gifts' to their new friends" (123). Zindel emphasizes, then, that the disclosure in which Maggie has taken part has cost her social status, damaged her reputation, and threatened her ability to pursue new friendships.

Like *A Little Friendly Advice*, Zindel's novel creates a contradictory construction of friendship by simultaneously warning against disclosure while crafting a narrator-reader relationship that depends upon the narrator's willingness to share thoughts, feelings, and—perhaps most importantly, in this case—secrets. Here again, the narrative constructs an understanding of the reader as a "safe" friend, one who cannot use the narrator's disclosure against her. At the same time, *The Secret Rites of Social Butterflies* further problematizes this contradictory portrayal of friendships by implicating the reader in the secrets being shared among Maggie and the other Revelers while demanding that the reader accept Maggie as a trustworthy friend. Indeed, just as Victoria uses information to control those around her, the narrative of this novel implicitly controls the reader through the disclosure of information about characters who exist exclusively for the purpose of having secrets. In many ways, then, the narrative construction of the relationship between Maggie and the reader follows the dangerous example of the Revelers' problematic treatment of enforced intimacy even as Maggie claims to be criticizing it.

In the prologue, as she briefly summarizes the story that she is about to share, Maggie directly addresses the reader: "I can't expect you to understand everything completely yet. If I told you the details right now, I'll bet you would feel as surprised as I did the day Victoria told me the Revelers existed. But don't worry: like me, you, too, will come to see the light, or shall I say, the writing on the wall" (1). In this moment of narrative self-consciousness, as she promises to explain these somewhat cryptic remarks, Maggie establishes the foundation for a relationship between herself and the reader based on Maggie's ability to inform and enlighten. Indeed, by acknowledging that the reader cannot "understand everything completely yet," Maggie claims a degree of authority while suggesting that the reader must trust that Maggie will share that authority as she tells the story. Because she also assumes that the reader will share her initial naïveté about and interest in the Revelers and their secrets, Maggie gestures toward the possibility of the reader experiencing an affinity for her and her experiences. Maggie's implicit hope that the reader will trust her—established when she tells the reader not to worry—is repeated throughout the novel as she unveils more of her own story along with the secrets she and the Revelers have collected. She even explicitly demands the reader's trust near the end of the novel when, during the party, Maggie allows herself to be distracted momentarily from guarding the door that conceals the Wall. Maggie says, "This is the only time I let my eye wander from the NO TRESPASSING! sign. I swear" (247). By attaching the phrase "I swear" to a confessional instant, Maggie reinforces her hope that the reader will find her trustworthy.

Throughout the novel, furthermore, Maggie reveals to the reader certain thoughts and feelings—particularly regarding the fact that her new friends have more money than she does—that she does not share with Victoria and the others. Maggie also continues to relate to the reader her hesitations about the Wall, especially once Victoria has established that expressing those hesitations aloud may result in Maggie's exclusion from the group. At the same time, however, Maggie reveals the secrets that she gathers about her classmates and teachers not only to the Revelers but to the reader as well, thereby suggesting that her concerns about other people's right to privacy may be outweighed by her—and, she assumes, the reader's—curiosity. By including the many secrets that she and her friends gather, Maggie implicates the reader in the Revelers' activities, making the reader complicit with a system of disclosure that equates knowledge with power.

In the novel's final pages, Maggie reflects on the lessons she has learned about intimacy and friendship, continuing to borrow from Victoria's treatment of her. Although Maggie has clearly come to see Victoria as mean-spirited and selfish, she employs Victoria's reasoning regarding the necessity of disclosure in adolescent development. "I still feel like there's a struggle going on between the kinds of things kids really feel and the way our parents and other adults want us to feel," Maggie tells the reader, echoing the justification Victoria has earlier presented to her regarding the rituals of the Wall. She goes on to reveal, "I also haven't yet decided where I draw my own lines between what I want to keep private and what I feel is right to expose" (288). Although Maggie clearly seems to be relating to the reader, who she assumes faces a similar dilemma as a necessary rite of passage into adulthood, her claim of having struggled about what to reveal and what to conceal rings false as a conclusion to a novel in which the narrator has shown no hesitation in disclosing her thoughts and feelings.

Whereas most of the novels in this chapter focus on the development or maintenance of friendships, Lockhart's *The Boyfriend List* (2005), *The Boy Book* (2006), *The Treasure Map of Boys* (2009), and *Real Live Boyfriends* (2010) more closely examine the aftershocks of damaged or destroyed friendships. Although the titles suggest a concern with romance, and while ex-boyfriend Jackson, new friend Noel, and several other boys provide the organizational scaffolding for the novels,[10] the true source of narrator Ruby Oliver's anxiety has much more to do with her former best friends, Kim, Nora, and Cricket. After a series of events leads to Ruby losing Jackson to Kim, then losing all of her friends after accidentally kissing Jackson at a school dance, Ruby finds herself isolated, confused, and suffering from the panic attacks that lead to her seeing a therapist. Over the course of the four novels, she reflects on her relationships with her now former friends, especially Kim, while seeking to build or rebuild friendships that will hopefully provide a healthier experience of intimacy. However, this process proves complicated, particularly when Ruby begins to develop romantic feelings for her friend Noel, in whom her friend Nora has already expressed interest. As she faces these struggles with the help of her therapist, Doctor Z, Ruby also relies on the reader as a nonjudgmental outlet to whom she can explain her side of the story and express her feelings of anger, frustration, and hurt. Throughout the novels, Ruby simultaneously acknowledges the dangers of revealing herself while attempting to rebuild relationships through disclosure; more importantly, Ruby's continued willingness to make herself vulnerable to the reader allows Lockhart to offer a construction of intimacy that suggests that despite the potential dangers, seeking intimacy is ultimately worthwhile.

From the beginning of the series, Lockhart emphasizes Ruby's confusion and anxiety regarding the role and boundaries of disclosure within her friendships, which has resulted, at least in part, from the fact that her friendships with Kim, Cricket, and Nora had always depended on revealing and keeping secrets. For years, the girls recorded their thoughts and feelings in a notebook they called "The Boy Book," which—despite its ostensible focus on the opposite sex—set forth a series of expectations and guidelines for the girls' friendships. For example, a list entitled "Rules for Dating in a Small School" includes the command "Tell your friends every little detail! We promise to keep it just between us" (*Book* 16). Even after the events that lead to her becoming ostracized from these friends, Ruby finds herself bound by their old rules. When Jackson attempts to communicate with Ruby behind Kim's back, Ruby considers telling Kim because "I feel like it's what I'm *supposed* to do. Like that's the code we set up when we wrote *The Boy Book*" (*Book* 43). Although Ruby has always found it comforting to be able to share her thoughts and feelings—even about embarrassing romantic incidents—with her friends, these references to and excerpts from their old notebook demonstrate that, to some degree, the girls understood disclosure as compulsory; as a result, Ruby has not previously interrogated the potential danger of revealing so much to her friends.

Having learned the hard way that she must choose the type and degree of her disclosure carefully, Ruby also gradually becomes aware of the ways other people's revelations shape her relationships with them. For example, when Noel uses his asthma inhaler in front of Ruby and tells her about his illness, she wonders if he shares that information with everyone or if they "had some kind of moment. . . . a little intimate thing where he was letting me in somehow" (*Book* 12). In contrast to Noel's tendency to keep his thoughts and feelings to himself, Ruby notes her friend Meghan's habit of being too open, saying, "Meghan is loud about her personal life. . . . She'll tell you when she has her period, and she'll tell you every single sentence [her boyfriend] wrote in a note, even really private stuff" (*Book* 59). Like Colie, who uses Morgan and Isabel as contrasting examples about degrees of disclosure, Ruby attempts to gauge her own disclosure by considering the examples set by Noel and Meghan.

Her struggle to navigate these questions is highlighted by her relationship with Nora; as they work to rebuild their friendship, Nora reveals that she has a crush on Noel, for whom Ruby has also developed romantic feelings. At first, Ruby favors what she believes to be discretion by hiding her feelings and rejecting Noel when he asks to kiss her; eventually, however, she decides to reveal her feelings to Nora, believing that her honesty will strengthen their friendship. However, Nora makes Ruby feel guilty for her disclosure and, when Noel and Ruby are later caught acting on their mutual attraction, Nora once again rejects Ruby's friendship. It is not until Nora herself begins dating another boy in *Real Live Boyfriends* that she and Ruby are able to once again repair their friendship. The ups-and-downs in Ruby and Nora's friendship ultimately inform Ruby's growing understanding of the natures of friendship more generally. When Nora rejects Ruby's apology regarding Noel, Ruby is understandably upset; however, she is also able to observe, "I loved Nora. I had loved her for a long time, and there was still so much to love about her. But she didn't really love me back, did she? She had dropped me twice . . . rather than trying to understand why I'd acted the way I did" (*Map* 232). Notably, that Ruby frames her realization as a question signals her assumption that the reader's understanding of the situation will mirror her own.

As she comes to a better understanding of the role of disclosure in her friendships, Ruby also gains the confidence to reconsider those friendships and especially the ways in which they have come to an end. She also continues to struggle with the loss of her once best friend, noting, "I see Kim, and there is still an ache for the kind of friends we used to be. Because I don't have that with anyone, the way I did with her. And maybe I never will. Maybe friendships aren't like that when we get older" (*Book* 191). In this explicit acknowledgment of the changing nature of Ruby's friendships, Lockhart offers an important suggestion about the role of intimacy in adolescent women's relationships with each other—namely, that the type of disclosure that Ruby once enjoyed as central to her friendships must necessarily make way for more "mature" relationships based on more limited self-revelation.

Even as Ruby learns this lesson, however, she creates and maintains a level of open communication with the reader that reveals her desire to be able to offer complete disclosure regarding her experiences of and new understandings of friendship. To some degree, this openness is the result of Ruby's narrative self-consciousness; more than any other narrator discussed in this chapter, Ruby makes a point of detailing the process by which she tells her story. At the end of *The Boyfriend List*, for example, Ruby explains that she is writing down her thoughts—"which," she explicitly clarifies, "is the stuff you're reading now" (229)—on her mother's laptop; a similar passage at the end of the following novel reveals that her father has bought her a refurbished computer of her own, on which she has continued the writing process. That Ruby so actively draws attention to the telling of her story, and even identifies the shape of the story as a novel by repeatedly calling attention to the chapter structures, demonstrates the degree to which she stands as an immediate, engaging narrator with whom the reader feels welcomed to enter an implicit interpersonal relationship.

Unlike other narrators in his chapter, Ruby adopts something like a generalized, at times pluralized, "Dear Reader" approach to her disclosure. For example, she initially refuses to describe herself but almost immediately relents, saying, "Oh, all right. I know some of you are jonesing for a physical description, and let it not be said that I deprive my readers" (*List* 21). Rather than constructing the reader's role as one of ideal, exclusive confidante, Lockhart's novels offer the possibility that an anonymous, plural audience allows for a less threatening space for disclosure. Having learned about the dangers of revealing herself too freely to her closest friends, whose betrayal of her and her secrets left Ruby isolated and upset, Ruby seems to be actively creating a relationship with her readers that protects her from such vulnerability by virtue of the fact that she has made the choice to share these secrets more openly. By admitting to and clarifying the circumstances of the very situations that have lead to the loss of her friendships, then, Ruby reclaims control over those secrets.

While Ruby primarily understands her reader(s) as surrogate friends, trustworthy and understanding in a way that her real friends have frequently failed to be, she also offers insight into another potential construction of the reader made possible by narrative intimacy. By sharing with the reader her feelings for Noel—particularly when she feels that she cannot make that information available to characters within the text, especially Nora and Noel himself—Ruby expands upon the basic model of friendship discussed throughout this chapter. When Noel kisses her, Ruby offers the reader a detailed description that casts the reader as something of a voyeur:

> I took off my glasses and kissed Noel again. And again, and again . . . I had been wanting to kiss him for so long, and he wanted to kiss me, and the room spun again and the sordidness disappeared and it was just him and me, together. I jumped up to sit on the table and wrapped my legs around him and blocked out everything else but the feel of his body against mine. (*Map* 160, ellipses in original)

By providing such a detailed description of their kiss and her feelings, Ruby invites the reader into an intimate romantic moment, welcoming the reader's awareness and potentially shared feelings of her desire for Noel.[11] Ruby's evolving understanding of friendship and romance is reflected, then, in her changing construction of the reader; whereas Ruby first seeks a friend who will receive her disclosure without judgment, a reader (or readers) who will allow her to explain the situation that has led to her isolation, she eventually comes to rely upon the reader not only as a trustworthy friend but also as a voyeuristic confidante with whom she can share her romantic and sexual desires. The *Ruby Oliver* novels thus provide an example of how the basic model of narrative intimacy that takes its shape from concepts of friendship may be expanded upon so that the narrator and reader may become—as I discuss in the next chapter—partners in desire.

As the works discussed in this chapter indicate, novels for adolescent women reflect many of the claims made by psychologists, sociologists, and Camy Baker: specifically, friendships are necessary to maturation process, but often involve dangers to self-esteem and social well-being. The characters in these and many other novels reflect the ways in which revealing thoughts and secrets to friends may allow for greater experiences of trust and camaraderie, but that sharing too openly or being indiscreet about when or to whom one makes disclosures may result in conflict or exclusion. In particular, the possibility of being betrayed or rejected—most clearly represented in the situations of Maggie and Ruby Oliver but implicit in all of the friendships developed by the narrators in these novels—acts as a persistent warning against the degree of disclosure that is generally associated with intimate friendships. In keeping with the "double-edged sword" concept advanced by Wiseman, then, contemporary American literature for and about adolescent women frequently highlights the potential dangers understood to be inherent to young women's friendships even as they present these relationships as positive, necessary aspects of adolescent life.

Furthermore, the narrators discussed here each experience friendship and its potential challenges in different ways; however, each of them expresses concerns about the role of disclosure in their friendships even as they rely upon the reader as a friend to whom all thoughts and feelings can be expressed. The distinction between the fictional characters who represent the potential threats of too-complete disclosure—particularly those who do reject or betray the narrator—and the real reader who cannot misuse or exploit the narrator's disclosure draws specific attention to adolescent women's concerns about making themselves vulnerable even within their closest peer relationships. The implicit relationships between narrator and reader in these novels, meanwhile, models a sort of "ideal" interpersonal relationship—the narrator may reveal anything and everything to the reader without fear of being betrayed or facing unexpected consequences. The very boundary between fictional narrator and real reader that is blurred by direct address and anticipation of reader's responses therefore actively reinforces contradictory messages about intimacy.

Chapter 3

"He Couldn't Get Close Enough"
The Exploration and Relegation of Desire

As the novels discussed in the previous chapter demonstrate, the development of narrative intimacy in young adult literature can play an important role in modeling or reinforcing cultural norms about friendships between adolescent women. Beyond the world of fiction, psychologists and sociologists postulate that young women's platonic relationships also play a vital part in establishing the foundation for romantic relationships, despite (or perhaps because of) the challenges that young women face in navigating their friendships. According to Kara Joyner and J. Richard Udry, adolescent women "bring more intimacy-related skills to relationships [than adolescent men], due to their experiences of intimate contact with other females" (371). As well as providing a framework for beginning romantic relationships, Neil Korobov and Avril Thorne argue, "friendships also double as the everyday contexts in which an understanding of romantic experiences develop" (49).[1] In other words, the literature of self-help and popular psychology suggests a cultural expectation that young women's friendships may offer them models for the types and frequency of their disclosure in platonic relationships, as well as contribute to cultural demands regarding the boundaries of emotional and physical disclosure in their romantic relationships. In terms of narrative intimacy, in turn, the model that presents the narrator-reader relationship as a friendship likewise provides the foundation for the construction of narrative intimacy in texts that deal with romance, love, and sexuality.

Like friendships, early romantic relationships have come to be understood as crucial to adolescent women's development, particularly in terms of the ability to create lasting intimate attachments. Whereas friendships may be figured as "double-edged swords," romantic and sexual relationships are assumed to present young women with an even more pronounced set of demands and contradictions. Despite growing resistance to the persistent "girls want love, boys want sex" dichotomy—a construction based at least in part on a "division of sexuality from intimacy [that] parses out desire for sex as normal for boys and desire for relationships as normal for girls" (Tolman, "Female" 227)—adolescent women face expectations that they will and should develop romantic relationships while being discouraged from exploring or expressing their desire for physical intimacy. In *Dilemmas of Desire: Teenage Girls Talk About Sexuality*, Deborah Tolman argues that contemporary American culture expects and encourages girls' desires for love, relationships, and romance while ignoring their sexual desires. In turn, while navigating the division between the roles of love and sex in their lives, adolescent women tend to engage in extended discourse regarding their crushes, first dates, and other romantic concerns while in many ways remaining silent on the subject of sexuality; as Sharon Thompson succinctly notes, "talking romance is a female adolescent tradition; talking sex is not" (7).

Much of the discussion surrounding adolescent women's experiences of love and sexuality remains shrouded in what Catherine Ashcraft calls "the unexamined discourse of 'readiness'" (328). As Ashcraft notes, adolescents are often advised by adults to refrain from sexual activity until they are "ready" and told that one simply "knows" when one is ready for sex (328). Because this vague language offers no real guidance, while in many ways denying the possibility of further clarification or discussion, it "hinders teens' abilities to make sense of their sexual experiences and prevents adolescents and adults from having meaningful conversations about sexuality" (Ashcraft 328). In turn, the discourse of readiness that dominates discussions of sex leads to confusion regarding the emotional aspects of romantic and sexual relationships. Adolescent women, in particular, receive a series of ambiguous messages that suggest that, to paraphrase a cliché, no one can really *explain* love, but you'll know it when you feel it.[2] As a result, "many youth express confusion about what meaningful connection is all about, whether they are capable of such connection, and how they can move toward satisfying and fulfilling connection" (Paul, Wenzel, and Harvey 375). Confusion regarding the development of such connections can lead to experiences of isolation, especially for adolescent women; Ashcraft writes, "With little positive acknowledgment of the ways in which they might enjoy sex or their sexuality, girls are left to decipher these feelings on their own, wondering if they are the only ones who have them" (329). Indeed, the ways in which the discourse surrounding sexuality causes a sense of isolation may lead girls to look to popular media for guidance and instruction.

Although my focus in this discussion will be novels written for and about adolescent women, it is also helpful to bear in mind the cultural representations of adolescent love and sexuality in other media such as television, music, and movies, as well as in nonfiction texts aimed at both young women and their parents. Like novels, these works provide cultural models that provide insights into the expectations and demands faced by young women as they embark upon their first romantic and sexual relationships, navigating for the first time the complicated interplay of love and sex that continues to influence our understanding of women's desires. In particular, these models reinforce the discourse of readiness that has come to be a primary marker of adolescent women's understandings of and decisions about sex. In other words, films, magazines, and particularly, for the purposes of this discussion, fiction and nonfiction literature contribute to the larger cultural representation of adolescent women considering their readiness for both emotional and physical intimacy, particularly as they struggle to understand the relationship between the two.

To some degree, popular media presents the possibility of adolescent women enjoying sexual relationships—for example, many of the female characters on the television show *Gossip Girl* pursue healthy sexual relationships with their significant others. However, the more prevalent model of adolescent women's engagement with love and sex still tends to privilege traditional warnings against sexual behavior even as it emphasizes the importance of romance in young women's lives. Magazines such as *Teen*, *Seventeen*, and *Cosmo Girl* regularly feature articles and advice columns dedicated to flirting, catching the attention of young men through clothes and body language, and interpreting the subtle clues of attraction; television shows marketed at teen audiences, from *Dawson's Creek* to *One Tree*

Hill, frequently explore the ins and outs of teenage relationships; romantic comedies set in high schools generally conclude with the suggestion that the central relationship will continue indefinitely; and music aimed at a market of adolescent women—often performed by musicians who are themselves teenagers, such as Britney Spears in the 1990s and Taylor Swift a decade later—frequently focuses on crushes, dating, and love. Although conflicts and breakups play an important role in representations of teen relationships, adolescent women are also encouraged to be open to the possibility of committed, loving connections that last through high school and into adulthood.[3]

Despite the prevalence of such representations of the possibility of lasting love, the emotional connections that adolescents form are frequently dismissed by adults as "puppy love" or otherwise inconsequential. For example, in *There Are No Simple Rules for Dating My Daughter! Surviving the Pitfalls and Pratfalls of Teen Relationships* (2006), authors Laura J. Buddenberg and Kathleen M. McGee assert that "kids use 'feelings of love' to justify a lot of selfish, silly, and destructive behaviors: ignoring friends, blowing off homework, forgetting family obligations, wasting money, and having sex" (31). Here, the authors not only dismiss the possibility that young people may experience romantic love but also condemn the actions of young people as they attempt to navigate these new emotional and sexual experiences. Furthermore, in presenting sex as a "selfish, silly, and destructive behavior," they provide insight into a more general representation of adolescent sexuality as dangerous and discouraged. Indeed, teenagers are reminded constantly of the dangers of sex, particularly in terms of unplanned pregnancy and sexually transmitted diseases, by sexual education programs in high schools, pamphlets available in doctors' offices, and televised public service announcements. Although all adolescents face cultural messages about the dangers of sex, a pronounced double standard continues to pervade understandings about the role of sex in the lives of adolescent men and women. Whereas adolescent men may find greater social acceptance and popularity as the result of pursuing and engaging in (hetero)sexual activity, adolescent women face the possibility of censure and rejection. As a result, the dangers of sex in the lives of adolescent women move beyond the physical risks of pregnancy and disease; young women must also confront the threat of being labeled "slut" and excluded from peer groups as the result of sexual activity.[4]

Self-help and nonfiction books regarding adolescent romance and relationships, both for parents and for teenagers themselves, reinforce the confusing messages that encourage young people to seek romantic connections while discouraging the exploration of sex and sexuality.[5] In many cases, such denials happen implicitly, as the texts simply fail to address questions of sex; in other cases, information about teen sexuality is relegated to brief discussions of its dangers. In *Reviving Ophelia*, Pipher argues that young women are surrounded by "sexual chaos," and that, in order to counter the implied danger of that chaos, "they need to be told that most of what happens in relationships is not sexual. Relationships primarily mean working together, talking, laughing, arguing, having mutual friends, and enjoying outings" (210). Works such as *There Are No Simple Rules*, furthermore, specifically present adolescent women as having no real understanding of sexual desire. For example, the authors note that "when it comes to dating, girls like to look like runway models. . . . They don't realize the level of sexual flirtation and attraction they can generate when their dates see a lot of skin" (Buddenberg and McGee 90). Such assertions deny adolescent women's sexual agency and decision-making by explicitly dismissing the possibility that they are aware of the power of sexual attraction and may willingly seek to control that power.

Likewise, self-help books for adolescent women actively reinforce the construction that separates sexual desire from emotional connections along gender lines. Throughout *For Young Women Only* (2006), Shaunti Feldhahn and Lisa A. Rice (whose purported goal is to provide insight into the thoughts and actions of young men in order to help guide young women seeking romantic relationships) insist that their readers recognize "what *power* girls have in the lives of guys" (30, emphasis in original). However, Feldhahn and Rice's "insights" into the minds of adolescent boys actually seem designed to influence and change young women's behavior while reinforcing the belief that young men and women approach romantic relationships from opposing points of view. For example, one chapter is entitled "Body Language: His Physical Desires = Emotional Consequences for Both of You"—effectively denying the possibility that young women will experience physical desire themselves. Likewise, Kimberly Kirberger's *Teen Love: On Relationships* (1999) offers a pair of lists entitled "What Guys Want" and the considerably longer "What Girls Want" that reinforce the distinctions that associate physical desires with young men and emotional desires with young women.

Like self-help books about adolescent women's friendships, as well as young adult novels on the subject of both friendship and romance, works written to guide parents and teenagers through adolescent romance rely on narrative intimacy. As the authors of such works assert their expertise along with advice, they encourage the reader to engage in an implicit relationship that will theoretically influence the reader's own choices. Buddenberg and McGee rely on their ability to empathize with the readers' experiences, explaining that they each have daughters of their own and offering sentiments—such as, "As a parent, you love your daughter and want the best for her" (8)—that indicate the concerns that they believe they share with their readers. In *Teen Love*, Kirberger includes letters from teen readers, offering her responses to these letters as evidence of her role as a credible advice-giver in her relationship with readers. Indeed, some authors of nonfiction works encourage readers to act upon the intimacy established by their narratives by offering the possibility of relationships beyond the narrator-reader connection; for example, Deborah Hatchell, author of *What Smart Teens Know . . . About Dating, Relationships, and Sex* (2003), provides her email address and invites readers to email her with questions. While narrative intimacy most clearly plays a role in the explicit advice-giving aspects of such texts, it is important to note that the emphasis on an author's reliability allows for the elision of important information about sex beyond its basic physical dangers.

Although, as I have noted, adolescent women look to a variety of media for information about love, romance, and sex, young adult novels are among the most popular and powerful cultural representations of teenage relationships. In an article exploring the representations of female sexuality in adolescent literature, Anna Altmann notes, "Certainly these novels contribute to the moral climate in which girls learn ways to live their sexuality. And certainly young readers explore their worlds through books" (22). Linda K. Christian-Smith echoes this assertion, arguing that romance novels for adolescent readers "allow readers to reflect on their developing sexualities" (101). Furthermore, while romance has been a common theme for adolescent women readers for decades, much of the literature published prior to the 1970s focused exclusively on the early stages of a relationship and rarely, if ever, addressed sex.[6] When Judy Blume published *Forever . . .* in 1975, she actively resisted the literary traditions that punished adolescents for their sexual desires and behaviors by allowing narrator Katherine and her boyfriend Michael to act upon their sexual desires without experiencing pregnancy, sexually transmitted disease, or death.[7] Blume explicitly supports young women's exploring their desires while emphasizing the importance of preparing for sex by obtaining information and contraception. Following the publication of *Forever*

. . . , young adult novels about romance and sex have generally been more forthright about the development of emotional and physical intimacy in adolescent relationships. In association with self-help literature and other popular discourse, then, novels such as those I consider work to create and maintain a model of adolescent womanhood as it pertains to love and sex.

It is important to note that the novels discussed here, though involving and in some cases dependent upon romantic elements, are not strictly speaking romance novels. According to John Charles, Shelley Mosley, and Ann Bouricius, "Romance novels are not about sex. They are about committed, loving, monogamous relationships" (416). Furthermore, romance demands a "happily ever after" ending contingent upon the establishment or continuation of the central romantic relationship. Instead, the novels discussed here not only explore the development of relationships and the search for love but also allow for and often privilege the possibility of failed emotional connections and regret over physical intimacy. More importantly, these novels demonstrate the role of narrative intimacy in constructing or reinforcing cultural expectations about teen romance and sex. In Sarah Dessen's *Someone Like You* and Kristen Tracy's *Lost It*, the narrators grapple with their decisions regarding the loss of their virginity and the importance of emotional intimacy, while Sara Zarr's *Story of a Girl* outlines the potential consequences of engaging in a sexual relationship without first establishing strong emotional bonds. While these three novels portray the role of sex in ultimately unsuccessful relationships, Stephenie Meyer's *Twilight* saga and Rachel Cohn's *Cyd Charisse* trilogy both present narrators whose struggles with love, commitment, and sexual desire end in lasting, committed relationships.

To a large degree, the version of narrative intimacy demonstrated in these novels builds upon the qualities that allow for an understanding of the narrator-reader relationship as a friendship: the narrator still relies on the "logical gap" between fiction and reality in order to position the reader as a safe location for disclosure of thoughts, feelings, and experiences, and the reader is still generally understood as being an adolescent woman who will be able to identify with the narrator. At the same time, novels about love and sex rely more heavily on what Warhol refers to as "unnarration,"[8] the idea that "representation, in the form of mere language, is inadequate to convey the depths of emotion the characters and the narrator are presented as feeling" (*Having* 43–44). To some degree, this unnarration— a common feature in sentimental novels of earlier centuries—reflects culturally accepted understandings about specific emotions as outside of or beyond expression through language; in the cases of the novels I discuss here, I believe unnarration also serves to underscore a fundamental difference from the version of narrative intimacy constructed in novels about friendships. Adolescent women's friendships are framed not only as fundamental but also as fundamentally expressible, containable by language because the emotions associated with these platonic relationships are more common and familiar than those associated with romantic love and sexual desire. Readers are also generally expected to have enough experience with friendships themselves to relate to the language that narrators use to describe those relationships. Narrators' tendency to express difficulty in describing or defining their romantic and sexual experiences, then, changes narrative intimacy in that such unnarration, in Warhol's words, "signal[s] to the reader to fill in the blank with the emotions for which the narrator cannot find words" (*Having* 44). While readers' experiences with love and sex are assumed to be more limited than their experiences of friendship, such "cues" ask readers to "take an active part in co-creating the scene's affective power" (Warhol, *Having* 44), framing narrative intimacy as a cooperative process in which desire may be mutually explored by narrator and reader.

Furthermore, because of the narrator's specific concerns about love and sex, narrative intimacy comes to depend not only on the disclosure of desire but also on detailed descriptions of sexual activities and fantasies (which, unlike the emotions associated with them, are often understood as narratable). The at-times explicit depictions of sexual activity found in many novels for adolescent women may thus simultaneously inform and titillate young readers by providing them with details that might not otherwise be available to them. The potential for young readers to experience arousal or desire as a result of reading such novels, in turn, highlights the manner in which narrative intimacy may cast the adolescent woman reader as a voyeur and, more importantly, an implicit but welcomed participant in the sexual experiences of the narrator. As Freud, Foucault, and many others have established, voyeurism tends to be associated with secrecy, guilt, and social or psychological deviance. In particular, Freud identifies the "pleasure in looking" as a normal and necessary part of human sexuality—but if looking replaces sexual activity, he asserts, it becomes a perversion. However, as Annette Kuhn argues in *The Power of the Image: Essays on Representation and Sexuality*, the guilt associated with voyeurism may be mitigated or erased by the suggestion that the voyeur (in this case, the reader) has been acknowledged or, more accurately, welcomed or invited by one of the participants (43–44).

The possibilities of vicarious arousal demonstrated in novels such as those discussed in this chapter provide insight into growing cultural trends regarding mediated sexuality—in other words, the increasing dependence on sexual materials that allow viewers and readers to explore sexual desires without exposing themselves to the physical and emotional dangers of sex. While these trends are by no means limited to adolescent women, they do reflect the contradictory expectations surrounding intimacy in contemporary American culture.[9] More to the point, narrative intimacy relies on a construction of the adolescent woman reader as a safe partner in the narrator's desire because she shares in the narrator's experience without being able to exploit or threaten the narrator as the young men in the novels themselves so frequently do. In turn, because the narrators each reinforce messages about the importance of "readiness" and the need to withhold disclosure and sex itself, they act as immediate models for the reader's own experiences and concerns about sex. By casting the reader as voyeur and in many cases inviting the reader to experience desire simultaneously with the narrator, then, these novels acknowledge young women's experiences of and curiosity about sexual desire in the face of cultural warnings about sex. While this acknowledgment may in some ways subvert cultural norms by allowing access to information about and vicarious enjoyment of physical intimacy, the construction of the narrator-reader relationship in fact undermines this possibility by relegating such disclosure about desire to the "safe" space between narrator and reader.

Although written decades after the publication Blume's *Forever . . .* , Dessen's 1998 novel *Someone Like You* echoes many of Blume's messages about adolescent romance and sexuality. Like Katherine, narrator Halley explores her first serious, physically intimate relationship while pondering the larger implications and consequences of sex itself—embodied here by Halley's best friend, Scarlett, whose one sexual encounter has resulted in an unplanned pregnancy.[10] As Halley flirts with the possibility of losing her virginity to Macon, the alluring, mysterious boy she's dating, Dessen imparts a number of fairly traditional warnings about sex, ultimately arguing that teenage couples should not take part in physical intimacy unless they have already established emotional intimacy. Meanwhile, Halley's revelations to the reader not only allow her to articulate her fears, concerns, and confusion but also emphasize her reluctance to broach those subjects with Macon, a point that Dessen highlights in order to strengthen the narrative intimacy between Halley and the reader.

When Halley first meets Macon, she finds herself attracted to him precisely because he is a mystery to her. Even after they begin dating, Halley notices that "he didn't usually explain what he didn't have to," including the activities that keep him occupied when he's not with her (82). As Halley finds herself becoming increasingly attached to Macon, she continues to struggle with his tendency to conceal things from her; at one point, she says, "No matter how well I thought I was getting to know him, there was always some part of himself he kept hidden: people and places, activities in which I wasn't included" (106). In response to Macon's secrecy, Halley herself declines to reveal her thoughts and feelings to him, particularly in terms of their disagreements about sex. Although she believes that she is in love with him and feels a strong desire to express that love through physical intimacy, Halley hesitates to make those feelings known to Macon, choosing instead to wait until he confesses his own emotions to her.

As a result of their shared reluctance to develop their emotional connection and understanding of each other, their relationship centers on their physical attraction. From the beginning, almost all of Halley's knowledge about Macon is related to his appearance and his past behavior, although she frequently attempts to ignore the fact that he has been involved in several physically intimate relationships. Her discomfort with their disparate levels of sexual experience becomes evident when Halley reveals that "Macon was a great kisser—not that I had much to compare him to—but I just knew. I tried not to think of all the practice he'd had" (158). Later, when he attempts for the first time to unbutton her pants, she says, "I had a sudden flash, out of nowhere, that he had done this before" (182). However, even as she acknowledges Macon's sexual past as an indicator of his probable desire for a physical relationship with her, Halley hesitates to pursue their attraction further; her hesitation, in turn, causes friction in their relationship. The first time Halley tells Macon that she's not ready to have sex, he gets frustrated and leaves. Halley says, "Something was changing, something I could sense even though I'd never been here before . . . . I already knew I'd lose Macon, probably soon, if I didn't sleep with him" (182).

During a scene in which Macon leads a blindfolded Halley to a ledge overlooking a dam, Dessen illustrates both the differences between Macon and Halley's understanding of their relationship and Halley's growing awareness of her own sexual desire. Initially confused by Macon's insistence upon surprising her, Halley becomes exhilarated and frightened upon finding herself on the ledge: "I leaned forward, still dazed and blinking, to peer over the edge and finally see the water I'd been hearing gushing past a full mile below. It was like opening your eyes and finding yourself suddenly in midair, falling" (131). When she tries to leave the ledge, Macon "pulled me back in, kissing me hard, his hands smoothing my hair, and I closed my eyes to the light, the noise, the water so far below, and I felt it for the first time. That exhilaration, the wooshing feeling of being on the edge and holding, the world spinning madly around me" (131). Using the dam as a metaphor, Dessen figures the increasingly intense relationship between Halley and Macon as one that simultaneously frightens and excites her. More importantly, as the dam unleashes the water that it has been holding back, Halley begins to consider the possibility of unleashing her own feelings and desires. Halley's sexualized language here thus calls attention to a larger shift in her relationship with Macon as they pursue their physical relationship further.

As Halley struggles with the decision of whether or not to lose her virginity to Macon, she confronts and dismisses the guidance offered by her mother and her pregnant best friend, both of whom are employed by Dessen as voices of experience and wisdom. Halley's mother, concerned about Halley's relationship with Macon and, more generally, with Halley's newfound reluctance to talk about her feelings, notes that "I don't think you understand how easy it is to make a mistake that will cost you forever. All it takes is one wrong choice" (170). Scarlett, meanwhile, phrases her advice a little less gently: "Don't be a fool. Don't give up something important to hold onto someone who can't even say they love you" (221). Although both her mother and Scarlett discourage her relationship with Macon, Halley decides to sleep with him on New Year's Eve, but because of her continued uneasiness with this decision, she must be drunk and stoned first. She reflects on the disparity between her hopes and the reality, noting, "I kept thinking that this wasn't how I'd imagined it would be. Not here, in a smelly bed, when my head was spinning and I could hear the flush of the toilet in the room next door" (229). When the drugs and alcohol cause her to feel sick, she asks Macon to take her home before they actually have sex. Because Halley does not disclose her feelings of confusion and uncertainty, and Macon—focused on his own pleasure—does not consider the possible emotional concerns guiding her behavior, their failed attempt at physical intimacy reinforces the problems caused by their lack of an established emotional connection.

Only when Macon causes a car accident in which Halley is injured does their relationship offer the potential for a greater connection based on the revelation of feelings. After being rendered unconscious and hospitalized, Halley recalls "Macon holding my hand, tightly between his, and saying it finally, in the wrong place at the wrong time, but saying it. *I love you*" (234). Despite the fact that she has been waiting for Macon to express these feelings for months, Halley is troubled by the anger and lack of responsibility that led Macon to cause the car wreck and his failure to remain by her side during her recovery. When he finally appears outside of her house to reaffirm his affection for her and ask her to forgive him, Halley breaks up with him; she reflects, "He wasn't what I'd thought he was; maybe he never had been. I wasn't what I'd thought *I* was, either" (240). Ultimately, Halley's realization that "I deserved better. . . . I deserved to grow, and to change, to become all the girls I could ever be over the course of my life, each one better than the last" reinforces her decision not to lose her virginity to Macon and celebrates her potential to pursue relationships that allow for both emotional and physical intimacy (243).

Throughout the novel, Dessen develops the narrative relationship between Halley and the reader in order to highlight the problems inherent to Halley's reluctance to speak to Scarlett, her mother, and especially Macon about her feelings. In many ways, Halley seems to position the reader as a surrogate for the figures in whom she might ordinarily be expected to confide; because she does not find affirmation for her feelings and plans in those around her, Halley constructs an understanding of the reader as a confidante who will unquestioningly support her decisions. For example, after Scarlett advises her against sleeping with Macon, Halley expresses her disbelief, saying, "I couldn't believe her. All this talk about trusting myself, and knowing when it was time, and now she fell out from beneath me" (221–22). Not only does she perceive Scarlett's advice as a betrayal, but she also seems to assume that the reader will agree with this assessment and offer support in Scarlett's place.

At the same time, Halley's rejection of the advice offered by her mother and Scarlett, as well as her growing dependence upon the reader as her exclusive outlet for her hopes and fears in her relationship with Macon, allows Dessen to underscore the idea that Halley is not ready for sex, a point further demonstrated by Halley's lack of knowledge about the act itself. At the beginning of the novel, Halley admits to a lack of experience and understanding of sex. She recalls her former relationship with a boy named Noah, explaining that he "was my first 'boyfriend,' which meant we called each other on the phone and kissed sometimes. . . . He'd been all right for a start" (18). When Scarlett confesses that she is pregnant and explains that the condom fell off, Halley says, "I didn't understand, exactly; I wasn't very clear on the logistics of sex" (96). Later, when she and Macon debate their physical relationship, neither of them will use the word "sex," referring to sex simply as "it" (182). Even when she is on the verge of losing her virginity, Halley relies on euphemism, saying, "We were very close, almost there" (229). Halley's confessions about her own lack of experience and her reluctance to fully articulate her sexual experiences even to the reader—a form of Warhol's unnarration—signal her belief that the reader shares in her inexperience and confusion, which simultaneously allows Halley to feel more comfortable in her disclosure and marks the opportunity for the reader to more fully sympathize and engage with Halley's exploration of this new territory.

By emphasizing Halley's apparent lack of emotional and intellectual preparation for sex, as well as her unwillingness to speak about her feelings to any of the characters in the novel, Dessen provides insights into the silences that frequently govern teen relationships. At the same time, Halley's disclosure to the reader allows her to revel in her attraction to Macon without fear of judgment. She describes to the reader an almost obsessive interest in him, but she never explicitly confesses her attraction *to* him or even broaches the possibility of a date, allowing him to lead the progression of their relationship. This pattern of reticence continues even after Halley and Macon have embarked on their relationship. For example, when Macon asks her whether she ever thinks about having sex with him, Halley once again reveals more to the reader than she does to Macon: "'I think about it,' I said, running my fingers through his hair. He closed his eyes. And I *did* think about it, all the time. But each time I was tempted, each time I wanted to give up my defense and pull back my troops, I thought of Scarlett" (182). Halley's willingness to disclose her hesitation to the reader while remaining silent on this point in her conversation with Macon reveals her fear that he will judge or reject her concerns; in revealing these feelings to the reader, Halley acts upon her implicit belief that the reader will understand and sympathize in a way that Macon may not.

Her disclosure also allows Halley to explore the physical aspects of their relationship within the intimate space she has shared with the reader. Throughout the novel, indeed, Halley provides the reader with detailed descriptions of her physical encounters with Macon, suggesting the possibility of understanding the reader as a welcome voyeur. For example, she describes this encounter: "I felt his arms wrap around me from behind, his hand, cool, on my stomach, and in the dark of my parents' alcove, he kissed me. . . . I kissed him back, letting his hand slide up my shirt, feeling the warmth of his legs pressing against mine" (178). Halley's account invites the reader to experience this intimate moment with her, as she provides both a detailed setting and a thorough account of their movements. Although this interlude does not lead to sex, Halley admits to her feelings of desire and the increasing difficulty she finds in putting a stop to their make-out sessions, saying, "It all felt so good, and I would feel myself forgetting, slipping and losing myself in it" (180).

Even as her feelings and desires for Macon grow, Halley hesitates to fully reveal herself to him: "I felt closer than ever to telling him that I loved him, but I bit it back. He had to say it first" (209). In constructing this unspoken ultimatum, Halley reveals that she does not trust Macon, but she also cannot find the means to clarify what she needs from him in order to feel comfortable and secure in their relationship and the possibility of losing her virginity to him. Likewise, she confesses her lack of confidence in her decision to sleep with Macon, saying, "I told myself it was the right thing, what I wanted to do, yet something still felt uneven and off-balance. But it was too late to go back now" (215). By making these disclosures, Halley perpetuates a level of intimacy with the reader that she ultimately fails to achieve in her relationship with Macon. Dessen frames Halley's unwillingness to articulate these thoughts to Macon in order to emphasize her lack of readiness for the physical relationship she plans to enter. In turn, Halley constructs an understanding of the reader as a trustworthy, nonjudgmental confidante, one who will not challenge her decisions or make demands to which she is unprepared to accede. This construction of the reader and the ensuing development of an emotionally intimate relationship between Halley and the reader allows Dessen to implicitly argue for the possibility of finding satisfaction in the exploration of desire without risking physical or emotional threats that frequently accompany sex.

In *Someone Like You*, Dessen frames Halley's ultimate decision not to lose her virginity with Macon as the correct choice: because Halley cannot voice her true feelings and concerns, we understand, she is not prepared to fully explore physical intimacy. In *Lost It* (2007), Kristen Tracy explores similar territory. However, unlike Halley, Tracy's narrator, Tess Whistle, considers the relationship between emotional and physical intimacy only *after* losing her virginity. In the midst of a series of unexpected decisions on the part of her parents and best friend, Tess meets Ben, a new boy at school who quickly becomes the most dependable person in her life. After losing her virginity to Ben, however, Tess finds herself dumped and confused. Over the course of the novel, she recounts and attempts to unravel the series of events that led to her current unhappy state; in the process, she reveals not only her own confusion about love and sex but also the ways in which acting upon that confusion can lead to heartbreak. Even as Tess struggles to understand the role of disclosure and desire in her relationship with Ben, she openly discusses with the reader feelings and thoughts she withholds from Ben, using these confessions as a way to explore her own desires.

In the first lines of the novel, Tess reports that "I didn't start out my junior year of high school planning to lose my virginity to Benjamin Easter—a senior—at his parents' cabin in Island Park underneath a sloppily patched, unseaworthy, upside-down canoe" (1). However, on the first day of school, Tess notices Ben when he is assigned the locker below hers; when she becomes distracted by his "cute butt," she accidentally drops a can of apple juice on his head. To save face, she tells Ben that she's diabetic, a lie that becomes central to their relationship: Ben, himself a survivor of childhood cancer, feels drawn to and protective of Tess precisely because he believes that she will be able to understand his own experiences with disease. Ben's assumption of their mutual experience highlights Tess's struggle to establish proper boundaries around her disclosure to Ben of her feelings and experiences. Even as Tess perpetuates the lie about diabetes, she openly reveals many other details about her life, thoughts, and feelings, believing that such ready disclosure will strengthen their relationship without understanding that she may in fact be endangering it instead. For example, caught up in a daydream about her future, Tess informs Ben that she never wants to name a son John; this piece of information, presented in an offhand manner, results in Ben's startled response that he isn't really thinking about having children yet. Though Tess does not immediately realize it, such confessions of her thoughts and plans lead Ben to distance himself from Tess, worried that their relationship may be moving too quickly.

Despite the fact that they have known each other only briefly, Tess becomes convinced that she and Ben will enjoy a long-lasting relationship. At the same time, Tess's stubborn belief that she and Ben will fall in love and get married ignores some obvious signs that they are not an ideal romantic match. On one of their first dates, Ben makes a series of jokes that cause Tess to roll her eyes; she remarks to the reader, "Sometimes his attempt at humor was way too corny" (60). Just as she fails to appreciate his attempts at humor, Tess reports that Ben frequently misinterprets her own comments, assuming that she is joking when she is in fact serious. Later in the novel, when Tess begins to fear that Ben is losing interest in her, she takes her grandmother's advice to play hard to get. A crucial element of her strategy, furthermore, is to refrain from sharing her thoughts and feelings so openly. However, she notes an important flaw in this plan: "Abandoning my true self made me a little uncomfortable. I had to keep telling myself I was doing it for love" (147). Although the strategy does renew and strengthen Ben's interest in her, Tess worries because she has won Ben's affection only by concealing her true feelings and personality.

Tess's difficulty establishing and understanding a balance of emotional intimacy in her relationship with Ben is paralleled and complicated by her intense physical attraction to him and her lack of previous information or experience in dealing with sex. Because of her parents' conservative beliefs, Tess's knowledge about sex is limited to the at times questionable information that she has gleaned from conversations with her best friend Zena; furthermore, although Tess has planned to remain a virgin until marriage, she has not considered the physical interactions that might lead up to sex. As a result, Tess finds herself shocked by her own behavior in the early days of her relationship with Ben. After their first kiss, Tess reports, "I suddenly felt like I couldn't get close enough to him" (65). The next night, she finds herself kissing Ben on her parents' bed; when he struggles to unhook her bra, rather than stopping him, she takes her bra off herself. She explains to the reader, "I was lonely. This was new. I couldn't stop myself. I didn't want to stop myself. He made me so happy" (79). She also begins to indulge in a series of daydreams about her future life with Ben, and she even convinces herself that she can continue to lie to Ben about her diabetes at least until she is pregnant with their first child. These fantasies both allow Tess to confront her sexual attraction to Ben within her already established, though poorly informed, ideas about sex and reveal her struggle to understand the development of intimacy within a relationship.

However, when Tess pushes Ben to move beyond their early sexual encounters, he hesitates, again citing fears that their relationship is progressing too quickly. Only when Tess is involved in a bad car accident does Ben revise his opinions about their sexual relationship, as he informs her during a visit to her hospital room:

"I love you, Tess," he said. He stood over me, smiling, brushing his hand against my face. "I love you and I want this relationship to work. No more slowing down." I remember being shocked to hear somebody I wasn't related to profess their love for me. It felt good. Then it hit me. . . . He couldn't get close enough. (168)

As in *Someone Like You*, the potential tragedy marked by a car accident allows for the possibility of a faltering relationship becoming stronger; however, unlike Halley, who rejects Macon's belated profession of his affection, Tess rejoices in Ben's admission of his feelings; her early fantasies collide with her sexual desire as she finds Ben expressing the sentiments she had previously assigned to him in her daydreams. Indeed, she even echoes the phrase "couldn't get close enough," which she earlier uses to describe her own desires for Ben. As she revels in the pleasure of Ben's confession of love, she does not immediately register the potential consequences for their physical intimacy. In fact, the renewed possibility for sexual activity catches Tess off guard. When Ben reveals his plan to take Tess to his parents' cabin so that their "first time will be special," Tess confesses to the reader that she feels "overwhelmed, like I was on the verge of becoming a whole different person" (188). However, rather than sharing those feelings of confusion with Ben, Tess convinces herself that she wants to lose her virginity to him, sacrificing her plans to wait until marriage. She must question this decision only days later, when Ben learns that she has lied about having diabetes and breaks up with her.

Despite the fact that Tess struggles throughout the novel to achieve an appropriate level of disclosure with Ben—and ultimately fails to do so, deciding to withhold more than she reveals in order to maintain his interest—she presents herself as unfailingly honest in her relationship with the reader. In the first pages of the novel, Tess assures the reader that she is telling her story "in the spirit of full disclosure and total honesty," having recently become aware of how concealing important information can damage or ruin a relationship (4). Furthermore, as Tess recounts the progression of her physical relationship with Ben, she shares a number of intimate details about their activities with the reader. In the process, she makes the reader privy to the type of intimate knowledge that has only ever been shared with Ben. Early in the novel, for example, she marvels at the fact that "I let a boy see me completely naked, and by this I mean braless and without my underpants. I let a boy I'd known for less than four months bear witness to the fact that my right breast was slightly smaller than my left one" (3). As a result of her desire to achieve full disclosure, then, Tess strives to develop a level of emotional intimacy with the reader that she fails to achieve with Ben, despite the degree of physical intimacy that their relationship eventually involves. By emphasizing the role of narrative intimacy, furthermore, Tracy emphasizes the dangers of sex in the absence of a fully developed emotional connection.

To a large degree, the information that Tess withholds from Ben but confesses to the reader has to do with her own confusion and hesitations regarding sex. She recalls that when she was younger, she once wondered about her own mother's sex life; at the same time, she says, "I remember thinking that these were questions Tess Whistle should not, would not, and could not ever ask" (81). By slipping into third-person voice here, as she does at several other instances when attempting to discuss her understanding of sex, Tess signals her discomfort with acknowledging and discussing her own desires. When she does recognize her attraction to Ben, furthermore, she also registers her surprise that she feels that desire. For example, early in their relationship she says, "I always thought I would have been the kind of girl who said *slow down, no*, and *stop doing that right now*. But those reactions would've required me to use my brain. And during this time, that wasn't happening" (75). Tess's failure to anticipate (and struggles to navigate) her own desires allow her to, like Halley, project her belief that the reader shares in her inexperience; her surprise at her own actions, in turn, invites the reader to actively consider (or reconsider) her own ideas about sex and desire.

Even as Tess reflects on the ramifications of her physical relationship with Ben, revealing both her continued discomfort with some of her actions and her confusion regarding the correlation between revealing herself physically and emotionally, she frequently adopts a didactic tone in her direct address to the reader. For example, after recounting some of the details of her "first time," Tess asserts, "Yes, on December 27, I had sex with Benjamin Easter. And yes, first-time sex is a big deal," confirming both the details of the event and what she assumes to be the reader's understanding of the loss of virginity (196–97). Later, when she reveals that she is too embarrassed to ask Ben whether he has brought condoms, she is quick to note that her embarrassment "isn't a good thing. I mean, if you're ready to have sex, you should be able to say the word 'condom'" (198). She also provides information about the experience of sex itself, noting that "I hadn't counted on sex being so messy and moist and I wished that I'd brought a towel" (205) and remarking, "It's such a weird feeling to have somebody else inside of you. Even if you love him" (230–31). These comments not only reflect Tess's own lack of information about (and her lack of readiness for) sex but also suggest that the reader might likewise be caught off guard by the actual experience of physical intimacy. In many ways, then, Tracy uses the narrative relationship to echo traditional warnings about sex and readiness discourse.[11] That Tess seems to find the act more narratable than the emotions behind the act, furthermore, signals her ongoing dependence on the reader to relate to her emotional experiences more than to the sexual experiences she describes here.

Tracy emphasizes the narrator-reader relationship, furthermore, by including a subplot about literature and its role in sexual decision-making. Specifically, Tess's decision to have sex with Ben is mediated by her own reading of *Ethan Frome*, which convinces her that life is too fragile to delay or avoid such opportunities. Although Tracy ultimately suggests that Tess's reasoning is faulty, the reader is positioned in a manner quite similar to the one occupied by Tess: the reading experience is supposed to inform the reader's decision making, but in the case of *Lost It*, the message is decidedly *not* to have sex because life is too short. Furthermore, Tess's willing disclosure to the reader about her experiences of sex and desire allow Tracy to emphasize that emotional intimacy is crucial to the success of any romantic relationship. As Tess reveals herself fully to the reader, then, she constructs an understanding of her relationship with the reader as a safe location for such emotional intimacy; without the threat of rejection or regret, the narrator-reader relationship allows for the safe transmission of Tess's experiences of desire while providing a model of disclosure that does not depend upon vulnerability.

Whereas *Someone Like You* and *Lost It* focus on the indecision and confusion leading up to the narrators' ultimate decisions regarding sex, Sara Zarr's 2007 novel, *Story of a Girl*, primarily concerns the aftermath of narrator Deanna's disastrous first sexual relationship. Zarr explores the ways in which sex may be used as a replacement for other kinds of intimacy, as well as how acting upon sexual desires may result in the label of "slut," which continues to serve as one of the most powerful social warnings against sex. At the age of thirteen, Deanna began seeing her seventeen-year-old brother's best friend, Tommy; their secret relationship quickly progressed to sexual activity, despite Deanna's inexperience and the difference in their ages. When Deanna's father interrupted Deanna and Tommy having sex in the back of Tommy's car, their relationship became fodder for high school gossip. Three years later, Deanna still suffers from the bad reputation and emotional isolation that resulted from her relationship with Tommy. Throughout the novel, Zarr explores the questions of physical and emotional intimacy through the concept of the "slut," a label that defines many of Deanna's experiences. Although Zarr includes warnings against engaging in sexual activity outside of a committed relationship, she also offers insights into the reasons that Deanna seeks that intimacy, while Deanna's relationship with the reader allows her to explore her pain and confusion as she attempts to find an appropriate outlet for her desires.

In the novel's opening lines, as Deanna explains the circumstances under which her father discovered her having sex with Tommy Webber, she admits, "I didn't love [Tommy]. I'm not sure I even liked him" (1). Over the course of the novel, Deanna slowly unravels the relationship with Tommy as she attempts to come to terms with their new roles as coworkers at a local pizza joint. She recalls their first meeting in frank, unsentimental terms: "He looked at me and it was the thing I'd been waiting for but didn't know it. I don't mean anything corny like I fell in love or even into a crush or anything. . . . It was knowing someone else thought about me for more than one second" (65). While Deanna dismisses the possibility of a romantic connection here, she provides insight into her desire to be acknowledged by someone. Throughout their relationship, as Deanna later comes to recognize, she depended more on Tommy's attention than on the development of a relationship based on mutual interests and experiences. However, the need for attention that drew Deanna into her relationship with Tommy backfired when the gossip about her began to spread; rather than being ignored, Deanna found herself the center of attention as an infamous slut, cast by gossips as "a total nympho," "a complete psycho," and "beyond pathetic" (17–18). Three years later, as she continues to experience social rejection and even physical harassment from her fellow students, Deanna wishes she could avoid the attention that she unexpectedly gained by engaging in a relationship with Tommy.

Deanna's role as the school slut provides insight into her specific struggles with emotional and physical intimacy, particularly in the contradiction that being defined by physical intimacy results in her exclusion from the possibility of emotional intimacy. This perception echoes discussions in self-help literature and works of popular psychology. As Emily White notes in *Fast Girls: Teenage Tribes and the Myth of the Slut*, "To become a slut is not to be associated with a group or a tribe; rather, it is to be singled out" (58). Furthermore, White says, "The slut becomes a way for the adolescent mind to draw a map. She's the place on the map marked by a danger sign, where legions of boys have been lost at sea. She's the place where the girl should never wander, for fear of becoming an outcast" (21). Although Deanna feels her reputation as a slut is undeserved—as she says, "Technically, I'm not a slut, because there was only ever Tommy, but it's hard to defend myself on a technicality when things happened the way they did. It's not like I could get on the PA system and issue a rebuttal" (42)—Deanna experiences the isolation that accompanies such a reputation. Therefore, while she escaped the physical consequences of pregnancy and disease, Deanna continues to suffer from the emotional consequences of the relationship, which, in turn, reinforce her belief that emotional and physical intimacy are incompatible.

As Deanna tells her story, she reveals that the disparity between emotional and physical intimacy has been, at least in part, a result of her own choices. In her description of losing her virginity, Deanna provides insight into her fears of emotional intimacy, which ultimately outweigh her fears of physical intimacy. Although she describes the sex as physically painful, particularly because a stoned Tommy failed to consider her comfort and enjoyment, Deanna says that "the worst part was when Tommy saw that I was crying and he got all nice and *Hey Dee Dee, don't cry, it will get better, you look so pretty . . . come on now, Dee Dee, come on.* It was like he had something on me, like he'd seen deep into somewhere he didn't belong" (70–71). Even as she offers some vague idea of the physical experience of intimacy, Deanna's focus here is her emotional distance from Tommy, particularly her sense that she needs to maintain a greater degree of separation from him. In other words, in describing her impression that his being nice to her has resulted from his having too much insight into her as a person, Deanna reveals that the physical closeness she and Tommy achieved has had less of an impact on her than the possibility of developing a stronger emotional bond. While she and Tommy would go on to have sex on several other occasions, Deanna explains that she developed a means of displacing herself from the sex itself by making up stories in her head, many of which she later records in her journal. Indeed, on the night that she and Tommy were caught, Deanna focused on the story she was writing in her head rather than on the physical experience of sex.

When her summer job reunites her with Tommy, Deanna struggles to navigate her feelings of anger and frustration, particularly when he attempts to rekindle their former relationship. When she reluctantly accepts a ride home—and, at least momentarily, the possibility of renewing their physical relationship—Deanna finds herself confronting the contradiction between her physical actions and her emotional desires and, after kissing him briefly, ultimately realizes that pursuing a sexual relationship with Tommy would depend on distancing herself not only from him but also from her own emotions. She recognizes that she does not wish to become physically intimate with him again and, in coming to that realization, she seizes the opportunity to express her feelings. Angrily bursting from the car, she challenges him to explain his actions, and Tommy responds with a grudging apology. Deanna reflects that she "felt like I'd been waiting to say that stuff to Tommy my whole life" (128). By actively resisting her tendency to avoid emotional intimacy and rejecting the possibility of once again turning to physical intimacy in order to feel accepted, Deanna begins to understand the potential for healing in disclosure.

While her confrontation with Tommy certainly does not solve all of Deanna's problems, it does mark a shift not only in her relationships with other characters within the novel but also in her relationship with the reader. Throughout *Story of a Girl*, Zarr emphasizes Deanna's difficulty in revealing her thoughts and feelings to those around her; although the reader receives more information about Deanna's experiences and desires than do the characters within the novel, even the narrator-reader relationship is frequently challenged by Deanna's reluctance to disclose certain thoughts and feelings. Deanna freely discusses the details of her sexual relationship with Tommy, as evinced by her decision to begin her story with the night that she and Tommy were caught by her father, but struggles to articulate her feelings about that relationship or her desire for a better relationship with her family, particularly her distant father. For much of the novel, furthermore, Deanna reveals her thoughts and feelings at least partially in excerpts from her journal, using her writing as an intermediary between her and the reader; only when Deanna recognizes the necessity of open communication with those around her does she put aside her journal and rely exclusively on direct address to the reader, allowing for fuller development of narrative intimacy.

Deanna's struggles to understand emotional intimacy are underscored by the amount of information she withholds not only from Tommy but also from her best friend Lee. Upon Lee's arrival at their school the previous year, Deanna had taken advantage of becoming friends with someone who had not already heard all of the rumors; tellingly, though, Lee had to establish the possibility of intimacy before Deanna felt comfortable confiding in her. Deanna recounts one early conversation in which Lee "told me that her real dad's a drunk and she didn't know where he was, and I told her, that's okay, my dad hates me. When she asked me why, I told her about Tommy. It felt good to be able to tell *my* version instead of Tommy's" (9). Although Deanna claims to trust and confide in Lee, their relationship is challenged by Deanna's general tendency to withhold information and her jealousy of Lee's happy romantic relationship with Deanna's longtime friend, Jason. When Lee approaches Deanna for advice about sex, then, Deanna responds coldly, causing a fight.

After Lee leaves in tears, Deanna thinks about how she could repair the friendship. She initially focuses on a strategy that depends upon her willingness to disclose her own experiences. "I'd tell her about sex," Deanna says,

> the good stuff, like how it could be warm and exciting—it could take you away—and the not-so-good things, like, how once you showed someone that part of yourself, you had to trust them one thousand percent and anything could happen. Someone you thought you knew could change and suddenly not want you, suddenly decide you made a better story than a girlfriend. (79)

Although Deanna ultimately misses her chance to have this conversation with Lee, this reflection provides insight into her understanding of the relationship between emotional and physical intimacy. Like Halley and Tess, furthermore, Deanna constructs an understanding of the reader as somewhat inexperienced and naïve by aligning the reader with Lee, whose questions about sex prompt this response. In particular, her decision to reveal to the reader (though not to Lee) that she once trusted Tommy "one thousand percent" allows Deanna to make one of the first emotional declarations of the novel, while her use of the phrase "someone you thought you knew" reinforces her present understanding of the lack of emotional connection between Tommy and herself.

Because, for most of the novel, she refuses to speak openly even to her closest friends, Deanna relies almost exclusively on the reader as she attempts to untangle her confusion regarding intimacy. However, even her reliance on the reader is mitigated by her hesitation and concerns about rejection. Throughout the novel, excerpts from Deanna's creative writing journal, in which she projects her own thoughts, feelings, and memories onto a nameless surfer girl, give the reader exclusive insight into Deanna's experiences. Eventually, though, Deanna recognizes the limitations of such a projection. "I didn't want to write about the girl on the waves anymore," she says, yet she adds, "I was scared to write about anything else" (98). While her fears about recording her feelings momentarily reinforce the potential for distance between Deanna and the reader, her decision to put aside her journal actually acts as a means of drawing the reader closer. Because the journal has, for much of the novel, acted as a sort of filter through which she can express her memories, thoughts, and feelings, allowing her to reveal aspects of herself to the reader without actually addressing the reader, Deanna's realization that she must confront her fears about expressing herself allow her to form a more intimate connection with the reader.

Ultimately, Zarr considers the ramifications of sex without love not only in terms of social reputation but also in terms of distancing adolescent women from the possibility of emotional intimacy. In other words, although Deanna's relationship with Tommy certainly occurs in the absence of (and as a potential replacement for) emotional intimacy, once she has engaged in this relationship, Deanna finds herself denied other outlets of emotional connection. Even in her disclosure to the reader, Deanna struggles to reconcile her experiences of sex and her desire for emotional intimacy; only when Deanna becomes committed to repairing the damaged relationships in her life does she fully welcome the reader into her confidence. The narrator-reader relationship therefore emphasizes the isolating potential of sex, particularly the contradiction that physical intimacy may deny the possibility of forming other relationships.

Just as Halley, Tess, and Deanna struggle with their decisions about the loss of their virginity, Bella Swan—narrator of *Twilight* (2005), *New Moon* (2006), *Eclipse* (2007), and *Breaking Dawn* (2008),[12] the four novels that make up Stephenie Meyer's *Twilight* saga—grapples with the physical aspects of her relationships with true love, Edward, and best friend (and would-be lover), Jacob. As Meyer traces the progression of this supernatural love triangle, she offers a construction of intimacy that focuses on the uncontrollable and often overwhelming nature of love and desire. Bella, confronted with the challenges of romantic intimacy for the first time, responds to her feelings for both Edward and Jacob by attempting to conceal the intensity of her desires. At the same time, the objects of those desires work to gain authority over her feelings and actions by establishing rules and guidelines for their intimate interactions. Because she believes that both love and desire are beyond her control, Bella's attempts to confront questions of intimacy require her to seek a relationship in which she has agency over her expressions and exploration of love and attraction. Bella therefore relies almost exclusively upon her disclosure to the reader in order to explore her feelings for Edward and Jacob.

When Bella arrives in tiny Forks, Washington, to live with her single father, she immediately becomes fascinated with Edward, whose pale beauty catches her eye on her first day of school. Drawn by his beautiful face and perplexed by his mysterious, at times aggressively off-putting behavior, Bella seeks to create a relationship with Edward in spite of his warnings that he is dangerous; she collects clues and information, struggling to solve the mystery of Edward's behavior and to resolve her attraction to him. Even as she begins to suspect that Edward is a vampire, Bella rejects the possibility of keeping her distance from him because, she explains, "When I thought of him, of his voice, his hypnotic eyes, the magnetic force of his personality, I wanted nothing more than to be with him right now" (*Twilight* 139). That overwhelming desire does not abate after she confirms that he is a vampire; instead, Bella simultaneously acknowledges that "there was part of him—and I didn't know how potent that part might be—that thirsted for my blood" and that "I was unconditionally and irrevocably in love with him" (*Twilight* 195). Bella's certainty about her love for Edward leads to her making a series of decisions predicated on her understanding of their relationship as eternal, beginning with her plan to become a vampire and ending with her agreeing to marry Edward despite her own distaste for the institution of marriage.[13]

Despite Bella's unwavering insistence upon her love for Edward, her disclosure to the reader focuses almost exclusively on what would more accurately be described as her lust for him. From the first time she sees Edward, Bella offers a near-constant series of descriptions of his bronze hair, topaz eyes, white skin, musical voice, and sweet scent that demonstrate the primacy of his physical presence in her life. For example, she offers this description in *Twilight*: "Edward in the sunlight was shocking. I couldn't get used to it, though I'd been staring at him all afternoon. His skin . . . literally sparkled, like thousands of tiny diamonds were embedded in the surface. He lay perfectly still in the grass, his shirt open over his sculpted, incandescent chest, his scintillating arms bare" (*Twilight* 260). Three novels later, she remains enchanted by these physical traits, as demonstrated in this passage from *Breaking Dawn*: "I never got over the shock of how perfect his body was—white, cool, and polished as marble. I ran my hand down his stone chest now, tracing across the flat planes of his stomach, just marveling" (25). Throughout the saga, the most suggestive aspect of Bella's physical descriptions of Edward is her constant emphasis on his being *hard*; though she generally uses similes about rocks (particularly marble or diamonds, as in the quotes above), the attention Bella pays to the fact that Edward is perpetually hard suggests her implicit understanding that he is in a constant state of arousal to which Bella responds with physical desires of her own. That his rock-like body also represents a constant threat to Bella's physical safety suggests that Edward simultaneously embodies sex and danger.

Edward actively reinforces this construction of sex as dangerous by refusing to pursue a sexual relationship with Bella while she is human. Although Bella frequently seeks to extend their romantic interludes by clinging to Edward or, as their relationship progresses, even attempting to unbutton his shirt, Edward consistently and categorically refuses to consider the possibility that they might be able to have sex while she is still a human. Primarily, he frames his refusal to pursue a sexual relationship with her in terms of the physical threats to her safety, telling her, "You don't realize how incredibly *breakable* you are. I can never, never afford to lose any kind of control when I'm with you" (*Twilight* 310). Furthermore, because he explicitly wishes to "protect her virtue," Edward objects to the possibility of taking Bella's virginity before they are married. Ostensibly for Bella's protection, then, Edward claims control over her desire, denying her the physical relationship she begins hinting at in the first novel. In presenting Bella's sexual desire and her ensuing discussions with Edward regarding the intensity of their physical relationship, then, Meyer emphasizes the connection between sex and danger in order to suggest that Bella needs to control her desire.

Bella's friendship with Jacob Black echoes many of these warnings. Although Jacob's attraction to and desire for Bella are evident from their first meeting in *Twilight*, she actively ignores his advances and denies her own growing attraction to him. In order to highlight this attraction, Meyer presents echoes of Bella's descriptions of Edward in her construction of Bella and Jacob's relationship. In *New Moon*, for example, when Bella visits him for the first time in several months, she expresses surprise at his appearance:

> He'd passed that point where the soft muscles of childhood hardened into the solid, lanky build of a teenager; the tendons and veins had become prominent under the red-brown skin of his arms, his hands. His face was still sweet like I remembered it, though it had hardened, too—the planes of his cheekbones sharper, his jaw squared off, all the childish roundness gone. (131)

Although Bella does not admit to her attraction to Jacob until the end of the following novel, the degree to which she attends to his having "hardened" so clearly echoes her descriptions of Edward that the reader is immediately made aware of her desire for Jacob. Over time, as their friendship grows closer, Jacob begins to force the issue of their mutual attraction by confessing his love for her and insisting that she feels the same love for him. Jacob thus resembles Edward not only in his physical presence but also in his attempts to dictate the direction and exploration of Bella's feelings of desire.

Like the other narrators discussed in this chapter, Bella willingly discloses feelings and thoughts to the reader that she actively conceals from those around her, particularly Edward and Jacob. To some degree, Bella's need for a confidante is the result of the supernatural creatures who populate her world; because she cannot reveal the true nature of the Cullens or, later, the young people of the Quileute tribe, Bella must be cautious regarding her disclosure to the other characters in the novel. However, even before Bella learns about the existence of vampires and werewolves, she describes herself as quiet, a quality she claims to have inherited from her father, and largely resists offers to join a social circle in her new school. Unlike Deanna, who experiences isolation as the result of her sexual activities and reputation, Bella actively avoids the possibility of a social life. By casting herself as something of a wallflower, Bella emphasizes her unwillingness to reveal herself emotionally to those around her, a trait she immediately and constantly contradicts in her relationship with the reader. Therefore, despite the supernatural trappings of the series as a whole, Bella's reliance upon the reader as a trustworthy confidante resembles the narrative intimacy developed in the other novels discussed in this chapter.

Just as *Losing It*'s Tess reflects upon the relevance of *Ethan Frome* to her own experience, Bella enacts an engagement with the reading process, particularly in her tendency to align herself with legendary romantic heroines. At times, the allusions are general, as when Bella reflects on Edward's departure in *New Moon* in terms of fairy tales: "True love was forever lost. The prince was never coming back to kiss me awake from my enchanted sleep. I was not a princess, after all" (411). More often, Bella returns to familiar texts in order to confront her own emotions and fears. As she navigates the increasingly complicated relationships between herself, Edward, and Jacob, she turns to her well-worn copy of Emily Brontë's classic romance: "I was like Cathy, like *Wuthering Heights*, only my options were so much better than hers, neither one evil, neither one weak. And here I sat, crying about it, not doing anything productive to make it right. Just like Cathy" (*Eclipse* 517). By projecting her own feelings and experiences onto fictional characters, Bella demonstrates the potential power of narrative intimacy, inviting the reader to understand this relationship with Bella in much the same way that she understands her relationship with Cathy.

Furthermore, because Bella so frequently encourages the reader's attention to Edward and Jacob by offering thorough, detailed descriptions such as those discussed above, she offers a model of desire that invites the possibility of a vicarious attraction to both men. As both relationships begin to include increasing amounts of physical intimacy, furthermore, Bella continues to offer detailed accounts of every one of their kisses and caresses, positioning the reader as voyeur and participant in her physical relationships with Edward and Jacob. For example, in *Eclipse*, she describes an interlude with Edward, saying, "He pulled my face back to his, and my lips shaped themselves around his . . . he rolled till he hovered over me. He held himself carefully so that I felt none of his weight, but I could feel the cool marble of his body press against mine" (*Eclipse* 187). She likewise chronicles her physical encounters with Jacob, particularly their first real kiss: "My brain disconnected from my body, and I was kissing him back. Against all reason, my lips were moving with his in strange, confusing ways they'd never moved before" (*Eclipse* 527). As Bella describes the kiss over the course of more than two pages, she invites the reader into this disorienting experience of physical desire. In each case, Bella invites the reader into intimate moments as a means of exploring her own desire while offering the vicarious enjoyment of such closeness to the reader. At the same time, Bella's dependence upon narrative intimacy limits and defines the reader's experiences and explorations of desire, forcing the reader to occupy a space that is more removed, and thus safer from the potential threats of sexual desire, than Bella's. This relegation of the reader's desire reflects Meyer's more general use of the narrator-reader relationship to reinforce for the reader the necessity of distancing oneself from the dangerous temptations of desire.

In *Breaking Dawn*, the final novel in the saga, Meyer emphasizes the importance of establishing distance as a means of avoiding the dangers of desire by making a marked change in Bella's dependence on the reader. After marrying Edward, enjoying an enthusiastically "human" honeymoon with him, and discovering that she is pregnant, Bella no longer offers the reader disclosure that she conceals from others. In fact, the narration of her desire for Edward becomes increasingly vague as her ability to enjoy a sexual relationship with him flourishes; she indicates that she and Edward enjoy an active sex life, but she no longer welcomes the reader as voyeur. Furthermore, and perhaps more tellingly, Bella finally makes the conscious decision to share her thoughts and feelings as openly with Edward as she once did with the reader. Having discovered that her ability to conceal her thoughts from Edward is the result of a "mental shield," Bella learns to control the barrier that stands between her thoughts and Edward. In the novel's final pages, she pushes the shield away, welcoming Edward into her mind and showing him a series of memories of their time together. "Now you know," she tells him. "No one has ever loved anyone as much as I love you" (*Breaking Dawn* 753). With those words, Bella signals to the reader that her ongoing struggle to control her emotions and desires—the inspiration for the narrative intimacy that the first three novels of the saga actively cultivates—has officially come to an end. More generally, Meyer suggests that Bella's acceptance of the roles of wife and mother allow her to understand her relationship with Edward as an appropriate space within which to explore her desires and that, as a result, she no longer needs to rely upon the reader for this purpose.

Throughout this chapter, I have discussed adolescent women narrators whose struggles with love and sex center on the loss of their virginity; as a result, these novels have explicitly and implicitly implicated young women's lack of knowledge and experience in the challenge of making good decisions regarding emotional and physical intimacy. In contrast, Cyd Charisse—the frank, flighty narrator of Rachel Cohn's *Gingerbread* (2002), *Shrimp* (2005), and *Cupcake* (2007)—faces her decisions regarding love and sex with a degree of familiarity and a lack of anxiety that reflect the possibility of adolescent women recognizing and exploring their sexual desires in a positive, healthy way. Although Cyd Charisse (who comes to be known as "CC," a nickname I will use here for the sake of brevity) has experienced some of the dangers of sex firsthand, she more actively concerns herself with the pleasure of pursuing her desires. Indeed, CC actively rejects the type of angst that so many cultural examples associate with sex, wondering, "How come on TV shows where teens are having sex it's always such a naughty thing, or something that has to be talked about over and over until the characters finally get it on. [*sic*] In real life, it is not so hard" (*Gingerbread* 46). Over the course of the trilogy, Cohn portrays CC's enjoyment of sex both with her on-again, off-again boyfriend Shrimp and within the context of occasional "hookups." While the novels do include implicit warnings about the dangers of sex outside of a committed relationship, Cohn offers a portrayal of adolescent sexuality and the development of mature emotional intimacy that focuses on pleasure; in turn, CC's relationship with the reader allows for the exploration of sexual desire as a healthy part of female adolescence.

Throughout the trilogy, CC struggles to maintain and understand her relationship with Shrimp, a short, blond surfer/artist whom she repeatedly declares to be her "one true love." Their relationship, though ostensibly deeply felt, is unsettled and disrupted over the course of the trilogy by emotional and physical distance. *Gingerbread* chronicles their first breakup and CC's subsequent trip to New York to visit her biological father and two half-siblings; *Shrimp* follows her as she returns home to San Francisco and to a renewed relationship with Shrimp, which ends once again when she rejects his marriage proposal; finally, in *Cupcake*, CC returns to New York to consider her post-high school and post-Shrimp options, only to reunite with Shrimp when he arrives in New York to surprise her. Only at the end of this third novel, as Shrimp and CC finally address their plans for the future—both individually and together—does the relationship that has misfired so many times finally seem stable enough to survive yet another separation.

From the beginning of the trilogy, CC declares her deep emotional attachment to Shrimp while explicitly focusing on her physical attraction to him, a pattern that resembles the tendency demonstrated by Bella and Tess to focus on their partners' appearances. She initially describes their relationship with a sense of reverence and awe: "Until Shrimp, I didn't know it was possible to care so much for another person that your heart just wants to combust with happiness every time that you are around that person" (*Gingerbread* 10). Because her previous relationship had been essentially unhappy and unhealthy (based mainly on sex, casual drug use, and CC's misguided attempts to find social acceptance), this new relationship with Shrimp allows her to gain insights into the possibilities of a happier, healthier romance. At the same time, her descriptions of their interactions throughout the three novels tend to focus on his physical appearance—she particularly likes to see him in his tight wetsuit after he surfs—and their physical interactions, especially the closeness they achieve while lying next to each other. Therefore, although CC experiences happiness in their relationship, she has not yet fully explored the possibility of emotional intimacy, instead relying upon the comfort of their physical closeness as a sign of the strength of their relationship.

The distinction between the exuberant physical relationship they have enjoyed and the close emotional bond CC clearly wishes to share with Shrimp becomes most apparent when they are first reunited after their summer apart. CC describes their first meeting in terms of the surprising lack of comfort she experiences, saying, "Shrimp stood in front of me, and it was like our live awkward slo-mo moment. What were we supposed to do here? Do we even really know each other anymore?" (*Shrimp* 55). Although CC does not lose hope that the awkwardness will abate, she does express concerns about the apparent distance that remains between them upon being reunited. Noting that "he's, like, been inside me" and reflecting that "you'd think two soulmates would have more to say, but we were both silent after our greetings," she explicitly draws a connection between the physical intimacy that ultimately defined their earlier relationship and their failure to fully develop the type of emotional intimacy that would ease the awkwardness of their reunion (*Shrimp* 58). Like Tess, furthermore, CC demonstrates the difference between what she evidently perceives as the narratable physical experience and unnarratable emotional experience of intimacy.

When they officially reconcile, CC recognizes for the first time their failure to fully communicate, especially when Shrimp announces his intention to drop out of high school without consulting her. She says, "We'd been sleeping together, talking about our dreams together, assuming we had a future together, for months now, and this was the first I was hearing about all this? Now I felt like all the time we'd spent together since becoming a couple again was a lie" (*Shrimp* 211). Even when they break up again at the end of the novel, words fail them. She describes making love in the back of Shrimp's car, both of them remaining silent because "we didn't need words to finish this conversation. Hands, bodies, and lips could take care of the rest" (267). Throughout the first two novels, then, Cohn emphasizes the clear difference between the closeness that CC experiences through her physical relationship with Shrimp and the emotional distance that cannot be bridged through their mutual unwillingness to discuss important questions and feelings.

Only after Shrimp returns from New Zealand and arrives unannounced in New York do CC and her so-called true love finally pursue more honest, thorough communication as a means of cultivating a relationship that relies on more than their mutual physical attraction. Although their reunion begins with sex ("God, it felt holy-fantastic-great to mind-soul-body merge with Shrimp again," CC reports), their relationship faces challenges when they begin to acknowledge that they each have a great deal to learn about the other, starting with Shrimp's real name (*Cupcake* 178). Indeed, CC even considers the possibility that they should not attempt to reconcile again, and she only begins to feel secure in their new relationship when she confronts Shrimp about his plans for the future and her place in them. He talks for hours, after which she tells him, "I can't remember you ever telling me so much about yourself at once" (*Cupcake* 196). Shrimp's reply, "I can't remember you ever listening so much at once," captures the essential challenge their relationship has always faced: despite CC's willingness to express and explore her own desire, she has not always acknowledged her own or Shrimp's need to express and explore the emotions surrounding that desire and their relationship as a whole (*Cupcake* 196). When their relationship is again tested by distance—CC returns to New York, while Shrimp makes his way to Nepal—they decide to remain committed to each other. Their farewell differs drastically from their post-breakup sex at the end of *Shrimp*; whereas she reports the silence of their previous goodbye, in this case she says, "Our lovemaking encompassed the soul-kissing-touching-talking-until-the-sun-set-over-the-Pacific variety" (*Cupcake* 295). In other words, only after recognizing the value of expressing their emotions in conversation as well as through sex do CC and Shrimp achieve the type of intimacy that allows them to feel secure in their relationship. Their new emotional closeness, in turn, provides a stronger foundation for the relationship that will again be tested by physical distance.

While Cohn emphasizes the development of CC and Shrimp's relationship, she also considers the possibility of finding satisfaction outside of a loving, committed connection. Throughout the series, even as CC professes her belief that Shrimp is her "one true love" and that they are meant to be together, she openly and frequently admits to experiencing physical attraction to other men, at times engaging in "hookups" ranging from kissing to sex. From the beginning of the series, CC repeatedly expresses her belief that such short and "steamy" connections can be a healthy, enjoyable part of her life. Indeed, she admits that she and Shrimp both initially expected their connection to end after a one-night stand. At the beginning of the second novel, on the verge of a slightly drunken hookup with an Irish soccer player, she says, "I am okay with scamming on hot guys" (*Shrimp* 27). And as soon as she moves to New York City, she develops a plan that includes "wiggle room to allow for the probability that almost immediately upon embarking on my new Manhattan existence, I would jump into some sexual experimentation . . . like an experiment-fling with a really old and sophisticated guy, like maybe thirty years old" (*Cupcake* 3). In her willingness to participate in hookups, CC demonstrates Elizabeth L. Paul, Amy Wenzel, and John Harvey's assertion that "youth who engage in hookups often are not gaining experience with advanced levels of relationship functioning, such as affection and bonding" (386). Instead, she initially focuses on the physical enjoyment of such hookups, less concerned with the emotional aspects than superficial attraction.

However, as CC's understanding of the importance of emotional connection grows, she begins to reconsider the role of hookups in her life; in the process, she demonstrates psychological findings that "casual sexual experiences contribute to youth's learning about interpersonal relating and to their hopes, fears, and expectations about themselves as future relationship partners" (Paul, Wenzel, and Harvey 387). For example, when a newly single CC first hooks up with her friend Luis in New York, she enjoys being with a man to whom she has felt a strong, immediate physical attraction. While she says, "It felt so nice to kiss a guy again," she also admits that "the whole make-out session made me feel kind of sleazy. . . . It was so absent any kind of connection other than lust" (*Gingerbread* 123–24). Although CC recognizes that she does not enjoy their hookup as fully as she might have enjoyed a similar interlude with Shrimp, she does not immediately dismiss the possibility of finding pleasure in such a casual, physical connection. A year later, at the beginning of *Cupcake*, CC (single again) hooks up with Luis for a second time, this time having drunken, unprotected sex with him. On this occasion, however, CC becomes determined to explore the emotional possibilities of their connection, engaging Luis in a discussion about the potential for an unplanned pregnancy and embarking on a brief romantic relationship that ends in their realization that they should remain friends. When she and Shrimp reunite later in that novel, CC draws on her short relationship with Luis in order to strengthen her lasting relationship with Shrimp. Through her interactions with Luis, then, CC demonstrates the possibility of enjoying a purely physical connection while emphasizing the importance of learning from such experiences to develop intimacy in future relationships.

CC's occasional non-Shrimp hookups also allow Cohn to implicitly argue for some degree of discretion in the pursuit of sexual pleasure outside of committed relationships. Although CC freely admits to finding pleasure in flirting, kissing, and even having sex with people other than Shrimp, the novels offer some warnings about the dangers of sex. Prior to the events in *Gingerbread*, CC experienced an unplanned pregnancy that she chose to terminate; she avoids a similar situation in *Cupcake* by taking the morning-after pill. While CC expresses and sometimes acts upon her attraction to men other than Shrimp, then, the potential for pregnancy or other undesirable consequences that result from these trysts underscores Cohn's implicit argument that while sex based exclusively on physical attraction may be enjoyable, it presents risks that do not always accompany committed relationships founded on emotional connections. Only in her relationship with Shrimp does CC escape fears of unplanned pregnancy and morning-after regret. However, Cohn is careful not to overstate these dangers and in fact counters the suggestion that such dangers only occur in hookups by including a subplot in which CC's friend Helen and her longtime boyfriend respond to their own unplanned pregnancy with a successful early marriage.

The relationships CC cultivates over the course of the three novels vary in their degrees of emotional and sexual intimacy; however, the development of CC's character is dependent upon her willingness to disclose intimate thoughts and feelings to the reader. Although CC claims that she is "not the kind of girl to keep a diary with a lock and a key," noting instead that "I keep all my secrets in my head," all three novels adopt a conversational and at times diary-like tone of camaraderie and confidentiality (*Gingerbread* 50). Indeed, from the opening pages of the first novel, CC invites the reader into her confidence, alluding to the unplanned pregnancy and abortion she had experienced a year earlier. She reflects on her baby's due date and at one point divulges that the contents of her backpack include not only condoms and a prescription for birth control but also "a silver baby rattle I bought at the drugstore the day I found out for sure I was pregnant, that somehow I have never managed to remember to throw out" (*Gingerbread* 136). Although this experience influences her relationship with Shrimp, she does not actually tell him about it until halfway through the second novel in a conversation that further forestalls their romantic reconciliation. CC's tendency to withhold such important information from Shrimp highlights the openness with which she reveals that information to the reader; as a result, CC sometimes seems to frame her relationship with the reader as sturdier and potentially longer-lasting than her relationship with Shrimp.

To a large degree, the apparent openness of the narrator-reader relationship depends on CC's assumption of affinity between herself and the reader, towards which she frequently gestures through direct address and conversational language. For example, throughout the series, CC ruminates on the possibility of growing up to live on a commune; the rules of the commune vary, depending on her current romantic situation or family tension. At the end of *Gingerbread* she invites the reader to join her in a commune focused on the eating of ginger: "Think about it. Sustenance, so long as we keep the ginger roots cultivated, will be easy" (172). This invitation demonstrates both her sense of closeness with the reader and her belief that the reader will likewise find the idea of a ginger commune appealing. She also suggests that she and the reader share a desire for the same reward of that communal lifestyle, saying, "At the end of the rainbow in Cyd Charisse's Land of All Things Ginger, there will be a Shrimp" (172). This comment indicates a belief—reinforced throughout the series—that the reader will share in CC's attraction to and desire for Shrimp. Her invitation to engage in this exploration of desire is most explicitly extended to the reader when Shrimp arrives unexpectedly in New York; she instructs the reader to ignore questions of why Shrimp has arrived and instead to "focus on the important things. Look at his tight little surfer body, way leaner than you remember, by way of either stress or kiwi diet, you don't know, but surely you'd like to experiment on the differential of his body's equation" (*Cupcake* 170). This direct address to the reader not only draws attention to CC's own attraction to Shrimp but also acts as a moment of narrative self-consciousness within which CC is able to emphasize the affinity she assumes exists between herself and the reader.

By including the reader in her sexual encounters with Shrimp, as well as offering vivid details of her sexual fantasies, CC seems to be offering readers the chance to enjoy sex and sexuality in a lighthearted way, exploring desire without the risk of judgment on either her part or the reader's. In contrast to the other narrators discussed in this chapter, then, CC presents the possibility of understanding sexual desires and behaviors as healthy parts of adolescent womanhood that do not necessarily have to be tied to committed relationships. At the same time, the "happily ever after" ending that depends upon CC having finally established a lasting relationship with Shrimp echoes the larger cultural message embodied by both novels such as those I've discussed here and the nonfiction literature, television shows, films, and so on that construct adolescent women's negotiation of love and sex in terms of "readiness." In other words, CC—like Halley, Tess, Deanna, and Bella—must confront her emotional preparation for a committed relationship as a fundamental step in her larger progress toward maturation.

Despite the differences in the narrators' experiences and approaches to disclosure, both within the texts and in terms of the implied relationship with the reader, all of the works discussed here provide insight into a larger consequence of cultural demands about adolescent women and intimacy—namely, that by discouraging young women from exploring or expressing their sexual desires before they are "ready," cultural demands deny them the possibility of fully engaging in the sort of emotional intimacy deemed necessary for sexual relationships. This rhetoric of readiness, as well as the multitude of messages that underscore it, offers young women an impossible challenge, requiring them to determine whether or not they are "ready" for sex without allowing them to acquire the necessary evidence to support that determination. Novels such as those discussed in this chapter, furthermore, not only reflect but frequently reinforce these problematic expectations by crafting narrator-reader relationships that are fundamentally shaped by an awareness of societal concerns: even as narrative intimacy offers a location to explore desire and love, it echoes traditional warnings about the potential physical and emotional threats posed by sexual activity and reinforces the ambiguous discourse of readiness surrounding adolescent sex.

As I have shown, the development of narrative intimacy in novels dealing with teen love, romance, and sex depends upon the relegation of adolescent women's feelings about and experiences of sexual attraction and activity, while constructions of the reader as a trustworthy confidante and potential partner in desire allow for the development of an implicit connection that mimics cultural norms regarding romantic relationships. At the same time, because this implicit relationship cannot be betrayed or destroyed by the reader, narrative intimacy establishes a "safe space" for the narrative to develop without the potential for vulnerability that accompanies real-life relationships. In the process of bridging the gap between fictional narrator and real reader, then, narrative intimacy reinforces the importance of developing intimacy in "appropriate"—and, in this case, impossible—spaces in order to avoid the risks that such intimacy might otherwise pose.

Viewed within the context of cultural conversations about young women's engagement with sexual desire and experience, the narrator-reader relationship is in and of itself a didactic tool that echoes the traditional demands about love and sex faced by adolescent women in contemporary American culture. For both narrators and readers, adolescent women's engagement in narrative intimacy allows limited access to desire while reinforcing contradictory messages about emotional and physical inti-macy. In this way, contemporary adolescent literature about love and sex ultimately serves much the same purpose as the didactic texts made avail-able to American teens in the mid-twentieth century: while the details may be more graphic at times, the presentations of young women at the heart of these novels still generally discourage the emotional and physi-cal explorations of desire that would ostensibly "ready" them for further experiences of intimacy.

Chapter 4

"She Doesn't Say a Word"
Violations and Reclamations of Intimacy

In the previous two chapters, I have dealt with the explicit benefits and implicit threats of disclosure in adolescent women's interpersonal relationships; through portrayals of friendships and romantic relationships, I argue, narrative intimacy in contemporary American young adult literature acts as a model for measured disclosure, encouraging adolescent woman readers to consider the dangers of intimacy while actively engaging them in relationships that depend upon the narrator's ability to fully disclose her thoughts and feelings. In this chapter, I shift to a consideration of how explicit violations of intimacy—namely, abuse and assault—challenge both narrators' and readers' concepts of narrative intimacy. Examining novels in which the narrator is either the victim of or a witness to such violations, I consider the ways in which narrators use narrative intimacy as a means of reclaiming an understanding of and control over intimacy. Instead of treating the reader as a partner and friend, then, the narrators in these texts primarily treat the reader as a therapist of sorts, relying on the implication of confidentiality in order to reclaim rather than model intimacy. In turn, this type of narrator-reader relationship reinforces concerns about the threats of intimacy because it is figured as the only safe space in which the narrator can reveal her thoughts and feelings without further vulnerability.

The particular use of narrative intimacy in novels such as the ones discussed here signals a larger cultural concern about young women's vulnerability to abuse and assault, which has markedly increased in recent years.[1] Generally speaking, studies suggest that many adolescent peer relationships, particularly romantic and sexual relationships, involve some type or degree of abuse: nearly one quarter of teenagers report that they have experienced psychological, physical, or sexual abuse in a dating relationship (Noonan and Charles 1087). More specifically, according to recent studies, "between 9 percent and 12 percent of adolescents report being physically abused and 29 percent report being psychologically abused by dates in the previous year" (Foshee et al. 380). Assault, particularly rape, is also prevalent during adolescence. According to one study, "The greatest proportion of all reported rapes (32 percent) occurred between the ages of 11 and 17" (Raghavan et al. 225). In the face of such statistics, contemporary American culture has increasingly fixated on young women's vulnerability to such threats. As Ruth O. Saxton notes, "The Girl in popular culture is an endangered species—in her own house as well as on the streets, vulnerable to rape, abuse, violence inflicted by others, and subject also to self-inflicted violence" (xxi). The violations of intimacy that are experienced by the narrators of the novels discussed in this chapter, therefore, reflect constructions of and concerns about the threats faced by adolescent women in America.

Furthermore, the ways in which narrators relegate their confessions about their victimization draw attention to the increasing cultural awareness of a phenomenon that sociologists have labeled "second assault" and its relationship to victims' fear of being abused by the very systems that are meant to protect them. Many young women who experience abuse or assault struggle with the question of how and to whom to report the trauma because they fear that they will be met by doubt or victim-blaming; this response, or "second assault," may cause victims to relive the pain, confusion, and shame that accompanied the initial assault. Studies have found that public health and safety officials (as well as family members and friends) may perpetrate second assault by responding to the report with some failure to recognize or affirm the victim status of the woman reporting the crime. In turn, as Courtney Ahrens notes in her article "Being Silenced: The Impact of Negative Social Reactions on the Disclosure of Rape," many "women who initially break the silence and speak out about the assault may quickly reconsider their decision and opt to stop speaking" (264). In the face of possible second assault, then, many victims of trauma, abuse, or assault either silence themselves after one failed attempt to report their experience or may refrain altogether from any sort of confession or disclosure.

In response both to concerns about abuse and assault and to the perceived likelihood that young women will struggle to navigate the aftereffects of trauma, self-help literature about these subjects tends to focus on the process of healing and reclaiming a sense of safety and security. Although studies show that both adolescent women and adolescent men report experiencing abusive treatment at the hands of their romantic partners,[2] self-help literature about teen dating abuse is overwhelmingly addressed to adolescent women and their parents. A simple review of titles demonstrates this tendency, with texts such as *Saving Beauty from the Beast: How to Protect Your Daughter from an Unhealthy Relationship* (2003), by Vicki Crompton and Ellen Zelda Kessner, as well as *But I Love Him: Protecting Your Teen Daughter from Controlling, Abusive Dating Relationships* (2000) and *But He Never Hit Me: The Devastating Cost of Non-Physical Abuse to Girls and Women* (2007), by Jill Murray, explicitly identifying their focus on young women. Other books, such as Barrie Levy's *In Love and in Danger: A Teen's Guide to Breaking Free of Abusive Relationships* (1997), signal the gender of their expected audience by employing pink letters and hearts on their covers. The number of such works directed at female audiences reflects cultural expectations that women will be both more likely to suffer abuse and more likely to seek guidance from sources such as self-help literature.

As the previous two chapters have demonstrated, narrative intimacy is a common feature in self-help literature about and for young adult women; in texts regarding abuse and assault, efforts towards the establishment and maintenance of such intimacy are even more pronounced than in self-help literature about friendships or romances. In many cases, the narrative intimacy is particularly intense, frequently tied to the authors' experiences as victims or parents of victims.[3] The authors of books for parents generally seek identification with the readers by emphasizing their own family situations; Murray makes a point of telling the reader, "Like you, I have a teenage daughter" (*But I Love Him* 5). Books for adolescent women, conversely, rely less on the author's ability to empathize with the reader's experience and more on the development of a tone that reflects understanding; in one such text, *In Love and In Danger*, Levy praises the reader, writing, "It took a lot of courage for you to pick up this book" (27). Works for parents and young women alike rely heavily on questions, asking readers to consider or write journal entries in response. For example, Herma Silverstein's *Date Abuse* (1994) presents the reader with a list of questions that includes the following: "Did your date ever shove you in anger, dig fingers into your skin when grabbing you, or 'playfully' slap you? Are there bruises where your date punched you in the arm? Is it hard to talk about something your date did, even if it happened a long time ago?" (10). These questions, which ask readers to align their experiences with what they will come to see as signs of abuse, tend to be presented in a manner that suggests an understanding of the reader's struggle.

In its heightened efforts to establish narrative intimacy and provide for readers a safe, comforting location in which to explore their fears and concerns, self-help literature about abuse and assault also highlights a paradox that is particularly prevalent in this discussion. Although, as the genre's name indicates, these texts claim to offer readers the opportunity to help themselves, readers of self-help texts must depend upon and wholly accept the authority of the narrator who guides them through the processes of recovery and healing. Whereas literature regarding young women's friendships and dating relationships may offer readers advice and occasionally pose questions for consideration, such texts do not insist upon the degree of narrative intimacy seen in those discussed here, most of which present series of steps, checklists of suggested activities (such as "write a journal entry about your experience"), or lists of questions aimed at the reader's growing awareness of her own strength and ability to overcome hardship. Only by completing the steps presented by the author, these works suggest, will the reader overcome the pain and confusion that have resulted from her victimization. In other words, then, self-help books about abuse and assault depend on the reader's acquiescing to the narrator's control, allowing the narrator to fully define and demonstrate the experience of intimacy even as the reader herself seeks to gain control over her understanding of disclosure, trust, and safe relationships.

Just as self-help books explicitly align the process of reading with the process of healing, bibliotherapy, an approach to psychological treatment of trauma that began to develop in the early twentieth century, has been used to help readers confront abuse and assault by pairing readers with texts that are meant to help identify, isolate, and overcome certain feelings, beliefs, and thoughts. In *Using Literature to Help Troubled Teenagers Cope with Abuse Issues*, which offers commentary from therapists, teachers, and scholars of adolescent literature in order to demonstrate the specific usefulness of selected fiction and nonfiction texts in helping young readers overcome their experiences of abuse, Joan Kaywell explains that bibliotherapy is so useful "because it is much easier to talk about someone else's problems using words artistically conveyed by masterful writers" (xx). While bibliotherapy obviously has applications beyond the treatment of victims of assault and abuse, adolescent literature that addresses these subjects has frequently been employed in helping young adults overcome their traumatic experiences. For example, Janet Alsup identifies *Speak*, a novel about rape discussed later in this chapter, as a useful text for use in bibliotherapy because it "might 'speak' to teen readers and help them cope with problems such as dating violence, divisive peer groups and cliques, and feelings of isolation and alienation" (163).

While readers may in fact find comfort in their identification with a narrator whose experience echoes their own, the construction of the narrator-reader relationship in the texts discussed here is explicitly concerned with the benefits that the *narrator* receives from the relationship, specifically in terms of being able to disclose her experience without the threat of second assault. Furthermore, the development of narrative intimacy in these novels is marked by an initial distancing followed by a gradually increasing reliance on the reader as a safe space for disclosure. Narrative intimacy thus suggests a process of reclamation and reimagining in which the narrator understands herself as having regained control after having had her understanding of intimacy challenged or betrayed by the emotional, physical, or sexual abuse or assault.[4] To put a new twist upon the term, then, if these novels may be seen as instruments of bibliotherapy, it is the reader who is figured as therapist, a construction these novels emphasize through the use of narrative self-consciousness (to return to Lanser's language). By pointedly drawing attention to their awareness of themselves as storytellers, the narrators of novels such as those discussed here not only establish the evolving nature of narrative intimacy within the texts but also illustrate their own understanding of the narrator-reader relationship as akin to a patient-therapist relationship.

In suggesting the possibility of what might be called "reverse bibliotherapy," I share Michel Foucault's interest in the understanding of narrative as confession. Foucault asserts that "one confesses one's crimes, one's sins, one's thoughts and desires, one's illnesses and troubles; one goes about telling, with the greatest precision, whatever is most difficult to tell" (59). However, in contrast to Foucault's concern with the power relationships involved with confession, as well as his focus on confession as sexual behaviors and pleasures, the types of confession made in novels such as those presented in this chapter frequently reject authority figures and the possibility of sexual pleasure on the part of either speaker or listener. Rather than framing the reader as "the authority who requires the confession, prescribes and appreciates it, and intervenes in order to judge, punish, forgive, console, and reconcile," as Foucault does (61), I find it more helpful to consider the reader as one who participates in the act of witnessing along with the narrator. As Dawn Skorczewski has noted, "Unlike the implicit hierarchical framework of the confessional mode, the act of witnessing involves a shared engagement by the listener, in which one participant provides testimony and another is available to hear it. Both speaker and listener function together as witnesses, not judges, of traumatic experience" (166). This construction is particularly relevant to the concept of narrative intimacy precisely because it replaces Foucault's hierarchy with a relationship that both narrator and reader may understand as equal.

Because the narrator frequently turns to the reader before she becomes willing to make her confession to an authority figure within the text, this understood equality and sharing of the act of witnessing is crucial to narrative intimacy in texts about abuse or assault. However, reverse bibliotherapy still intersects with questions of power in sometimes troubling ways; while narrative intimacy may reduce or avoid problems associated with unbalanced power structures, it also raises questions about young women's (re)claiming of agency and authority in intimate relationships. Although the process of reclaiming intimacy seems to empower the narrator and offer the reader a positive model of healing and strength, the narrators' dependence upon the reader might in fact be seen as reinforcing adolescent women's vulnerability and general lack of control over intimacy because the only truly safe space for what is figured as a *necessary* disclosure—one without which the narrator cannot begin to heal—is the impossible relationship with the reader.

In constructing the role of the reader as therapist, authors such as those discussed here draw on contemporary representations of and assumptions about the therapist-patient relationship, particularly when the patient is an adolescent woman. Across popular culture, the frequency with which younger patients seek therapy as a means of navigating the struggles they face during adolescence has become increasingly prevalent. The television show *In Treatment* featured the character of an anorexic teen gymnast, while several of the books discussed here and elsewhere in this study involve adolescent woman characters—such as Ruby Oliver, whom I discussed in Chapter 2—who speak openly about attending therapy sessions. Generally speaking, cultural constructions of the therapy process draw on the idea that, through carefully placed questions and the occasional thoughtful commentary, therapists guide patients through a gradual process of breaking down metaphorical walls and working toward a state of better mental health. In *Reviving Ophelia*, Pipher, a clinical psychologist, describes her reliance on such a model of therapy in her work with adolescent women, noting, "Their voices have gone underground. . . . I need to ask again and again in a dozen different ways, 'What are you trying to tell me?'" (20). Most importantly, therapists are defined by their lack of judgment and maintenance of patients' confidentiality, both of which help to create a framework within which patients can develop the trust necessary to fully disclose thoughts and fears to their therapists. Even as narrators may implicitly rely on these conventional understandings of therapist-patient relationships, however, it important to note once again that hierarchical assumptions that might accompany that relationship when the therapist is an adult and the patient an adolescent are minimized or removed by the development of narrative intimacy, which casts the reader as similar to the narrator in age and situation.

In order to interrogate the development of narrative intimacy and the construction of the reader's therapist role in contemporary American fiction for adolescent woman, I examine six recent novels that explore the experiences and effects of violations of intimacy. The first three novels discussed in this chapter represent a progression of abuse in romantic relationships, from verbal and emotional abuse, as seen in Deb Caletti's *Honey, Baby, Sweetheart*, to physical abuse in Sarah Dessen's *Dreamland* and sexual abuse in Niki Burnham's *Sticky Fingers*. I then turn to Louisa Luna's *Brave New Girl*, which follows the narrator's experience of acquaintance rape, and Laurie Halse Anderson's *Speak*, which deals with the aftermath of the narrator's being raped by a near-stranger. Finally, I discuss Courtney Summers's *Cracked Up to Be*, which considers the ways that witnesses to such violations may also struggle to reclaim control over intimacy. Though each of the novels discussed here presents a different type of abuse or assault, certain narrative patterns that exist across the texts highlight the particular construction of the narrator-reader relationship as a means of the narrators' reclaiming control over and understanding of intimacy.[5]

In contrast to the constructions of reader as friend and as partner in desire, the narrator-reader relationships discussed here continue to rely upon the understanding of the reader as a trustworthy confidante but are less interested in developing affinity between narrator and reader; indeed, because they generally work from the assumption that the reader will not be able to fully understand the traumatic experiences they eventually disclose, narrators (at least initially) present themselves as *different* from the reader, often figuring themselves as models or warnings that should reinforce for the reader how to avoid falling prey to similar events of abuse or assault. Therefore, in contrast to the narrators discussed in the previous two chapters who have generally been both immediate and engaging, the narrators here—while still immediate, frequently using present-tense narration—in many cases work to prevent the reader from knowing them too intimately until they have established a framework or familiar ground, defining the narrator-relationship as "safe" for themselves before fully disclosing their experiences, thoughts, and feelings to the reader. In particular, they rely on the previously mentioned narrative self-consciousness and a more general dependence on foreshadowing as means of forestalling intimacy. These efforts, which are particularly pronounced reminders of Lamarque's logical gap, emphasize the degree to which the narrator's understanding of intimacy has been disrupted. The eventual complete disclosure to the reader—which generally happens halfway through the novel, most notably in novels featuring one central incident of abuse or assault—acts as a rehearsal that helps the narrator gain the courage to make that disclosure to characters within the novel. Finally, each of these novels present ostensibly happy endings based on the idea that, having achieved disclosure and thus reclaimed a sense of control over intimacy, the narrator is rewarded by the promise of new or renewed relationships, either in stronger bonds with family and friends or in the possibility of a new, healthier romance.

Like the narrators discussed in the previous chapter, furthermore, those presented here often rely on unnarration as they attempt to capture their experiences of violation. Here again, though, the dependence on unnarration reflects a shift in the construction of narrative intimacy; whereas narrators of novels about love and sex typically employ the inability to express their feelings as a means of welcoming the reader's involvement in the development and exploration of intimacy, narrators of novels about abuse and assault rely on unnarration to more fully indicate gaps in narrative intimacy that will gradually be filled. In other words, when narrators who have experienced violations of intimacy use unnarration, the reader is not signaled to participate with the narrator in imagining some inexpressible but generally positive feelings but instead to recognize the struggle for expression as a crucial element in the narrator's act of witnessing her trauma. As the narrator finds the language and, more importantly, confidence to express thoughts and feelings that she has previously sought to conceal or repress, unnarration becomes less necessary and plays a less important role in the narrative intimacy that develops between narrator and reader.

Emotional and verbal abuse, studies indicate, are the most common and least reported types of abuse in adolescent dating relationships.[6] Such abuse, which frequently precedes physical or sexual abuse and which many people—adolescents and adults alike—fail to recognize as a violation, can take on a variety of appearances. Bobbie K. Burks includes in her definition the following: "ordering around: exerting control over a woman to keep her at a power disadvantage"; "denial (of abuse by the abuser): blaming the victim or telling the victim or others that the abuse never happened"; and "coercing the victim into illegal activity" (16–17). In *Date Abuse*, Silverstein simplifies the definition to "any behavior that leaves the other person feeling hurt inside" (13). Because emotional abuse often manifests as jealousy and possessiveness, as an abuser may believe that these behaviors "give him control over the person he loves" (Levy 32), many young women fail to recognize these signs as abusive, instead interpreting them not as controlling but as indications of their partners' love for them.

As a result of cultural models that present jealousy and possessiveness as signs of romantic attachment, the line between romance and emotional abuse can be difficult for some young women to discern. In Deb Caletti's 2004 novel, *Honey, Baby, Sweetheart*, narrator Ruby McQueen finds herself in an emotionally abusive relationship with Travis, a rich boy with a bad reputation. In many ways, Travis resembles Macon, the bad boy with whom Halley becomes involved in Dessen's *Someone Like You* (discussed in Chapter 3); however, while Macon's own behavior is at times risky or even potentially criminal, he purposely does not involve Halley in that aspect of his life. Travis, on the other hand, actively draws Ruby into his dangerous behaviors and activities, controlling her through manipulation and pressure. Caught up in the excitement of being with him, Ruby consciously decides to be the "fearless" girl that Travis wants her to be; quickly, however, she discovers that his expectations place her in situations that are at the very least anxiety inducing and are often dangerous. As Ruby reflects on the relationship, she attempts to unravel the complicated network of control and acquiescence that she initially understands as evidence of Travis's love. Although Ruby does engage with the reader from the opening pages, depending heavily on direct address, she only gradually allows her disclosure to become intimate in nature. In the process, Ruby clearly defines the narrator-reader relationship as a space in which she can reclaim her sense of intimacy without further vulnerability to the angst that marks her relationship with Travis.

Ruby's first awareness of Travis comes in the form of his motorcycle parked on his front lawn, destroying the grass; she reflects, "That should have told me all I needed to know right there" (1). Seeing Travis and his motorcycle as an opportunity to shed her label of "the Quiet Girl," Ruby flirts with him and makes a series of unguarded decisions, beginning with her accepting a ride on his motorcycle. As Travis drives at over 100 miles per hour, Ruby clings to him and, she says, "I was struck solidly with the knowledge that I was somewhere I shouldn't be, way beyond my depths, in a very wrong place. I wanted off" (33). Rather than confessing to her anxiety, however, Ruby takes a cue from an offhand remark made by Travis and decides that she can be fearless "if that's what he thought I was. I could be a lot of things I never considered before" (35). She immediately decides to cultivate this persona, even though, as she notes, "I didn't know this person who was talking. I wasn't even sure I liked her" (37). Before her relationship with Travis has even fully begun, then, Ruby has already registered a degree of confusion and fear that will mark their interactions from that point forward.

Early in the novel, Caletti foreshadows the control and danger that Travis will come to represent in Ruby's world. Before he has even learned her name, Travis gives Ruby a gold necklace; instead of fastening it around her neck, however, he initially loops it around her wrists, creating makeshift handcuffs, and presents the first explicit ultimatum of their relationship—"Give me a kiss to say thank you"—before releasing her (39). Then, Ruby says, "He unfastened the necklace, slid it into the pocket of my jeans. [He said,] 'Don't say no. Or we might not be friends anymore'" (39). Although Travis speaks and acts playfully, both his words and his behavior indicate his need for control; his slipping the necklace into her pocket rather than handing it to her, furthermore, signals a willingness to test boundaries. Ruby, in turn, responds to these mild demonstrations of power by understanding them as flattery, accepting the necklace despite her reasonable misgivings about taking such a lavish gift from someone she has just met. She also notes that the necklace's slippery texture, which she describes as "that bad feeling, that wrong feeling," is unpleasant to her, indicating her implicit discomfort with both the necklace and the relationship with Travis (75).

The speed with which the relationship progresses, Travis's taking control over their shared activities, and his claiming authority over Ruby's feelings all provide insight into the development of emotional abuse in adolescent romantic relationships. The escalation of their shared activities from daredevil stunts to petty theft illustrate a progression of emotional abuse as well: in her discussion of emotional abuse, Burks writes that coercing a partner into illegal activity, as Travis does, "is an ultimate expression of the power the perpetrator has over his or her victim" (17). A few weeks after their initial meeting, Travis takes Ruby for a walk on some nearby train tracks. While she initially enjoys the excursion, her happiness turns to fear when a train begins to approach and Travis will not let her leave the tracks until the train is dangerously near (73). Ruby's initial fear and anger at Travis's behavior are met and defused by Travis's reframing his actions as romantic; silencing her protests, he shows her that their hearts are now beating in time with each other (74). By focusing on the sexualized imagery of a passing train and the rhythms of Travis's and Ruby's hearts, Caletti suggests that Travis has effectively linked sexual desire and danger, a point that is emphasized by Ruby, who notes, "From that day onward, we went too fast, frighteningly fast" (74). Soon, Travis raises the stakes of their relationship and her willingness to be "fearless" by bringing Ruby along with him as he robs a house. Though he initially lies to her about the purposes of their visit, Travis eventually reveals to Ruby his pockets full of stolen jewelry. He responds to her protests by saying, "You know what we're doing here" (95), thereby not only involving her in his crime by bringing her to the house but also framing her as a willing participant, suggesting that she would be in as much trouble as he if they were to be caught.

Although Ruby tries to avoid Travis after that night, he corners her just days later in a greenhouse at the nursery where she works. Ruby's conflicted reaction—"I needed Travis out of there, and in some way I felt down, down, deep, I just plain needed Travis" (119)—reflects her more general confusion about their relationship, particularly the continuing connection between danger and desire. He asserts his control over her yet again by drawing attention to her vulnerability, grasping her arms in his hands and saying, "I miss your wrists. They're so small they're breakable" (118). He follows this veiled threat by commanding, "One kiss and we'll leave. Baby, come *here*" (120). Ruby does as he says, but her anxiety over doing so is highlighted by her fear that he will crush the fragile orchids that surround them. By projecting her fears onto the flowers, which have traditionally represented feminine sexuality, Ruby signals her own anxieties about the boundaries of sexual intimacy being breached by Travis's claiming control.

Unable to break away from Travis despite her growing anxiety about their relationship, Ruby finds herself once again involved in his illegal activities when he takes her to back to the nursery and coerces her into telling him where her boss keeps the keys to the cash register. Having betrayed the trust of Libby, her boss and a close family friend, Ruby finally recognizes the degree to which she has isolated herself from her friends and family as a result of her unhealthy relationship with Travis. In an effort to reclaim control over her understanding of intimacy by rejecting that isolation, Ruby reopens the lines of communication with her mother, who herself has been involved in an unhealthy relationship with Ruby's selfish, absent father for years; with her help, Ruby manages to extricate herself from Travis's control. When she calls to break up with him, he laughs and says, "I don't believe you. I got you wrapped around my finger," to which she replies, "Fuck off," before slamming down the phone (266). Ultimately, then, Travis's most explicit claim of control over Ruby and her decisions allows her to gather her anger and confidence in order to finally reject him.

This final break from Travis occurs only at the end of the novel, when Ruby's trust in narrative intimacy makes possible her reclamation of control over intimacy in the face of Travis's violations. Throughout the novel, Caletti draws attention to Ruby's construction of the narrative, emphasizing her awareness of the act of storytelling. In the process, Caletti highlights the parallels between Ruby's relationships with Travis and the reader in order to establish Ruby's evolving understanding and eventual reclamation of intimacy through the narrator-reader relationship. From the beginning of the novel, Ruby speaks frequently and directly to the reader, introducing herself in the opening pages and inviting the reader to look past her "quiet girl" exterior. She offers as an example the confidence she shows while reading aloud during English class: "That's when you wonder if there might be more to me. More than a glimpse of my coat flying out behind me as I escape out the school door towards home.

At least that's what I hope you think" (5). This address to the reader suggests the possibility of knowing Ruby, but she does not yet offer the reader anything more than superficial information, suggesting that she needs to lay the groundwork for further disclosure before actually sharing with the readers the qualities to which she alludes with the phrase "there might be more to me."

Likewise, Ruby initially maintains some degree of distance by drawing attention to the fact that she is relating a story; indeed, the degree to which she employs narrative self-consciousness signals her understanding of the reader's playing the role of therapist. By including sentence tags such as "like I said" and "as I said" throughout much of the novel, Ruby emphasizes that her disclosure is a gradual process during which she slowly builds up the amount of information she wishes to share with the reader. Such phrases also serve as signs that Ruby is becoming more open with the reader, as when she initially expresses her own discomfort about the new persona she cultivates under Travis's control: "She was fearless, all right. But to tell you the truth, she was making me nervous" (37). The phrase "to tell you the truth," which Ruby uses several times over the course of the novel, demonstrates her need to explicitly identify for the reader moments of more complete disclosure. She also compares her disclosure to the reader explicitly to her inability to speak to Travis about her real feelings. During their first reckless motorcycle ride, she says, "A shout, *Slow down!* stuck in my throat. I didn't, couldn't, let it out. Here it is—I was afraid of looking stupid, which is, of course, when you do the most stupid things of all" (34). Again, the phrase "here it is" acts as a sort of textual "deep breath," as though Ruby must gather the courage to confess to her fears of looking stupid.

Furthermore, Ruby's tendency to foreshadow elements of her relationship with Travis through her reliance on symbols such as the necklace indicates her need to gradually establish a framework within which she can trust the reader to receive her disclosure without the threat of judgment or blame. As a result of Ruby's hesitation, the reader and narrator are not immediately experiencing the story as a shared space; instead, Ruby defines the space in order to ensure that the reader remain in the role of therapist rather than welcoming the reader's identification and sharing of the experience. Once Ruby feels comfortable enough to make such preliminary confessions to the reader, her narration becomes increasingly frank, providing insight both into the process of her reflecting on her feelings about Travis and into the ways that her relationship with the reader makes such reflection possible and productive. Ruby especially comes to depend upon the narrator-reader relationship in order to interrogate feelings she experiences but never expresses to Travis. For example, though she never tells Travis that she loves him, Ruby says to the reader, "I decided I must be in love with Travis Becker. Something that horrible and wonderful had to be love, because what else could it be?" (76). As Ruby unravels her conflicted feelings about her relationship with Travis, she actively resists the possibility of welcoming the reader as a partner in her desire; unlike narrators who present their sexual desires and experiences to a voyeuristic reader, Ruby dissects her decisions and desires in order to reclaim a sense of control over the relationship. When she describes him, she makes a point of denying the reader's possible desire for him by identifying him as dangerous.

Ruby's gradual process of revealing herself to the reader is highlighted not only by her continued struggle to understand her relationship with Travis but also by her reluctance to speak even to characters within the novel with whom she normally has a close relationship. For example, when Libby attempts to draw Ruby into a conversation about Travis by admitting to her own mistakes in a past romantic relationship, Ruby declines to discuss Travis aloud; instead, she divulges to the reader that "Libby was right. The stuff with Travis was getting bigger than me, overtaking who I was" (78). That Ruby feels more capable of disclosing these fears to the reader than to Libby both reflects the degree to which she has come to rely on narrative intimacy and her conviction that even her formerly close relationships do not provide her a safe location for such a confession. The one attempt Ruby makes to disclose her concerns and fears about her relationship with Travis to someone in the novel further underscores her confusion about intimacy and perceived need for such a safe space. When she speaks to Joe Davis, the pastor at the local church, she shares with him much of what she has already told the reader about Travis and their relationship; indeed, her disclosure to him seems to be possible only because she has already revealed it within the confines of the narrator-reader relationship. Even as her decision to speak to Joe suggests a growing sense of control over her disclosure and the bounds of intimacy, she also makes a point of asking him, "This stays between us, right?" and drawing on a memory of "something I once heard about minister-patient confidentiality or something like that" (102). By aligning narrative intimacy with a confidential, therapy-like interaction, Ruby draws attention to the ways in which she treats the reader as a sort of therapist as well.

Throughout *Honey, Baby, Sweetheart,* Caletti clearly establishes the manner in which emotional abuse can destroy one's sense of control, trust, and intimacy. Ultimately, as Ruby draws on the confidence and security she has developed through her increasingly intimate relationship with the reader, she fully separates herself from Travis and begins to consider the possibility of enjoying interpersonal relationships based upon disclosure and trust. Her relationship with her mother, in particular, improves as Ruby becomes more willing to discuss her feelings about her parents' tumultuous relationship; that both Ruby and her mother finally resolve to break free of the bad romantic cycles in which they find themselves suggests their mutual need for intimacy as a source of strength. The novel ends on an optimistic note, as Ruby seems to be embarking on a relationship with a paragliding instructor who can teach her how to fly. Because she has been able not only to reevaluate Travis and his treatment of her but also to reconsider the nature of intimacy through her relationship with the reader, Ruby is ostensibly in a stronger position than at the beginning of the novel; her flirting with the skydiving instructor signals her readiness for a romantic relationship that will not threaten her or violate her boundaries as her relationship with Travis has.

The controlling, manipulative traits Travis displays in Caletti's novel never turn into direct physical abuse; however, current psychological and sociological research emphasizes findings that emotional and verbal abuse frequently precede physical abuse in young people's romantic relationships. Sarah Dessen follows the trajectory from emotional abuse and controlling behavior to physical violence in her 2000 novel *Dreamland.* Reeling after her older sister Cass runs away from home, sixteen-year-old Caitlin O'Koren embarks on a passionate relationship with Rogerson, drawn by his mysterious air and dangerous reputation. Despite the fact that he has had run-ins with the law and continues to sell drugs, she falls in love with him quickly and initially understands his constant presence as affectionate rather than jealous and stifling. As his controlling attitude transforms into physical abuse, Caitlin finds herself unwilling to end the relationship even in the face of near-constant threats of violence. Withdrawing from her family and friends, Caitlin discloses the abuse only to the journal that Cass left behind for her and, more completely, to the reader, using these inviolable outlets of disclosure as a means of reclaiming her understanding of the nature of intimacy.

Just as Ruby links danger and desire, Caitlin aligns the experience of love with the presence of pain, beginning with the tiny scar over her eyebrow, a souvenir from a childhood fight with Cass that has come to represent their close emotional connection and clear understanding of each other. When Cass begins dating a young man named Adam, Caitlin watches Cass's expressions of love and passion with disdain, even telling Cass, "If I act like that, be sure to put me out of my misery" (14). In connecting love and misery, here Caitlin signals an already problematic understanding of the nature of love and intimacy; when Cass runs away just weeks later to live with Adam in New York, Caitlin connects her own pain to Cass's experience of love. The night that Caitlin meets Rogerson is also marked by danger and physical pain. During a halftime performance, Caitlin, a cheerleader, falls from the pyramid and hurts herself. She decides to attend the after party nonetheless; on the way, she encounters Rogerson for the first time at a gas station, where she notices his dreadlocked hair and green eyes. When he approaches her, she says, "My head felt fuzzy and strange, and I wondered if maybe I *had* whacked it on the way down" (51), once again linking the possibility of pain and love. Later that night, when he has driven her home and she has ended up braless after a heavy make-out session, Caitlin thinks, "One tumble off the pyramid and look how far I'd fallen" (59).

Along with her uncharacteristic decision to "hook up" with a boy she has just met and may never see again, Caitlin begins to adjust her entire personality to meet what she understands to be Rogerson's expectations. Early in their relationship, Rogerson tells Caitlin, "I knew you were trouble. . . . Could tell just by looking at you" (57). As Caitlin is in fact the *opposite* of trouble—well-behaved, obedient, a good student, and a cheerleader—Rogerson's statement reflects his desire to understand her in his own terms. Just as Ruby takes a cue from Travis's description of her as "fearless," Caitlin reacts with a desire to be the person Rogerson wants her to be. Reflecting that "for all he knew, I could be the kind of girl that smoked. I could be anything" (60), Caitlin begins smoking both cigarettes and pot, skipping school, and isolating herself from her parents in order to present herself as "the kind of girl" Rogerson wants. In acquiescing to what she perceives to be Rogerson's desires, Caitlin begins to work within a framework of control that increasingly allows Rogerson to exploit her attempts to please him.

From the beginning of their relationship, Caitlin notes behaviors and comments that foreshadow the eventually dangerous nature of her relationship with Rogerson. After only two dates, Rogerson becomes a near-constant presence in her life: "He drove me home every day. He came over from [his school] at lunch to take me out and called me every night—usually more than once—and then again before I went to bed" (90); he insists on her coming along with him as he visits his drug clients and, on the nights that she stays home, "he'd always drive by my house at least once, slowing down and just idling, engine rumbling, until I went outside to talk to him" (111). Caitlin's reaction to these behaviors—which, she explains, she initially interprets as flattering rather than frightening or controlling—reflects what Katherine Suárez notes is a tendency among adolescent women in abusive relationships to "misinterpret . . . jealousy as a sign of love" (429). Dessen also hints at Rogerson's violent inclinations by casting him as a victim of abuse himself. During their first official date, Caitlin witnesses Rogerson being slapped by his father, an event that immediately causes their relationship to become more intense: "I never told anyone what happened at Rogerson's. But from then on, we were together" (89).

This foreshadowing also highlights the manner in which Dessen draws on the work of sociologists and psychologists in tracing the development of abuse in Rogerson and Caitlin's relationship. In particular, Dessen illustrates the "cycle of abuse," which was first identified by Lenore E. Walker in her 1979 text *The Battered Woman*. Through Rogerson's passive aggressive tendencies and the couple's more general lack of communication, Dessen portrays the first phase, tension-building. Once the cycle has begun, the other three phases—acting out, reconciliation, and calm—are set into motion. Because Caitlin does not initially acknowledge that Rogerson's treatment of her during the tension-building phase may become abusive, she is caught completely off guard by his first violent response to her. A sullen Rogerson, in response to Caitlin's jokingly calling him a "big baby," punches her in the face (143). As she reels from the pain and shock of the attack, Rogerson tells Caitlin that he loves her for the first time. In turn, Caitlin says, "I could have just gotten out of the car and walked up to my house, leaving him behind forever. Things would have been very different if I had done that. But the fact was that I loved Rogerson" (146). Because of her conviction that love and pain are inextricably linked, then, Caitlin remains in her relationship with Rogerson even as he becomes increasingly violent. This first incident, furthermore, marks Caitlin's explicit decision to hide the truth from her parents; when she lies about the mark on her cheek, explaining that she has slipped on their icy sidewalk, she rejects the possibility of disclosure to—and thus help from—them.

Dessen also draws on recognized patterns of abuse in Caitlin's acknowledgment that, after the first few incidents of physical abuse, "Rogerson had taken to only hitting me where I could cover it: arms, legs, shoulders" (164). As the abuse escalates, Rogerson persistently refuses to accept responsibility for his actions, saying, "This isn't my fault. . . . It isn't, Caitlin. You know what you did" (156). This victim-blaming, as well as Caitlin's willingness to accept that blame despite the fact that she has committed none of the transgressions for which Rogerson punishes her, reflects what studies have found to be common elements in abusive relationships. Following each act of violence, furthermore, Rogerson apologizes and treats her with kindness—common elements of the reconciliation phase in Walker's cycle of abuse—only to return to acts of anger and aggression within a matter of weeks. In the midst of this violence, Caitlin responds by further modifying her behavior and appearance to meet Rogerson's demands, hoping to secure as much "safe" time as possible between attacks. When Caitlin decides to lose her virginity to Rogerson—an event that, she says, "hurt, too, but in a different way, one I'd been expecting" (165)—she even more firmly cements her understanding of the intertwined nature of love and pain. Caitlin's experiences of sex provide further insight into her struggle to navigate intimacy; she is not coerced into sex by Rogerson, but instead actively pursues sex as a means of convincing herself of Rogerson's affection for her. She says, "I told myself that this was the closest you could get to another person. So close their breaths became your own. So I gave him all of me, believing I could trust him" (166). Their sexual relationship thus serves multiple purposes for Caitlin: it allows her to experience what she believes to be true intimacy; it allows her a reprieve from his violence; and it ushers in (at least temporarily) the fourth—or calm—phase of the cycle of abuse.

The increasingly frightening nature of Rogerson's behavior leads Caitlin not only to seek comfort in drug use but also to isolate herself from the family and friends who might try to separate her from her boyfriend. The possibility of ending the cycle only appears when Rogerson's abuse culminates in an act of public violence: in a jealous rage, he attacks her on her front lawn in full view of the guests Caitlin's parents have gathered for a party. Noting that "it was the first time he'd done it out in the open" (215), Caitlin surrenders to the abuse, curling into the fetal position as he punches and kicks her. Even as Caitlin registers her weakness and submission to the pain Rogerson inflicts, she expresses her belief that she needs him, saying, "He had taken everything. But he had been all I had, all this time. And when the police led him away, I pulled out of the hands of all these loved ones, sobbing, screaming, everything hurting, to try and make him stay" (218). Her inability to distinguish between the pain Rogerson has caused and her pain at the thought of losing him demonstrates the degree to which Caitlin's understanding of intimacy has been challenged and ultimately destroyed by Rogerson and his exploitation of her trust. Rogerson goes to jail, and Caitlin's parents send her to a rehabilitation center—ostensibly, Caitlin enters rehab because of drugs, but she acknowledges that the real addiction she needs to overcome is her dependence on Rogerson. Caitlin's response to Rogerson's arrest suggests that Dessen is actively engaging with a concept of what psychologists call addictive love, which is marked by insecurity, changes in personality (particularly the use of alcohol or drugs as a coping mechanism), and feelings of fear and guilt. Brenda Schaeffer notes that "love addiction can range from an unhealthy dependency sanctioned by society to violence and abuse abhorred, but nevertheless promulgated, by that same society" (9–10). That Caitlin specifically requires therapy to overcome addiction, then, demonstrates the degree to which her relationship with Rogerson has altered her understanding of intimacy and its place in her other relationships.

As Caitlin chronicles the relationship from its passionate beginnings to its violent end, she depends upon the gradual development of intimacy within the narrator-reader relationship as a means of reconstructing an understanding of intimacy that allows for love and trust without the threat (or promise) of pain. Her hesitant but growing dependence on the reader as a safe space for disclosure suggests that Caitlin understands the reader as occupying a therapist-like role, a point that is emphasized by her eventual relationship with an actual therapist at the rehabilitation center. Like Ruby, Caitlin initially depends only on superficial disclosure, addressing the reader but refraining from the full expression of her thoughts, feelings, and fears. The reliance on foreshadowing in the opening chapters particularly suggests Caitlin's hesitation to disclose her concerns to the reader. As she offers clues to the potentially dangerous nature of her relationship with Rogerson, Caitlin hints at but does not explicitly acknowledge her growing awareness of Rogerson as a threat. The use of foreshadowing here, then, acts as a sort of narrative "cry for help," allowing the reader to recognize that there is cause for concern in spite of the fact that Caitlin has not yet gathered the courage to express that point.

Caitlin's changing descriptions of Rogerson also demonstrate the shifting nature of her relationship with the reader. Initially, Caitlin focuses on Rogerson's physical appearance and air of mystery, using descriptions of him to work through the immediacy of her attraction to him and the danger that she eventually comes to experience in the form of abuse. Though their physical relationship progresses quickly, reflecting the intensity of her attraction to him, Caitlin does not welcome the reader as a voyeur or partner in her desire; she offers no detailed descriptions of their kisses and acknowledges the loss of her virginity without any discussion of the decision-making process that preceded it or any details about the event itself. In this way, Caitlin clearly frames her desire for Rogerson as understandable but inaccessible to the reader, simultaneously demonstrating her hope that the reader will understand the initial attraction while deliberately removing the reader from some of the most intimate moments of her romance with him.

Dessen also emphasizes the manner in which a lack of communication not only plays a role in abusive relationships but more generally contributes to the destruction of intimacy. From the beginning of their relationship, Caitlin and Rogerson avoid discussing abuse, both his at his father's hands and hers at Rogerson's. As a victim of abuse himself, Rogerson provides a model of silence that Caitlin immediately follows when he becomes abusive. She also doesn't speak to her parents, her best friend, or her neighbor Boo (who she believes may have suspicions about the relationship), choosing instead to conceal her bruises with clothing and lie about the wounds she cannot hide; she explains to the reader that "I couldn't tell anyone. As long as I didn't say it aloud, it wasn't real" (171). As she comes to depend more heavily on the reader, Caitlin reveals anxiety about her relationship with Cass that reflects her fears about intimacy in general; because she is determined to hide the abuse from those around her, she confesses to the reader that she cannot speak to Cass when she calls on the phone because she feels sure that Cass will know immediately that something is wrong. Instead, she addresses Cass only within the confines of her journal, saying, "I don't know if you'll ever read this. Maybe I won't want you to. But something's happening to me and you're the only one I can tell" (161). Though Caitlin is ostensibly addressing Cass, this journal entry in fact reinforces the point that only the reader is privy to Caitlin's increasingly thorough considerations of her feelings and fears.

Like *Honey, Baby, Sweetheart*, Dessen's novel demonstrates the narrator's need to come to a stronger sense of disclosure, trust, and intimacy in general through her relationship with the reader before she is able to reconnect with the characters within the novel. Dessen traces Caitlin's slowly developing willingness to open up to the reader in order to highlight the impact that this has on her relationship with others; after having isolated herself and hidden her suffering from her friends and family, Caitlin ultimately relies upon narrative intimacy as a space in which to reclaim a sense of control over her life and her disclosure. Her gradual decision to make full disclosure to the reader allows Caitlin to claim a degree of authority over her experience, as it requires her to declare her own intentions, as well as to understand herself as having the power to decide how, when, and to whom she reveals herself. At the end of the novel, having chosen to disclose her experiences of abuse to her therapist in the rehabilitation center and, more importantly, to her mother, Caitlin is rewarded by the return of her older sister. Their reunion signals Caitlin's renewed willingness to pursue an intimate, trust-based relationship with Cass, the one person she most wanted to tell and the one to whom she felt least capable of speaking about the abuse.

Caitlin's relationship with Rogerson acts as an illustration of the progression from emotional to physical abuse, a progression which also has implications for other types of abusive relationships. Recent studies of sexual abuse within romantic relationships—which is generally defined as any sexual activity (including but not limited to rape) that is achieved through force or coercion—argue that such abuse frequently follows an established pattern of emotional or verbal mistreatment. In her 2005 novel, *Sticky Fingers*, Niki Burnham considers the development and potential consequences of sexual abuse in what the narrator initially believes to be a healthy romantic relationship. When Harvard-bound high school senior Jenna Kassarian resists her boyfriend Scott's pressure to have sex, she finds herself the victim of the date-rape drug; though Jenna's best friend saves her from being raped, Scott's decision to spike Jenna's drink with Rohypnol represents a violation of the boundaries she has drawn and her own understanding of their intimate relationship. As Jenna unravels the series of events that leads to the attempted rape and dissolution of her romance with Scott, she comes to depend upon the reader as a means of redefining and reimagining the problematic nature of that relationship.

Throughout the novel, the question of physical intimacy—specifically, the loss of Jenna's virginity—challenges what Jenna believes is an otherwise strong romantic relationship with her boyfriend of more than a year. Although Jenna thinks of smart, athletic, and popular Scott as nearly perfect and thus too good for her, his treatment of her throughout the novel suggests unrecognized verbal abuse. For example, when Jenna receives notification of her early acceptance to Harvard on the same day that Scott learns that he has not been accepted, she initially finds him supportive of her achievement. However, when she hesitates to accept his invitation to celebrate that night, citing her need to finish homework and study for a test, Scott chides her, saying, "You just can't let go, can you?" (18). Though Jenna bristles at his tone, she conceals her feelings and ultimately agrees to "relax" for the night. Her acquiescence to this first demand leads to a second, more problematic confrontation regarding their sexual relationship. Rather than taking her bowling, as he originally suggests, Scott takes Jenna to their normal "spot" to make out in his car. When she asks him twice to slow down, his response reflects the degree of control he demands as well as his lack of respect for the boundaries Jenna attempts to maintain. Instead of slowing down, he responds by pushing further ahead: "'Aren't you having fun?' he teases, easing his fingers just low enough to make me squirm" (25). Even after Jenna removes his hands, Scott continues to push, suggesting that if Jenna does not want to lose her virginity in a car they can rent a hotel room. When she continues to express reluctance, he says, "You're killing me, Jen. I want you so bad, and we've waited forever" (30). Scott's specific use of the word "we" here suggests his reframing of Jenna's refusal to have sex as a betrayal of a mutual agreement that they have never actually reached.

During this conversation, Scott's attempts to persuade Jenna to surrender to his desires reflect his willingness to test and efforts to redefine the boundaries of their relationship. Even as she expresses her concerns to Scott, Jenna reveals that he has been able to persuade her to do other things that are outside of her comfort zone:

> He runs his hand up under my white T-shirt, then gives me one of his wicked little Scott smiles I know is intended to make me cave in. It worked a few weeks ago, when he convinced me to bail on seventh period (there was a substitute) and go out to a movie to celebrate our one-year anniversary, even though I'd never skipped class before. But this is an entirely different situation. (29)

That Scott has convinced Jenna to engage in other activities that she regards as risky suggests that he, like Travis and Rogerson, has at times claimed control over Jenna's agency and attempted to redefine her behavior and personality. Jenna's assertion that "this is an entirely different situation," in turn, reflects her unwillingness to evaluate Scott's actions as potentially manipulative or abusive.

As time passes, Scott's insistence upon pursuing a greater degree of physical intimacy becomes more pronounced. Even as he apologizes for pressuring her, Scott makes a more explicit claim of authority over their physical relationship, telling her, "I think we're ready now. And before senior year is out, we're going to take that final step. I know it" (48). Though he once again frames his point in terms of "we" and their mutual readiness for sex, Scott effectively claims complete authority over what should be a decision based on both his and Jenna's feelings and desires. He also denies her the opportunity to refute his assertion, changing the subject before Jenna can respond; instead, she is left to note to the reader, "Guess that's the end of that conversation" (50). In response to Scott's dismissal of her doubts, Jenna attempts to adopt an equally confident stance regarding their sexual relationship; her willingness to acquiesce to Scott's framing of her own readiness for sex hints that, just as Ruby and Caitlin attempt to be the girls their boyfriends want them to be, Jenna will abandon her previous standards and behaviors in order to meet Scott's expectations.

Burnham also highlights the abusive nature of Scott's behavior by emphasizing the ways in which his treatment of Jenna exacerbates her growing struggle to maintain intimacy in her other relationships. Even as Jenna works to have control over the boundaries of her sexual relationship with Scott, she faces unprecedented challenges in her relationship with her best friend, Courtney, who has recently lost her own virginity and whom Jenna catches shoplifting. As Jenna tries to engage Courtney in conversations about these events, Courtney creates a distance that confuses and hurts Jenna. When Jenna happens upon Courtney and Scott in the middle of a fight, she becomes even more concerned. Although Scott claims that he and Courtney were simply talking about college applications, Jenna admits to the reader that she doubts his story: "My gut is telling me that the [college] thing is totally made up, that something else is going on and he just doesn't want to spill the beans" (144). In the face of this doubt, however, Jenna begins to distance herself from Courtney rather than Scott, believing that she can trust him over her best friend.

Despite her discomfort and confusion, Jenna refuses to identify Scott's treatment of her as problematic, instead expressing her belief that "he can't help but pressure me, at least a little bit" (117). That "pressure," which Jenna accepts as a natural part of their relationship rather than as a form of verbal abuse, takes a new form on the night of the New Year's Eve party. Although Jenna has expressed her lack of interest in drinking and parties in general, she agrees to go along with Scott's plans; she even drinks half of the beer that Scott gives her before admitting to herself that "drinking this stupid, nasty-tasting beer [is] a bass-ackwards way of making it up to

Scott for not having sex with him" (232). Within moments, however, Jenna begins to feel the effects of the beer: "I'm suddenly feeling totally light-headed and spacey, like I'm drunk. Even though I know I can't possibly be" (235). Soon after she registers her confusion over the impact of the small amount of alcohol she has consumed, Jenna finds herself vomiting in the bushes and passing out.

When she wakes up in the hospital, Jenna learns that Scott has slipped Rohypnol into her drink. Courtney fills in the gaps in the story: she overheard Scott talking to someone about buying the drug; when she confronted him in the fight that Jenna witnessed, he initially denied everything, then explained that he was looking for a way to help Jenna relax; after Courtney threatened to tell Jenna, Scott blackmailed her with the knowledge that she shoplifted. To Jenna, Courtney says, "Your boy-friend—a guy I really, really liked until a couple of weeks ago—is a total asshole. And it's about time you knew it" (258). Overcoming her initial disbelief, Jenna realizes that all of the information Courtney shares with her neatly fills the holes in her earlier conversations with Scott; in addition to his spiking her drink, then, Jenna realizes that he has actively deceived her and threatened her relationship with Courtney. Because she has so long acceded to Scott's framing of intimacy, this realization forces Jenna to reconsider the nature of their relationship, his treatment of her, and the trust she has placed in him.

This reconsideration, Burnham implies, begins with a general avoid-ance of contact and communication; because Scott's abuse has threat-ened Jenna's sense of control over the role of intimacy in her life, she struggles—both in her relationship with Scott and in her relationship with the reader—to reestablish comfortable boundaries of disclosure. After being released from the hospital, Jenna avoids Scott by chang-ing her schedule at school and refusing to take his phone calls. When he finally does reach her by phone and tries to apologize, she tells him, "Scott, you don't even want to know what I think about you right now" (261). To the reader, she completes her thought by explaining exactly what she does think:

> That I'm hurt. That I feel cheated and lied to. That all he ever really wanted was to get into my pants, and that when I made him wait too long, he figured he's get in there one way or another.
> That he couldn't possibly have loved me. (261)

Her unwillingness or inability to reveal these feelings to Scott acts as Jenna's ultimate realization of the problematic nature of their relationship. That she does feel capable of sharing these feelings with the reader, however, demonstrates the degree of narrative intimacy Jenna gradually cultivates in the face of the violation of intimacy she experiences at Scott's hands. Although Jenna's initial disclosure to the reader is marked by her unwillingness to acknowledge the warning signs of Scott's abusive nature, by the end of the novel—where this passage appears—she has come to rely upon the reader as a trustworthy confidante; through her increasingly open disclosure to the reader, furthermore, Jenna manages to reclaim a sense of control and comfort that Scott violates in his attempts to achieve sexual intimacy in spite of Jenna's boundaries.

As Jenna works through her conflicting emotions and desires regarding the loss of her virginity, she develops her relationship with the reader as a carefully detached one, relying on rhetorical questions and superficial disclosure. Even when tackling a particularly important question, as she does when she says, "I have to wonder—can you love a guy, really and truly love a guy, and not want to sleep with him? Okay—not *not want* to, but to question whether it's the right thing to do?" (54), Jenna resorts to hedging and hesitation rather than directness. Her question simultaneously signals a lack of certainty, as though she is responding to an imagined need for clarification, and more generally suggests her treatment of the reader as a sort of therapist to whom disclosure can be made as a means of untangling her confused thoughts and emotions. Over the course of the novel, Jenna admits with increasing frankness that she has doubts and misgivings about her relationship with Scott that add to her more general lack of readiness for sex. She only occasionally notes her pleasure; more often, she is focused on her distress and anxiety, frequently noting that these feelings stand in direct contrast to how she believes she should be feeling. As in *Honey, Baby, Sweetheart* and *Dreamland*, then, the moments at which Jenna discusses her physical relationship with Scott are not presented as voyeuristic opportunities but as occasions on which the narrator alerts the reader to the potential threat presented by her romantic partner.

Although the relationship between narrator and reader becomes markedly more intimate, Jenna remains hesitant to discuss her doubts and concerns with those around her, particularly her cousin Mark, with whom she has a strong friendship. Although Mark offers her advice and demonstrates his willingness to listen to her, she second-guesses her responses to his emails and ultimately sends back only generalized responses to his often very specific questions. For example, after Mark sends her a lengthy email giving her (unsolicited) advice about sex, Jenna replies with an email that says, "I'll leave you in suspense about my thoughts" (166). To the reader, however, she reveals the confusion she feels as the result of Mark's email, saying, "I mean, do I admit that Scott has been pressuring me for sex? Or do I tell Mark he's way wrong?" (174). Jenna's hesitation in speaking about her feelings and concerns to Mark reflects her implicit awareness of the ways in which Scott has threatened her views of intimacy. At the same time, as Jenna clearly distinguishes between thoughts that she can reveal to Mark and thoughts that she willingly reveals to the reader, she signals the possibility that she understands the reader, who is assumed to share her age and gender, to be a more appropriate outlet for her disclosure than the slightly older Mark, who may in fact threaten Jenna's already tenuous grasp on intimacy by insisting upon levels of disclosure with which she is uncomfortable.

Jenna comes to rely even more on the reader because of the suspicions created by Courtney's behavior and Scott's lies about it, which make Jenna question whether she can trust Courtney despite their history together. Although Jenna and Courtney are able to repair their relationship after Courtney confesses her knowledge about Scott, Jenna maintains a careful distance, relying more heavily on the reader than on Courtney even a year after the events narrated in the novel have taken place. In the epilogue, specifically, Jenna tells the reader that she has a new boyfriend, to whom she was introduced by her cousin and who has not pressured her to do anything outside of her comfort zone. She notes that she hasn't mentioned this boyfriend to Courtney yet, although she has been dating him for a few months. This ongoing distinction between her disclosure to the reader and to other characters in the novel acts as an indication that she is still working on rebuilding her understanding of intimacy; furthermore, because her friendships have been tested along with her trust in her relationship with Scott—a common theme in books about abuse and assault, as other novels in this chapter demonstrate—Jenna continues to rely on the reader as a safe space even as the novel ends.

In fact, narrative intimacy extends beyond the final pages of *Sticky Fingers*: Burnham includes an author's note, which directly addresses the reader and offers information and advice about date-rape drugs. Burnham specifically asks the reader to become familiar with a list of "several things you can do to protect yourself and your friends from these kinds of attacks" and encourages the reader to take it upon herself to research the subject further (277). Burnham thus explicitly reinforces—in ways that the other novels discussed in this chapter do not—the idea that Jenna should be understood as a model or warning for the reader, who is encouraged to use both Jenna's experience and Burnham's advice in order to avoid falling victim to such an experience herself. In a manner similar to self-help literature on the subject, then, Burnham asks the reader to follow her instructions, simultaneously depending upon narrative intimacy in order to ensure the reader's trust and asking the reader to acquiesce to her instructions in order to avoid the risk of an intimate violation. This parallel to self-help books suggests that Burnham is actively working within a set of concerns about young women's vulnerability to such abuse or assault that are constructed, at least in part, by such texts.

In the novels discussed thus far, narrators have worked within patterns of abuse that, over time, lead to their isolating themselves from those around them and only slowly regaining the assurance, through the development of narrative intimacy, to confide in those around them. In the case of the three texts in the following discussion, however, one central violation—namely, a rape either experienced or witnessed by the narrator—results in a break that often manifests as a total silence on the part of the narrator. In Louisa Luna's *Brave New Girl* (2001), narrator Doreen Severna struggles to navigate her feelings after being raped by her older sister's boyfriend. From the first time she meets Matthew, thirteen-year-old Doreen is intrigued by and attracted to him; when he winks at her, she says, "I feel a little twist inside my stomach" (4). Although Matthew is several years older than she is, he pursues what is at first an apparently platonic relationship with her that is increasingly marked by his testing of boundaries and ultimately results in his raping her. In response to the series of events that lead from Doreen initially considering the possibility of intimacy with Matthew to his violating that intimacy, she struggles to establish consistent narrative intimacy with the reader.

Soon after Matthew begins dating Doreen's older sister, Tracy, he initiates a series of strange, invasive interactions with Doreen. She describes him asking to come into her room, and, she says, "I watch him looking at everything, touching everything a little bit. He keeps talking to me but doesn't face me. He just stares at my wall, my CDs, the little picture of [her best friend] Ted that was taken when we were in the seventh grade" (6). Because Doreen is made uncomfortable by his presence and his authoritative approach, his actions mark the first breach of Doreen's comfort zone.

On another occasion, when he is waiting for Tracy, Matthew sits in the living room with Doreen, just staring at her. Her attempt to justify this strange behavior—"I don't know what his trip is, but he is really into staring at people. I don't think he does it to be rude, though"—further demonstrates her inexperience with, and difficulty in navigating, appropriate boundaries (13). Matthew later tests the limits further by asking Doreen to trade shirts with him. While Doreen admits that she is confused by this request, she agrees because "it seems like this trade means a lot to him. He really wants my shirt" (27). After she puts on his shirt, he turns and stares at her in a way that causes Doreen to "want to wrap myself in a blanket or something" (28). Though she acknowledges that he often makes her feel uncomfortable, she implicitly accepts her discomfort as the result of her own awkwardness and inexperience rather than on any act on his part.

In the midst of this confusion, Matthew once again invades the space of Doreen's room, this time when she's asleep. When she wakes up to find him sitting on her bed, her confusion intensifies: "We both just sit there, and I'm really wondering where the hell everybody is. Not because I want to talk to any of them or anything, but it's just that every time I'm with Matthew, or I see him, he makes me feel like we're telling each other secrets or something" (46). Doreen's sense of their interactions as secret-keeping comes into clearer focus the next time she wakes up to find him in her room. Having once again violated Doreen's privacy by entering her room without permission, Matthew tests another boundary by telling her that he likes her more than Tracy and kissing her. Caught off guard by his words and actions, Doreen can do little more than register what is happening: "And then he's kissing me inside my mouth, his tongue moving all slow—I can feel it against my teeth, and it's sort of shocking" (103–4). Her use of penetrative language points to Doreen's discomfort with Matthew's blurring of physical boundaries. He, in turn, is clearly aware that his actions are a violation because he covers her mouth, saying, "Shhh," to indicate that she should not tell anyone about the kiss (104).

Unsure of how to interpret or respond to Matthew's actions, she begins to entertain fantasies in which he breaks up with Tracy and becomes Doreen's boyfriend; drawing on her limited sexual knowledge, Doreen imagines the possibility of a physical relationship with him. In the face of these imaginary interactions, Doreen becomes even more conflicted when Matthew rapes her, struggling to even classify the event as a violation. When she wakes up from a dream to find Matthew on top of and inside of her, Doreen expresses her ongoing uncertainty, saying, "I don't even know how it started. Now even" (123). Matthew, on the other hand, demonstrates a clear awareness of and control over the situation: "And when I hurt so bad like someone was stabbing me I opened my mouth to say shit or something, he covered my mouth too. Shh. You're so perfect, Doreen" (124–25). The parallels between this and the earlier, limited violations—specifically demonstrated by her reliance on the language of penetration and his actively silencing her attempts at speech—intensify Doreen's confusion and guilt, as she did not reject or report his earlier advances. After the attack, Doreen struggles with both the emotional and physical effects of the rape. She throws her bloody sheets into a dumpster, but she decides not to take a shower or even wash off the blood that runs down her leg.

More than any other narrator discussed in this chapter, Doreen struggles to establish some stable sense of intimacy both before and after her experience of an intimate violation. Because of her young age and relative isolation from both her family and her peers, Doreen has not yet established any fully developed ideas about or understandings of intimacy when the rape occurs; her attempts to navigate her feelings and fears after that violation of intimacy, therefore, are more challenging because—unlike Ruby or Caitlin, for example—she has no solid examples or experiences of intimacy to which to return. Her relationship with the reader therefore reflects Doreen's ongoing confusion about the limits of disclosure and trust. Consequently, rather than relying on foreshadowing and other techniques that narrators such as Ruby and Caitlin use to maintain an initial distance from the reader, Doreen alternates between engaging and distancing the reader, at some moments disclosing more than the reader may expect while at others actively resisting any sort of narrative intimacy.

For example, in the opening lines of the novel, Doreen reports a series of instructions, insults, and demands that people present to her before telling the reader, "I don't say anything and just leave, because it's just easier" (2). This contradictory assertion—a claim of silence that appears on the first of approximately 200 pages of her narration—signals to the reader the degree to which Doreen may struggle with her understanding of disclosure. This challenge is further demonstrated in Doreen's own framing of her closest friendship as limited in its opportunities for disclosure and intimacy; Doreen tells the reader, "Ted doesn't understand that you can just forget things when you want to. It's a game. Just think like a little kid does and pretend something. Pretend you weren't in the room or pretend it wasn't you or pretend you were just the table or something instead of a body" (11). Doreen's description of her ability to establish distance even from herself reinforces the difficulties she presents to the development of intimacy even before the rape occurs, while her assertion that "Ted doesn't understand" the concept that she is explaining suggests that Doreen hopes to establish some common ground with the reader that she has not been able to fully develop with Ted. Within a few pages, Doreen underscores this suggestion with her admission that "Sometimes, when I'm listening to music, when I listen to the Pixies, I feel like I could scream . . . and then I think I'm pretty crazy and I can't ever tell anyone I have those feelings. Not Ted. Not anyone" (16). Again, by noting that the information she shares with the reader is not something to which Ted has been made privy, Doreen allows for a degree of intimacy with the reader that she does not seek or achieve with the characters within the novel.

At the same time, Doreen's focus on alienation and anger, revealed in the quotations above, allows her to hold the audience at a distance. In a two-page passage in which every sentence begins with the word "fuck," Doreen further demonstrates her isolating tendencies and expresses her anger at everything in her world (122–23). The final sentence—"And fuck you, too"—potentially alienates the reader, particularly because it includes the reader in the list of things that make Doreen unhappy; at the same time, the direct address to the reader is engaging, representing the possibility of inclusion. In other words, even as she insults the reader, she acknowledges the reader's presence and her disclosure to that reader. Indeed, Doreen seems to be presenting the reader with an implicit challenge to pursue narrative intimacy in spite of her resistance. Because Doreen seems initially to assume that the reader will dismiss and ignore her, as the characters within the novel tend to do, she only gradually allows for the possibility that the narrator-reader relationship may be a safe space for disclosure. Even when she does begin to confide in the reader, however, she does so in a manner that, because of its frequent stops and starts, more closely resembles the relationship between a patient and therapist than a friendship.

When she begins to notice Matthew's attention, however, Doreen becomes more willing to disclose her feelings and concerns to the reader, perhaps because of her increased awareness both of the possibility of intimacy and of her own lack of preparation for such intimacy. The first time Matthew kisses her, she tells the reader, "It feels like my stomach's dropping out, like wind is blowing through me, and I feel myself getting wet and I get embarrassed because of it and don't want him to know" (104). Doreen's explicit awareness of her sexual desire, as well as her embarrassment and wish to conceal it, marks the distinction between what she shares with the reader and what she feels willing to share with those within the novel. She exhibits a similar struggle with the boundaries of disclosure when she first attempts to articulate the experience of her rape:

> All I know is. All I know is nothing. All I know is there were rumors. All I know is that I didn't want to open my eyes really. All I know is that I couldn't move. All I know is that I still don't think I can move. All I know is that there's a big tear now and every time I close my eyes I think I can hear it happening—like a thousand pieces of paper being ripped in half. (123–24)

Doreen's repetition of the phrase "all I know" signals her doubt, even in her own ability to remember and define the trauma; it also echoes the passage earlier in the book in which she repeats the word "fuck." In this case, rather than alienating the reader through direct address, Doreen seems to be relying upon repetition as a means of seeking clarity and support, as she might in a session with a therapist.

Throughout the second half of the novel, Luna draws attention to the manner in which Matthew's violation of intimacy leads to Doreen's inability to seek connection with those around her through open communication; this refusal to disclose her experience, in turn, reflects Doreen's more general fears regarding victim-blaming and second assault. When an opportunity arises to tell Ted about the rape, for example, Doreen feels a fleeting impulse to reveal the situation to him: "What I almost say is, He fucked me, Ted, and I really didn't have anything to do with it, and I thought I wanted him to, but it hurt really badly and he didn't ask if he could, he just started and I was just lying there letting him" (169). Although Doreen lets the moment for disclosure pass, her ability to articulate these thoughts to the reader signals the first time that she fully acknowledges her lack of control over the situation and becomes open to the understanding that she has been raped. In addition to making this revelation to the reader, Doreen signals her ongoing struggle to navigate the boundaries of intimacy and trust by reaffirming to the reader, "I was about to tell [Ted], I swear," a claim that reveals both her defensiveness and her awareness of the reader (169). Even as she demonstrates her ability to make disclosure to the reader, however, Doreen's fear of second assault prevents her from confiding in her closest friend; instead, she insults and antagonizes him, actively constructing a distance between them rather than depending on and potentially deepening the intimacy in their relationship.

Only after Doreen rehearses her disclosure about the rape to the reader does she finally acknowledge it to her parents, who fail to recognize the few hints she tries to offer them prior to her confession. For example, after the rape, Doreen makes the explicit decision not to shower, something that directly contradicts what she has revealed to the reader to be a habitual attention to cleanliness; that no one notices her dirty hair and unwashed face highlights the degree to which Doreen is isolated from and ignored by everyone but the reader. Luna also reinforces the realistic dangers of disclosure after a violation of intimacy: Doreen's disclosure to her family, which begins accidentally but allows her to fully reveal Matthew's assault, involves a moment of second assault when Tracy laughs at her. When her father looks to Doreen to confirm this information, however, she immediately realizes that he believes her, which effectively prevents her from silencing herself again. This gives her the courage to open the lines of communication with her normally incommunicative father, for which she is later rewarded with the promise of healing and hope when her father gives her clean white sheets for her bed. Having established the narrator-reader relationship as a safe space for disclosure and the possibility of intimacy, then, Doreen begins to draw on the example of narrative intimacy in order to create stronger relationships with those around her.

In its depiction of acquaintance rape, *Brave New Girl* illustrates that— as studies such as Gloria Cowan's "Beliefs About the Causes of Four Types of Rape" have repeatedly found—adolescent women are much more likely to be raped by an acquaintance, friend, or dating partner than a stranger. Nonetheless, cultural representations of and concerns about rape perpetuate a still prevalent fear of rape at the hands of a stranger, such as the assault at the center of Laurie Halse Anderson's 1999 novel *Speak*. Anderson follows narrator Melinda Sordino as she struggles to recover from being raped by a stranger at a party that took place just weeks before her freshman year of high school began. Prior to the rape, Melinda had been part of a close-knit group of friends; when her phone call to the police led to the party being busted, however, Melinda found herself abandoned by those friends, particularly Rachel, her former best friend. Rather than explain the reason that she contacted the police, she isolates herself and accepts that it is her fate to be ostracized. Throughout her freshman year of high school, Melinda documents her thoughts and observations, often

alluding to the trauma she has experienced but not explicitly acknowledging it until more than halfway through the novel. Melinda thus gradually reclaims control over her voice, rehearsing disclosure to the reader
before enacting her new sense of empowerment by speaking out in the
final pages.

Although it is evident from the opening pages of the novel that Melinda
has experienced a traumatic event, she does not begin to make explicit
references to the rape for several chapters; even when she does allude to it,
furthermore, she relies upon code rather than immediately identifying her
attacker and the nature of the attack. For example, when she passes her
rapist, a senior named Andy, in the halls, she refuses to name him: "I see
IT in the hallway. IT goes to Merryweather. . . . IT is my nightmare and I
can't wake up" (45). Her use of the pronoun "it" suggests her unwillingness
to fully acknowledge the violation Andy committed; that she capitalizes it,
however, indicates the centrality of the event. She therefore draws attention simultaneously to the violation and to her inability to fully disclose it.
Likewise, throughout the first half of the novel, Melinda demonstrates an
inability to voice the word "no" even in nonthreatening contexts. When
the gym teacher asks her to show the basketball players how to shoot free
throws, for example, Melinda finds herself unable to refuse despite her
lack of interest in the activity. This inability to articulate refusal, particularly by simply saying "no," signals the nature of the violation and foreshadows Melinda's eventual disclosure.

That disclosure comes only after a series of events that both force
Melinda to recall the attack and reveal the necessity for the reader to
occupy a therapist-like role. The most vivid example involves the dissection of a frog in science class, which leads to a flashback that clearly
demonstrates the depth of Melinda's trauma and the degree to which her
inability to speak about her experience continues to affect her life and
relationships. As she watches her lab partner David pin the frog, Melinda
describes it in language that allows her to present the parallels between
the frog's situation and her own: "He spreads her froggy legs and pins her
froggy feet. I have to slice open her belly. She doesn't say a word. She is
already dead. A scream starts in my gut—I can feel the cut, smell the dirt,
leaves in my hair" (81). Melinda's personification of the frog, as well as the
abrupt shift from the narration of dissection to the memory of her own
attack, illustrates her struggle to navigate and articulate her memories;
she must displace the traumatic experience of rape onto the frog before
she can allow herself to acknowledge her own experience of having been

metaphorically cut open by the attack. When her recollection of the rape causes her to pass out, however, Melinda claims aloud that she is simply sick from the process of dissection rather than taking the opportunity to disclose the information to a concerned doctor. The reader-as-therapist, then, occupies the only space in which the psychological and emotional damages caused by Melinda's rape can be clearly seen and understood.

Only in the middle of the novel, after she has established a framework of foreshadowing and allusions, does Melinda actually reveal the details of the rape to the reader. In a vignette entitled "A Night to Remember," which plays on a common prom theme in order to draw attention to the ways in which hopes of romance are transformed into a painful assault, Melinda recalls meeting Andy, a handsome senior, at the party. After a couple of beers and a few moments of what could barely be called conversation, Andy begins to kiss her. She recounts an exchange in which Andy asks her, "Do you want to?"—explicitly noting that even in her confusion she responds aloud with the word "No" (135). Andy persists, pushing her to the ground and covering her mouth with his own mouth or his hand. In response to his physically silencing her, Melinda says, "In my head, my voice is as clear as a bell: 'NO I DON'T WANT TO!' But I can't spit it out" (135). Because this moment builds upon incidents she has already narrated, the significance of her ongoing inability to say the word "no" highlights the shift in the nature of her disclosure to the reader.

Furthermore, although Melinda does not dwell on her alcohol consumption, the fact that she and Andy both drink beers prior to the rape both reflects the real-life prevalence of alcohol consumption in sexual assaults among adolescents—according to one study, "It is estimated that approximately one-half of assault cases involve alcohol consumption by the perpetrator, victim, or both" (Rickert, Vaughan, and Wiemann 497)—and implicitly calls attention to a more general fear of second assault, as victims who admit to alcohol or drug use often find their stories met with a degree of suspicion or doubt. Indeed, Melinda's own experiences of disclosure reflect the very real possibilities of victim-blaming and second assault. After disclosing the details of the rape in "A Night to Remember," Melinda gathers the courage to reveal the rape to a character within the novel—specifically, her former best friend, Rachel, who has recently begun dating Andy. From the beginning of the novel, Melinda expresses her sense of loss at the broken friendship: "If there is anyone in the entire galaxy I am dying to tell what happened, it's Rachel" (5). In an attempt to prevent Rachel from becoming Andy's next victim, Melinda reaches out to her in a note; even in writing, Melinda is hesitant to make the disclosure: "*I didn't call the cops to break up the party*, I write. *I called*—I put the pencil down. I pick it up again—*them because some guy raped me. Under the trees*" (183). While Rachel first expresses sympathy when Melinda explains that she's been raped, she becomes angry and calls Melinda a liar when she identifies Andy as her attacker. While this exchange confirms Melinda's belief that people won't accept her story, the experience of making the admission in the first place is presented as crucial to her ability to speak out against Andy when he corners her and attempts to attack her again.

Indeed, throughout the novel Anderson attends to Melinda's gradual progression of reclaiming her voice, progressing through written word into speech as she reclaims her understanding of intimacy and control over disclosure. Particularly because she suffers a second assault, Melinda relies almost exclusively upon the narrator-reader relationship as a means of both coming to terms with the violation and attempting to navigate a new understanding of and control over intimacy. Melinda's treatment of the reader as therapist, furthermore, is marked by her gradual progression from hesitation to full disclosure. Her reluctance to speak about the rape is initially enacted in her limited disclosure to the reader: "I am not going to think about it. It was ugly, but it's over, and I'm not going to think about it" (5). Even once she has described the assault, however, Melinda continues to doubt her own interpretation of the events, as she demonstrates when she says, "If my life were a TV show, what would it be? If it were an After-School special, I would speak in front of an auditorium of my peers on How Not to Lose Your Virginity. Or, How Seniors Should Be Locked Up. Or, My Summer Vacation: A Drunken Party, Lies, and Rape" (164). Both her displacement of the disclosure to the imaginary audience of her peers and her question, "Was I raped?"—which she addresses directly to the reader—signal her need for affirmation and support (164). At the same time, this passage suggests that she is only able to entertain the question at all because she has already described the attack to the reader.

This gradual reclamation of control over disclosure and intimacy ultimately provides Melinda the strength to fight off Andy when he corners her and attempts to rape her again. At first, she is unable to articulate anything beyond a "no" that is revealed only to the reader, an echo of the "no" she both thought and spoke at the party; however, this time her silent "no" is followed by a loud, angry "NNNOOO!" that she says "explodes" from her (198). Having regained her voice through her disclosure to the reader, Melinda is able to reclaim both her physical safety and a sense of control over her experience: "IT happened. There is no avoiding it, no forgetting. No running away, or flying, or burying, or hiding. Andy Evans raped me in August when I was drunk and too young to know what was happening. It wasn't my fault. He hurt me. It wasn't my fault" (198). Melinda's use of clear, unambiguous language and her repetition of the sentence "It wasn't my fault" signal a newfound strength and confidence regarding her experience and her ability to heal from that trauma. In the final lines of the novel, Melinda draws upon this confidence as she opens up to her art teacher, Mr. Freeman, about rape in a moment that demonstrates her sense of control over disclosure and intimacy. The final words of the novel are, notably, "Let me tell you about it" (198).[7]

Notably, while all the narrators in this chapter express some degree of isolation from those around them, the experiences of Doreen and Melinda are marked by not only isolation but near-total *silence*. These two characters' dependence upon silence—or, perhaps more accurately, their shared belief that speech is not an option—suggests that rape is understood as so great a violation that it makes any sort of intimacy temporarily impossible. Only through the gradual development of narrative intimacy, which itself requires these narrators to overcome fears and confusion in order to reclaim what was an already tenuous grasp on the concepts of disclosure and trust, can Doreen and Melinda begin the process of speaking out to and receiving comfort from characters within the novels themselves. Once they break their silence, however, these narrators find themselves rewarded with the same types of hope and optimism that meet Ruby, Caitlin, and Jenna, represented in these novels by Doreen's father's gift of new white sheets and Melinda's opening up to the art teacher who has supported her.[8]

Even when the narrator herself is not the direct victim of the assault, the awareness of and indirect involvement in someone else's victimization can shake or destroy her understanding of intimacy; Courtney Summers's 2009 novel, *Cracked Up to Be,* thus illustrates Crompton and Kessner's assertion that young women who see or know of assaults suffered by their friends may respond with similar feelings of violation, guilt, and fear (203–5). After the rape and disappearance of her best friend, Jessie, privileged Connecticut teenager Parker Fadley attempts to isolate herself from her family and friends in the hopes of eventually disappearing altogether. Having developed a drinking problem, an anxiety disorder, and suicidal tendencies, Parker struggles to get through each day, a challenge that is further complicated by constant reminders of her former "perfect" self. As she stumbles towards the end of her high school career and the perceived escape it represents, Parker slowly reveals to the reader the circumstances that so drastically altered her personality and behavior. Parker does gradually offer the reader information about Jessie and her disappearance; in the process, she demonstrates that her own unwillingness to disclose these facts and feelings has been the direct result of her belief that free disclosure and her own abuse of intimacy caused the tragedy in the first place.

At the beginning of the novel, Parker explains that she has been attempting to alienate her friends and family since Jessie disappeared, relying primarily on a drinking problem and a suicide attempt to achieve that goal. "At first," she explains, "I drank to be caught. It was the start of my great campaign to distance myself from everyone" (31). Though Parker initially found success with this approach, she says, "I hadn't counted on my family and former friends conspiring against me" by interpreting her behavior as a cry for help and looking to intervene (31). Her "former friends," in particular, serve as a reminder of Parker's past as a popular cheerleader and straight-A student. Reflecting on her former pursuit of popularity, Parker explains, "I didn't want to be popular because it was easier; I wanted to be popular because in high school that's the best thing you can be: perfect. Everything else is shit" (70). Her self-imposed isolation and constant efforts to alienate everyone around her, therefore, represent a near-total reversal of her previous attitudes and behaviors. At the same time, Parker's reflections on her "old" self demonstrate that even before Jessie's disappearance, she may have struggled with intimacy, as she valued perfection and popularity over close friendships.

Her efforts to distance herself from those around her rely on two seemingly contradictory impulses: the first is to ignore her friends and family, the second to actively challenge their attempts to reach out to her through belligerent over-sharing. In other words, when she is not responding to them with silence, Parker goes out of her way to cause discomfort for those around her by speaking awkward truths. For example, when her ex-boyfriend confesses that he still has feelings for her, she responds by saying, "Why? I did awful things to you and I'd do them all over again" (33). By using uncomfortable or displaced disclosure, Parker attempts to push people away rather than drawing them closer. Parker also struggles with intimacy and disclosure when a new student, Jake, attempts to begin a relationship with her. Although Parker reluctantly acknowledges her attraction to Jake, and she does find some relief in his not having known her prior to the events that caused her to develop her current attitudes, she wavers when it comes to pursuing a romance with him. In turn, Jake's frustrations with her erratic behavior cause him to push for a greater degree of disclosure than she is willing to give. In his attempts to understand her better, he goes so far as to ask her if she was raped: "I've been trying to figure out why you're as fucked up as you claim you are. Is that what it is?" (88). Parker tells him that she was not raped, but she does not offer any sort of explanation for her being, to use his words, "as fucked up as [she] claim[s] to be." She eventually begins to date him—even though, as she tells him, "I know you deserve better" (118)—but still does not fully trust the possibility of a truly intimate relationship with him or anyone else.

Throughout the novel, Summers actively constructs parallels between Parker's treatment of the characters within the novel and her treatment of the reader; the gradual distinctions between the type and manner of disclosure allows her to highlight Parker's growing reliance upon the narrator-reader relationship as a therapeutic space within which she can grapple with her feelings of anger, guilt, and isolation. Summers achieves this most effectively in her portrayal of Parker's relationship with the school counselor, Ms. Grey. Although Grey offers Parker a confidential space for disclosure, assuring her, "This is your space. Feel free to say anything. You have my word that it won't leave this room. I want you to trust me. In learning to trust me, I learn to trust you, and from that trust we go forward" (17), Parker actively rejects and manipulates her efforts. While Parker initially withholds her thoughts and feelings from the reader as well, her gradual willingness to make disclosures to the reader—some of which explicitly call into question Grey's methods and motives—signals her need for a space in which she can in fact "feel free to say anything." While the implicit parallels between Parker's treatment of Grey and her treatment of the reader demonstrate her need to understand narrative intimacy as an opportunity for confession without the fear of judgment, her more general dependence on abrasive, sarcastic language as a means of alienating those around her indicates the difficulty Parker experiences in developing that intimacy. By relying on the same tactics she uses with her family, friends, and teachers, then, Parker challenges the reader rather than welcoming the possibility of disclosure.

Summers also emphasizes the development of the narrator-reader relationship and Parker's reclaiming intimacy through it by drawing parallels to Parker's evolving friendship with Jake. Because he did not know the "old" Parker, Jake is in some ways a prime candidate for her disclosure; even so, she stops short of telling him things, often completing her thought via narration to the reader rather than fully opening herself to him. For example, when Jake asks her how close she was to succeeding in her suicide attempt, she tells him, "I don't know," before adding to the reader, "Not close enough" (181). Eventually, Parker surrenders to her desires both for Jake and for some experience of intimacy, having sex with him despite her belief that it is a mistake. Rather than offering the reader a voyeuristic description of their night together, she describes the event in simple, tragic terms, saying, "It's terrible in its gentleness and he's just wasting it on me" (182). The next morning, although she finds herself surprised by the comfort she finds with him, Parker rejects Jake and the possibility of continuing their new romance, a move that marks a shift in the intimacy that she chooses to perpetuate and develop with the reader. In other words, her attempt to reclaim control over her understanding of intimacy through an ill-advised sexual encounter does not work, but it does allow her to reflect and rely on her relationship with the reader, from whom she no longer works to distance herself.

Along with Parker's move away from the sort of hesitation and alienation that continue to mark her relationships with characters in the novel, her growing dependence on the narrator-reader relationship is demonstrated by her increasing willingness to offer the reader information about Jessie's disappearance. Over the course of the novel, Parker offers a series of eleven flashbacks to the party from which Jessie disappeared, each of which builds upon the information that was revealed in the previous flashback. The number and construction of the flashbacks, furthermore, allows Summers to emphasize Parker's reluctance to establish *any* new relationship, even one with the reader. That Parker recounts the flashbacks in the same present-tense voice that she uses throughout the novel also indicates the immediacy with which she continues to experience the confusion, fear, and anger that marked the night of the party and Jessie's disappearance. Eventually, Parker's flashbacks reveal the last conversation she had with Jessie before the rape and murder. After being chided by Chris about her inability to relax at parties, Parker made the then-uncharacteristic decision to get drunk; in the middle of the party, she stumbled onto Jessie's boyfriend Evan kissing another girl in the kitchen. Drunk and disconcerted, Parker escaped outside, where Jessie found her trying to regain control over her senses. A concerned Jessie told Parker, "You're not responsible for everything, Parker. You can't control the way things end up. Stop trying" (109). These oddly prophetic words triggered Parker's anger, which had already been building as the result of Jessie's having told

Chris and their friends about Parker's increasingly common panic attacks. In response to Jessie's attempts to comfort her, Parker blurted out, "Evan's cheating on you with Jenny Morse. They're fucking" (110). This disclosure, inspired not by Parker's friendship for Jessie but her anger and desire to hurt her, led to Jessie's drinking too much and hooking up with the "clean-cut frat boy with an ugly mouth and dead eyes" who would rape her and drag her into the woods later that night (192). Having fully described this series of events, Parker explicitly links Jessie's disappearance with her own disclosure; when she found out that Evan was cheating, she says, "I was happy because I wanted to hurt Jessie for caring that I spent junior year hiding out in the girls' room between periods, hyperventilating. She wanted to help me and I wanted to hurt her for it" (207). Parker's belief that her use of disclosure as a weapon caused Jessie's death therefore laid the groundwork for her isolating herself from (and resisting the possibility of intimacy with) those around her.

Only when Jessie's body is found nearly a year after she first disappeared does Parker fully acknowledge the silence she has chosen and maintained. She recalls finding Jessie's bracelet in the woods two weeks after she went missing: "I think it's there for me because I killed her and I take it and I wear it so I never forget even though I'll never forget and I never say a word to anyone because if I hadn't said anything in the first place none of this would have—" (193). The run-on sentence that stops abruptly before Parker fully articulates her thought signals that even in this revealing moment, she struggles to reveal herself. Within pages of this disclosure to the reader, however, Parker finds it possible to reveal these details to a character within the novel, disclosing to Evan the events that surrounded Jessie's disappearance. When he attacks her, verbally and physically, Parker reveals to the reader that this pain is in fact what she has been seeking all along: "All I can think is *yes*" (198). Only after revealing the truth to the reader and then to Evan can Parker express the reasoning that has led to her silence:

> All I know is that I went to a party and I was the catalyst for every horrible thing that happened there and after and I don't know why I didn't say anything later and I don't know how to fix it and I'm afraid of what happens next, so I have to keep doing it this way until it's right again, but I don't know how to make it right again because I'm always wrong.
>
> I'm a bad person. (207)

Beyond the simple confusion of her involvement in the trauma that ended her friend's life, Parker struggles to articulate the impact that violation has had on her understanding of herself. Parker's conviction that she is a bad person who deserves to suffer is presented as a means of seeking comfort from the nonjudgmental reader who, because of the logical gap between fiction and reality, cannot respond with the accusations and physical attack that Parker claims to want. It is the reader's inability to respond at all that satisfies Parker's desire for a safe location for disclosure—it offers no possibility for betrayal, as she feels she betrayed Jessie.

In the final pages of the novel, Parker suffers one last panic attack and finally tells Grey everything, after which she begins the process of healing more explicitly. She notes how quickly everything begins to move, "from the moment in the hall telling Grey the truth to her creaming herself and telling my parents to them crying to the news slowly traveling through the school and not everyone thinks it's my fault" (211). She begins seeing a psychiatrist, and she concludes the novel on an optimistic note that involves the possibility of a renewed, healthier romance with Jake. At the same time, Parker's optimism is not unchecked; she says to the reader, "I know that's not the way life happens. There are no tidy resolutions. Ask me if I think it was my fault, if I think this heaviness will ever go away" (213). Through this direct address to the reader, Parker signals her desire that the line of communication remain open even after the book ends; this implication of ongoing communication further aligns the narrator-reader relationship with the actual therapy process.

As these six novels illustrate, narrators who experience abuse or assault frequently rely upon the reader in a manner that differs from the constructions of friendship and voyeurism seen in the novels discussed in earlier chapters: rather than beginning with the basic assumption of affinity and identification, in these novels, narrative intimacy is first challenged and eventually reclaimed through the process of the narrator's use of the reader as a therapeutic space. Even in this space, the narrators often hesitate, relying on foreshadowing and other elements to forestall their disclosure. These novels suggest that the violations the narrators have experienced cause not only isolation but real struggles to open up even within the safest possible space; narrative intimacy, in turn, develops much more slowly and requires the reader to accept the role of therapist. This construction of the reader's role is highlighted by the number of narrators who find themselves in therapy or therapy-like situations, particularly because in many cases, even those nonthreatening spaces are not available to them until they make an initial disclosure to the reader.

Through the construction of the adolescent woman reader as therapist, which allows authors to explicitly draw on cultural associations regarding the therapy process while avoiding the implicit power hierarchies commonly associated with confession, these novels also present narrative intimacy as the device through which hopeful conclusions can be reached. Because the reader's location outside of the text allows the narrator to disclose her experiences without fear of judgment or betrayal, the narrator is able to make disclosure without the fear of second assault that frequently prevents disclosure to characters within the novel. Only after having forged a connection with the reader in an inviolable space do these narrators find themselves able to connect or reconnect with characters within the novel. The narrator-reader relationship, with its echoes of the patient-therapist relationship, therefore model the possibility of healing and empowerment through intimacy. However, the same aspects of narrative intimacy that provide the possibility of empowerment for the narrators also problematically inform the expectations of the reader. By projecting onto young readers the expectations of a therapist-like role, such novels reinforce cultural contradictions: even as they offer portrayals of young women reclaiming intimacy, the expectations of narrative intimacy insist that the readers understand themselves as receivers rather than disclosers of information. In other words, while the novels demonstrate the potential benefits of disclosure for the narrators, they limit the reader's ability to necessarily identify with the process of disclosure itself.

More generally, the emphasis placed on the narrator-reader relationship as the only location for disclosure underscores a larger system in which young women are understood as vulnerable to the sorts of abuse and assault that occur within the novels. In particular, the development of narrative intimacy in these novels reinforces problematic ideas about young women as victims, as the narrator-reader relationship is not initially founded on affinity (as it is in the cases discussed in Chapters 2 and 3) but on the assumption that the reader will not be able to recognize or understand the narrator's trauma. In effect, this presents a construction of the reader as one who has *not* experienced this kind of violation and in fact suggests that the narrator's experience should help the reader recognize the warning signs that might help her avoid becoming a victim herself. Thus, as readers fulfill the role of therapist and allow the narrator to "speak" out through confessions and disclosure in order to achieve healing and hope, they engage in a network of expectations about gender and age that in fact reinforce young women's sense of vulnerability and the potential dangers of intimacy.

Chapter 5

"What if Someone Reads It?"
Concealment and Revelation in Diary Fiction

In the previous three chapters, I have considered the potential benefits of and threats to intimacy presented by young women's interpersonal relationships; generally, narrators' attitudes toward disclosure have been marked by their awareness of their vulnerability to such risks, while narrative intimacy has developed as a model or reflection of a contradictory expectation that young women should both seek intimacy and refrain from becoming too intimate with anyone. The model of storytelling employed by the narrators I have discussed thus far, furthermore, has placed less emphasis on the specific mode of communication than on the impulse driving that communication. While Ruby Oliver, discussed in Chapter 1, makes note of the laptop on which she is recording her story, most narrators depend upon a more vague use of narrative self-consciousness that clearly indicates their awareness of the storytelling process and their audience without identifying how their disclosure is being communicated. In this chapter, I shift from a focus on the *type* of disclosure being made to a closer examination of one common *location* for disclosure—namely, the diary, which has come to be closely associated with adolescent womanhood in contemporary American culture—and to the ways in which fictional adolescent women diarists actively anticipate readers in spite of the ostensibly private nature of the diary form. Because the diary itself represents both disclosure and concealment, as a diarist relies upon her diary as a space within which to reveal secrets for the express purpose of concealing them from others, fictional diaries provide the most overt opportunity for narrators to address their desire for a safe space within which to confess thoughts, feelings, and secrets they wish to conceal from other characters. In turn, as narrative intimacy in diary novels depends upon the narrators' paradoxical expectations that the private diary will have at least one reader, the genre offers a useful means of considering the contradictory expectations surrounding adolescent women's experiences of intimacy in contemporary American culture.

Though young women's personal diaries have been published and read by large audiences for centuries, suggesting that this "private" medium has frequently been understood as being anything but, the diary in contemporary America largely exists as a symbol of privacy and secret keeping. Indeed, diaries created for and marketed to young women frequently feature small (and often easily broken) locks and keys to ensure that the contents be kept secret.¹ More generally, popular culture frequently represents young women writing furiously in pink notebooks that are then stashed under mattresses or in underwear drawers in the hopes of being kept secret from the prying eyes of parents and siblings. Such expectations of young women as diarists are reflected in nonfiction literature that offers advice about how to go about writing—and concealing—a diary. In *Totally Private and Personal: Journaling Ideas for Girls and Young Women* (1996), author Jessica Wilber—herself a teenager—says, "There are many good reasons for keeping a journal at this stage of your life and forever. It's a good release when you're angry, sad, troubled, or even wonderfully happy. It's your safe haven for exploring your feelings and dreams" (1–2). Wilber goes on to note, "Remember, you're the only one reading your journal, so don't worry about what other people might think" (17), and she offers suggestions (such as developing a code, using "invisible ink," or drafting a Privacy Contract with parents) for keeping contents private. The book also includes some of Wilber's own journal entries as well as her mailing address; these gestures toward narrative intimacy invite the reader into a relationship that belies the privacy of the journal form. In *Write It Down!: A Girl's Guide to Keeping a Journal* (1999), Erica Smith reinforces these statements as she instructs readers to select the type of journal carefully, to decorate and personalize it, and especially to find a safe place to hide it. Noting that "on any list of things that are important to you, privacy is probably right at the top," she offers a list of "snoop-proofing maneuvers" to keep parents and siblings from reading the diary (Smith 24).

To some degree, however, the emphasis on privacy found in late twentieth and early twentieth century considerations of the diary relies on relatively recent assumptions about the form. As Deborah Martinson notes, around the beginning of the nineteenth century, "'Girls' in their adolescence were encouraged to keep 'nonproductive' diaries as an accomplishment, something like needlepoint, that did not take away from their femininity but could embellish their routine domestic duties" (4). In contrast to more technical diaries (such as ship captains' logs), the diaries of adolescent women began to record not only the events of day-to-day life but also the private thoughts, hopes, and longings of the diarists. At the same time, the popularity of published diaries, both real and fictional, increased, a trend that Trevor Field credits to the rise of the cult of sentimentality and a general awareness of young women as an audience drawn to sentiment, emotions, and romance (32). By the turn of the twentieth century, young women's diaries were published so regularly that Oscar Wilde remarked upon the trend in *The Importance of Being Earnest*. When Algernon asks Cecily if he might read her diary, she refuses because "it is simply a very young girl's record of her own thoughts and impressions, and consequently meant for publication. When it appears in volume form I hope you will order a copy" (II.1). Her response, while obviously humorous, illuminates the complex relationship between young women and their diaries, particularly the often contradictory impulse that one's personal, private "thoughts and impressions" are somehow destined to become accessible to a public readership.

Although Cecily's comments directly reflect a publishing trend of the eighteenth and nineteenth centuries, they also foreshadow a pattern of adolescent women's diaries becoming popular reading for broad audiences that continues more than a century later. Anne Frank's *Diary of a Young Girl*,[2] which has never been out of print since its original publication in 1952, has given way to counterparts such as the mid-'90s *Zlata's Diary*, which is also a war diary; a series of "real" diaries "edited" by Beatrice Sparks, the best known of which is *Go Ask Alice*;[3] and, more recently, works such as *The Notebook Girls: Four Friends, One Diary*, which was coauthored by four adolescent women. Despite the contemporary insistence upon young women keeping their private thoughts under "lock and key," then, the publication of such diaries acts as a very visible reminder that what may begin as a chronicle of secret thoughts and feelings may yet become a much less private venture.

These publishing trends not only reflect an ongoing, if evolving, understanding of the diary as potentially public but also a general understanding of the diary form as feminine. While many men have certainly kept diaries—and some of these diaries, such as Samuel Pepys's, have likewise gone on to be widely published and read—the form has increasingly been associated with women. To some degree, this association results from the larger cultural expectations of authors and authorship: in eras when women were discouraged from writing more masculine forms, many women writers turned to diaries because, as Judy Simons explains, "The female tradition of personal writing simultaneously invites opportunities for expressive release, guilt, and fictive construction. The diary form undoubtedly permitted women a degree of freedom of expression that was inhibited elsewhere, while still retaining some of its clandestine character" (255). As diaries have become an object of literary study, in turn, they have typically been understood as feminine because, Rebecca Hogan notes, their fragmentary nature and the lack of "the architectonics of shape or plot" sets them apart from the more "masculine" structures and cohesion of novels and other prose narratives (96). Furthermore, Hogan argues, the immersive, immediate nature of the diary has influenced critical responses to it, as "the privileging of details in the diary form gives it a structure and perspective which have been culturally and historically seen as feminine" (99).

The privileging of privacy likewise marks the diary as feminine, as the details recorded in the typical diary extend beyond the day-to-day realities of life to include emotions, memories, and concerns that are culturally linked to women. Although the diary stands as a symbol of privacy, however, the process of writing and keeping such a "secret" document requires at least some consideration of a potential audience. For some diarists, indeed, the potential audience is one of the motives for keeping a diary in the first place; as Joan R. Neubauer notes, two of the primary reasons for keeping a journal are providing a legacy for future generations and serving as the foundation for a memoir or autobiography (4). In turn, Adrienne Shiffman asserts that an "awareness of a possible readership, present or future, determines both the journal's subject matter and its approach and consequently calls into question the whole status of the diary as a private literary construct" (96). Despite the author's possible (and possibly even professed) intention that the diary and its contents remain private, then, most diarists write with an awareness that the diary may one day be read by themselves or someone else and may even secretly desire a public readership.[4] However, even if the diarist has no intentions of making the contents of the diary public—if the audience in question is limited to the author's future self, in other words—diarists have a tendency to construct a reader to whom to direct their writing as a means of offering some shape to the type, tone, and amount of disclosure they make.

Because the diary writer is also in almost every case the diary's primary (anticipated or real) reader, the relationship between narrative positions made available by the diary form is an inevitably complex one, resulting in what Jennifer Sinor calls an "inextricability between writer, reader, and text" (39). The assumption that the author and reader will be one in the same leads in some cases to the use of "circumscribed, even coded language," and authors of such private diaries frequently make little or no effort to provide context for the references they make to places, people, or occasions (Bloom 26). At the same time, the construction of diaries as private writings leads to the seemingly paradoxical expectation not only of *a* reader but of an especially *active* reader; as Sinor explains, "Because the form of diaries is less immediately accessible to readers and because reading diaries requires piecing together information, the reader of diaries must make more choices, become more involved than she would if reading a more accessible text" (39). While Sinor emphasizes the work of real readers in navigating the often confusing language of private diaries, her discussion also indicates the possibility of narrative intimacy through the diarist's expectation that a potential reader will be willing to face the challenges of such a personal narrative. This consideration of the potential relationship between author and reader in truly private diaries also provides insights into the even greater potential for narrative intimacy in diaries whose authors not only construct but actively anticipate readers. When a diarist does expect that her narratives will be read—leading to what Lynn Z. Bloom calls "public private diaries"—she typically employs techniques that signal an awareness of audience, including

> the employment of foreshadowing/flashbacks; emphasis on topics rather than chronology; repetition of philosophical themes and pervasive issues; character depiction; scene setting; and the use of integrative metaphors, symbols, and other stylistic devices. All of these techniques help to develop and contextualize the subject, and thus aid in orienting the work to an external audience. (Bloom 29)

In contrast to the diarist who expects that she will be her only reader, then, the diarist who expects an audience constructs the narrative in ways that invite readers, rendering the diary—and thus the diarist—accessible rather than mysterious.

Just as the awareness of a possible, if not necessarily known, reader influences the construction and content of real diaries, the possibility of an audience has a direct impact on the tone, content, and boundaries of disclosure explored by fictional diarists. In *The Diary Novel*, Lorna Martens asserts that "the private and confidential nature of the writing in most fictional journals, necessarily opposed as it is to the public form of readership represented by the novel, underpins both the intention and the achievements of their writers" (161). Put another way, novels written as diaries bring into conversation with one another the expectations of private forms and the demands of public ones. In turn, "instead of a narrator who creates a narrated world and addresses himself to a fictive reader, we have a narrator who takes himself as subject and is his own reader," which results in the real reader of the diary novel being in many ways aligned with the narrator (Martens 5). At the same time, many fictional diarists move beyond this limited concept of the reader as future self in order to create a more inclusive idea of audience. Specifically, in the case of the diary novels discussed here, the reader is constructed as an adolescent woman and, initially, a stranger, though in most cases the diarists gradually adopt a familiar tone and refer back to earlier recorded incidents in such a way that they clearly believe the reader will recognize and understand the references. It is important to note that, like Anne Frank, many fictional diarists explicitly distinguish between the diary as object and the reader of the diary. Just as Anne creates a friend, "Kitty," to whom she can direct the contents of her notebook, many fictional diarists use "you" and other direct address to refer to the reader rather than the diary. The diary is thus not the reader—and cannot be the reader—because it is the space that the narrator and reader share.

As is the case with the novels discussed in previous chapters, the fictional diaries discussed here demonstrate the authors' dependence on Lamarque's "logical gap" between fictional narrator and real reader as the foundation of narrative intimacy. Fictional diarists' tendency to construct an understanding of the unknown reader who becomes a familiar confidante, then, signals the desire for an audience who can receive disclosure without responding with judgments or criticism.[5] Furthermore, as H. Porter Abbott writes, "The principal advantage of diary fiction . . . is the *immediacy of the writing itself"* (29, emphasis in original); in other words, even if the narrated event is in the past (of any distance), the act of narration is immediate. Martens likewise notes that the diary novel "emphasizes the time of writing rather than the time that it is written about. . . . This present-tense progression tends to dominate the subject matter, so that the diarist usually writes about events of the immediate past—events that occur between one entry and the next—or records his momentary ideas, reflections, or emotions" (4–5). The immediacy of the writing not only shapes the content of the diary novel but also has a direct impact on the construction of the reader as implicitly involved in the diarist's decision making: an awareness of a present or future reader influences the diarist's choices regarding what to *do* as well as what to *write*. That diarists almost necessarily employ narrative self-consciousness (most frequently by documenting the time and place of their writing) further signals the diary novel form's particular usefulness in the creation of an implicit intimate relationship between narrator and reader. Narrative intimacy in diary fiction thus allows readers perhaps the most explicit example of the decision-making process behind disclosure and, in turn, intimacy, as diary writers frequently address their choices to withhold certain pieces of information from those around them, for fear that the information they report to their diary alone might cause problems in those relationships.

The types of narrative intimacy I have discussed in the previous chapters remain relevant in diary novels, which allow for a construction of the reader that is more generalized but no less intimate than in novels that construct the reader as friend, partner in desire, or therapist. In her book for adolescent women diarists, Smith describes keeping a diary as "having a secret friend you can tell everything to—someone who listens and doesn't pass judgment" (6–7); for many young women, in turn, the "everything" they feel encouraged or compelled to reveal includes details of their romantic feelings and experiences, from first crushes to first kisses and beyond. The diary can also act as a location for the sort of disclosure and discussion of personal feelings frequently associated with therapy; indeed, Philippe Lejeune identifies as one of the primary functions of the diary "to release, to unload the weight of emotions and thoughts in putting them down on paper." Because the diary novel is generally positioned as an inclusive chronicle of a period of time rather than a focused discussion of a limited series of events, furthermore, the unknown reader that many fictional diarists construct may in fact be called upon to fulfill any or all of these roles (at times simultaneously) over the course of a novel.

This constructed reader is, moreover, expected to identify with the narrator, as anticipated affinity remains a crucial aspect of narrative intimacy in works such as those discussed here. Precisely because they struggle with their interpersonal relationships, fictional diarists typically extend invitations to readers in order to create some form of connection that depends upon mutual understanding. Unlike true private diaries, which frequently do not make an effort to ensure continuity, clarity, and coherence, diary novels merge the conventions of public private diaries and typical novels—using, as Bloom notes above, techniques such as foreshadowing, metaphor, and a focused interest in pervasive themes—in order to provide a somewhat paradoxical sense of accessibility to the constructed reader. In turn, the reader's awareness of the diary's status as fiction allows for a violation of privacy that would be unacceptable within the context of most real interpersonal relationships. Here I return to Richard Walsh's treatment of fictionality, first discussed in my introduction; I refer particularly to his assertion that "fictionality is neither a boundary between worlds, nor a frame dissociating the author with the discourse, but a contextual assumption by the reader, prompted by the manifest information that the authorial discourse is offered as fiction" (36). Because the reader can approach these texts with a full awareness of their fictionality, the violation of privacy that would normally be associated with the reading of one's personal diary is somewhat mitigated and, in fact, encouraged as a necessary step toward an intimate relationship with the narrator.

In order to explore the construction of narrative intimacy in diary fiction for adolescent women, I discuss contemporary American novels that adopt the form of a diary, journal, or notebook intended for the purpose of private disclosure and secret keeping. Meg Cabot's *Princess Diaries* series and Megan McCafferty's *Jessica Darling* series offer fairly traditional treatments of the diary novel: in both cases, the teen diarist relies almost exclusively on her diary as a means of navigating the struggles of high school life and pondering the challenges of young adulthood. In Margaret Peterson Haddix's *Don't You Dare Read This, Mrs. Dunphrey*, the narrator in question initially keeps her diary as a school assignment; the novel follows her progressive acceptance of the diary as a safe space for disclosure even as she submits the notebook to her teacher on a weekly basis. The final two novels discussed here, Julie Halpern's *Get Well Soon* and Alyson Noel's *Cruel Summer*, complicate some of the conventions of diary fiction by drawing on epistolary form in order to further emphasize questions of privacy, secret keeping, and narrative intimacy. Although their specific reasons for keeping a diary vary, each of the narrators discussed in this chapter provides insight into larger concerns regarding disclosure and discretion that reveal the degree to which they have internalized cultural expectations about intimacy.

In Meg Cabot's popular *Princess Diaries* series (2000–2009),[6] narrator Mia Thermopolis comes to rely on her diary as her constant companion and sole confidante. The series begins just days before Mia, a high school freshman, learns that she is a princess and the future ruler of a small (fictional) European principality and follows her through high school as she attempts to balance school, her social life, and daily "princess lessons" with her overbearing grandmother. A self-professed freak with big feet and small breasts, Mia comes to rely on her diary as the only space within which she can be completely honest about her feelings, from her anxiety over her mother's burgeoning relationship with Mia's algebra teacher to her crush on her best friend Lilly's older brother, Michael, and her general uncertainty that she has the qualities and desire necessary to rule a kingdom. Regardless of her immediate conflicts and concerns, Mia expresses an ongoing struggle with the limits of honesty that comes to dictate the organization and inclusion of details throughout the series, though the structure and consistency of Mia's diary entries undergo a notable change over the course of the series as a whole.

From the beginning of the series, Mia acknowledges (and sometimes obsesses over) her own tendency to lie to those around her about her thoughts, feelings, and experiences. Indeed, the first line of *The Princess Diaries*—"Sometimes it seems like all I ever do is lie" (1)—establishes this theme, while the passage that follows offers insights into the type and goal of lies that Mia frequently finds herself telling:

> My mom thinks I'm repressing my feelings about this. I say to her, "No, Mom, I'm not. I think it's really neat. As long as you're happy, I'm happy."
>
> Mom says, "I don't think you're being honest with me."
>
> Then she hands me this book. She tells me she wants me to write down my feelings . . . since, she says, I obviously don't feel I can talk about them with her.
>
> She wants me to write down my feelings? Okay, I'll write down my feelings. I CAN'T BELIEVE SHE'S DOING THIS TO ME! (*Diaries* 1)

The contradictory assertions that Mia makes to her mother and to her diary (regarding her mother's romantic relationship with Mia's algebra teacher) substantiate Mia's claim regarding lies and establish a pattern that continues throughout the series. The motive behind this specific lie—protecting her mother's feelings, an unselfish gesture on Mia's part—signals Mia's more general understanding of dishonesty as a version of appropriate behavior. In other words, Mia's lies, both those she makes outright and those she makes by omission, reflect her belief that complete honesty is potentially hurtful or selfish. The diary, then, most immediately offers her a location within which she explores honest, complete disclosure without disrupting her relationships with those around her.

The passage above also demonstrates the immediacy with which Mia embraces the diary, both as an object and as a concept; the journal accompanies her to school, meetings with her royal father and grandmother, and, on at least one occasion, church. The diary's omnipresence is marked both by the narrative self-consciousness Mia employs by constantly noting the date, time, and location of her writing process and by the inclusion of material other than private entries—for example, because Mia often writes in her diary during the school day, her personal disclosure about events in her life is frequently interrupted by her algebra notes or French phrases. Mia becomes so dependent upon the diary as an outlet that she even writes about events as they occur, providing truly immediate narration of her experiences. In *Princess in Love*, Mia documents her entire thought process as she tries to decide how to respond to a note she has just received from her hapless boyfriend, Kenny, who has recently confessed that he loves her. As he waits for her to respond, Mia writes,

> Oh, God. *Now* what am I supposed to do? He's sitting here next to me, waiting for an answer. In fact, that's what he thinks I'm writing right now. An answer.
>
> What do I say?
>
> Maybe this is my perfect opportunity to break up with him. *I'm sorry, Kenny, but I don't feel the same way—let's just be friends.* Is that what I should say? (*Love* 59)

This entry continues as Mia considers her options, particularly the possible repercussions of breaking up with Kenny (who also happens to be her biology partner) right before the school dance and their final exams. Mia even goes so far as to begin drafting the breakup note in her diary before the bell rings to end their class. Throughout the series, such immediacy marks Mia's diary as a crucial element in her ability to navigate both her relationships with characters in the novel and her relationship with the reader, to whom she directs questions that indicate a desire for a sympathetic listener who might even be able to offer her advice.

Not only does she adopt this type of conversational address to an unidentified "you," but she also offers descriptions of people, places, and events that would not be necessary if she believed the diary's content would never be made available to anyone but herself. Though she herself is a native New Yorker, Mia frequently provides descriptions of local venues such as the Central Park Zoo and even offers directions to various tourist attractions, suggesting that she wishes to make her setting clear and accessible to a reader who is not familiar with New York—a reader other than herself. She also offers detailed physical descriptions of the people around her, referring to qualities such as her father's shiny bald head, her grandmother's tattooed eyebrows, and Lilly's resemblance to a pug. As time passes, Mia comes to rely less on descriptions of her friends and family members, which suggests a belief that the reader has already developed a familiarity with these characters, and begins making references and allusions to past diary entries. In the process, the *Princess Diaries* series reflects one of the most important qualities of public private diaries, indicating an expected reader by avoiding the kind of "coded" language associated with written works that are truly intended to be private.

Although Mia frequently chooses to write while surrounded by her friends and family, she seems to believe that the private nature of the diary will dictate other people's acceptance of her need for privacy and even expresses annoyance when those around her ask what she is writing, read over her shoulder, or complain about her writing while they are trying to speak to her. For example, after expressing a particularly vehement thought, Mia notes, "Oh, my God. Lilly just leaned over to see what I was writing and saw that last part. That is what I get for using capital letters" (*Pink* 19). Even as she resists others' efforts to insert themselves into her diary-keeping, however, Mia frequently signals a more general, implicit understanding of a potential reader, particularly in her tendency to make comments that suggest she is considering a reader other than her future self. While Mia does become comfortable with the idea of *a* reader, it is important to note that she reacts differently when confronted with the possibility of *specific* readers, as evinced when her English teacher, Mrs. Spears, requires them to begin keeping a journal to be submitted at the end of each week:

She has got to be joking. Like I am going to allow Mrs. Spears to be privy to my innermost thoughts and emotions. I won't even tell my innermost thoughts and emotions to my *mother*. Would I tell them to my *English teacher?*

And I can't possibly turn *this* journal in. There's all sorts of stuff in here I don't want anyone to know. (*Spotlight* 6)

Mia resolves to start a fake journal for her teacher, despite the fact that she quite explicitly began keeping a diary in the first place so that she would have a place to be honest about her thoughts and feelings. Mia has immediate concerns about her teacher's judgments and criticisms of her diary's contents because this audience does not offer Mia the distance that the implicit, impossible relationship with the reader does. Her impulse to protect the contents of her private diary, particularly the "stuff . . . I don't want anyone to know," privileges her relationship with the reader as the one space within which she feels comfortable making certain assertions and confessions.

The consequences of Mia's struggles with honesty become the primary focus of each of the ten novels in the series; in particular, Mia's failure to be honest with her best friend, Lilly, and her eventual boyfriend, Michael, form the central, organizing points of several novels. To some degree, Mia's forthrightness about her inability to be fully honest with her closest friends acts as a means of reinforcing her dependence upon narrative intimacy. For example, early in the series, Mia confesses to the reader, "I could never tell Lilly, but secretly I sort of want to be Hilary Duff. Once I had a dream I *was* Hilary" (*Diaries* 167); immediately after admitting this, she adds, "Isn't that an embarrassing thing to admit?" (*Diaries* 167). The reference to Duff signals Mia's expectation of affinity, as she assumes that the reader will be familiar with the famous teen singer/actress; in turn, the phrase "I could never tell Lilly" explicitly distinguishes between Mia's understanding of her best friend and the reader as friend, while her acknowledgment that this particular confession is potentially embarrassing demonstrates her belief that she can make this disclosure to the reader without fear of being teased or judged. This moment also reflects the tension that troubles Mia and Lilly's friendship throughout the series, largely as the result of Mia's romantic attachment to and eventual relationship with Lilly's older brother Michael. Although Mia admits her crush to the reader early in the series, she also explicitly rejects the possibility that she can speak to Lilly about it: "I'd *never* want Lilly to know that I feel that way about her brother. She'd think it was weird" (*Diaries* 60).

When Michael confesses his own romantic feelings to Mia at the end of the third novel, the focus of Mia's diary entries shifts from her lies to Lilly to concerns about her ability to be honest with her new boyfriend. In *Princess in Waiting*, Mia endangers her relationship with Michael by taking her grandmother's advice to emulate Jane Eyre by withholding information and playing hard to get (87). Although Mia eventually realizes the flaws in the Jane Eyre plan, she continues to struggle with her disclosure to Michael throughout the series, particularly in terms of her feelings for him. Despite his assurances that he loves her, Mia frequently hesitates to reciprocate; to the reader, she explains, "I mean, it's embarrassing, telling the person you love that you love them. It shouldn't be, but it is" (*Waiting* 95). Mia's inability to tell Michael the truth acts as both a means of perpetuating the pervasive theme of honesty that informs the series as a whole and as reminder that the diary and its constructed reader are made privy to more details about Mia's feelings than those closest to her.

Mia's complicated concerns about honesty eventually lead to the downfall of her romance with Michael as tensions over their physical relationship build. The reader is also made aware of Mia's fears about sex in ways that Michael is not. While Mia explicitly tells Michael that she is not ready for sex, she does not fully explain the reasons behind her hesitation (which include her fear of taking her clothes off in front of him, a concern that she freely expresses to the reader). This awkwardness regarding sex and embarrassment at voicing her feelings for Michael indicate a lack of readiness on Mia's part for both the emotional and sexual intimacy that their relationship may potentially entail, which ultimately (and ironically) leads to the end of their relationship when Mia overreacts to Michael's admission that he is not a virgin. The depression Mia experiences after their breakup, in turn, perpetuates her struggles with honesty, particularly when she begins seeing the unfortunately named Dr. Knutz. Indeed, Mia frequently reports to the reader the questions he has asked and the analogies he has used to help her confront her struggles in order to offer thoughts and opinions that she has withheld from him during their sessions. Frustrated at the lack of progress she has made towards feeling like herself again—which she expresses towards the end of the novel, writing, "God. I just . . . when am I going to start feeling BETTER? When am I going to get out of this hole Dr. Knutz PROMISED me he'd help me out of?" (*Mia* 210, ellipses in original)—Mia must eventually recognize the possibility that expressing her feelings to someone other than the unknown reader of her diary may allow for the possibility of healing. Like the narrators discussed in Chapter 4, then, Mia begins to understand her disclosure to the reader as a sort of rehearsal for disclosure to Dr. Knutz and, more generally, her parents and friends as she reclaims a feeling of normalcy.

Mia's increasing willingness to make disclosure to the characters in the novel is marked by a shift in her relationship with the reader. This is signaled in part by changes in the immediacy of Mia's narration; in the first four volumes, Mia writes many times each day, and there is no more than a few days difference between the end of one novel and the beginning of the next. However, as the series continues, Mia's writing becomes less consistent: more than two months pass between the end of the fourth volume and the beginning of the fifth, for example. And as she grows older, the length of time that passes between volumes grows considerably—more than eighteen months pass between volumes nine and ten. As the amount of time that passes between entries increases, Mia's willingness to make complete disclosure to the reader likewise undergoes a transformation. This becomes particularly evident in her chronicling of her reunion with Michael in the final novel of the series; as she and Michael overcome their past obstacles, Mia becomes more reticent regarding their physical relationship. When she loses her virginity to him on prom night, she writes, "I don't want to go into too much detail about what happened between us here in his loft last night, because it's private—too private even for this journal" (*Forever* 369). For the first time, as she reaches new levels of intimacy with Michael, Mia creates the kind of distance from the reader that her concerns about honesty have caused her to maintain from the characters within the novels themselves. In marking this shift from complete disclosure to an explicit concern with discretion (which is similar to Bella's sudden reticence about her physical relationship with Edward at the end of Meyer's *Twilight* saga), Cabot seems to suggest that Mia has outgrown the need to rely on her diary as an outlet for all of her thoughts, feelings, and experiences. That the series ends just a few pages later with Mia's graduation from high school underscores the suggestion that the diary is an object uniquely suited to young women as they navigate cultural demands regarding concealment and revelation; the narrative intimacy developed throughout the series, then, ends as Mia becomes an adult.

Like *The Princess Diaries* novels, the five novels that make up Megan McCafferty's *Jessica Darling* series (2001–2009) follow their narrator as she struggles to navigate the problems of school and social life; however, whereas Princess Mia's saga ends with high school graduation, Jess's story continues through college and into her early adult life. In the first novel, *Sloppy Firsts*, Jess begins writing a journal as a means of expressing her sadness at her best friend Hope's moving away and documenting her day-to-day frustrations with everyone else in her life. However, like Mia, Jess quickly comes to depend on her diary as the only safe space in which to disclose not only her loneliness but also a series of secrets she keeps from everyone, including—and in some ways especially—Hope. The five novels follow Jess over the course of ten years, as she attempts to make sense of her feelings for the enigmatic Marcus Flutie, decide where to attend college, and figure out what she should do with what seems to be a useless degree in psychology. Throughout the series, McCafferty emphasizes Jess's attention to detail in her descriptions of the places, people, and situations she encounters, which not only reflects the immersive, accessible nature of Jess's diaries but also highlights the potential for narrative intimacy that such immersion encourages.

From the beginning, Jess demonstrates an awareness of and concern about the potential that the contents of her diary may be read. Early in her diary-keeping process, Jess addresses this question to the reader: "Who is this for, anyway? Who are you? Who actually found this notebook and cares enough to read it? You must have little to do. Wait. Are you *me* twenty-five years from now? Too weird. Stop thinking, Jessica" (*Firsts* 122). In this moment, she implicitly aligns the reader with her future self even as she expresses some degree of discomfort with the idea that even she herself will revisit this diary's contents. Soon, however, her disclosure takes on a congenial, familiar tone as she increasingly relies on direct address to a reader who is decidedly *not* her future self, as demonstrated when she instructs the reader to "go ahead and Google me" (*Thirds* 38). More importantly, Jess actively seeks affinity with the reader by calling upon what she assumes to be shared knowledge, opinions, and desires. These affinity-seeking moments vary from fairly superficial pop culture references, such as her note that "as you know, [MTV's *The Real World*] returned to none other than New York City for its tenth season" (*Second* 190), to highly personal confessions, as when she describes a sexual fantasy, writing, "In the X-rated version, there is no wardrobe or intelligible dialogue. The plot is best left to your (okay, *my*) prurient imagination" (*Thirds* 20).

While Jess ultimately welcomes the possibility of an unknown reader with whom she assumes to share common interests, the series also offers examples of how she reacts to readers other than the one she imagines.

In *Sloppy Firsts*, Jess reacts with surprise when her teacher refers to an essay that Jess had written about Hope months earlier; the comment, Jess writes, "reminded me that someone actually *read* what I wrote" (193). More to the point, she admits, "I had shared something personal, and the very idea of it made me kind of queasy" (193). That she feels so uncomfortable recognizing the intended audience of a public discourse makes her concerns about the privacy of her diary more pronounced. For this reason, when Jess enrolls in a summer writing course that requires her to keep a journal, she decides to create a second diary "that was highly censored, unlike [her] personal journal, which isn't censored enough" (*Second* 33). As this comment indicates, Jess's concerns about the degree of disclosure she makes in her personal journals remains a theme throughout the series. She makes occasional attempts at self-censorship and sometimes notes her surprise at the depths of her disclosure, writing comments such as "Jesus Christ. I can't believe I just wrote that" (*Firsts* 249). Indeed, she becomes so self-conscious about the contents of her diary that she decides to destroy it, as she explains in the opening pages of the second novel, *Second Comings*:

> My last journal was the only eyewitness to every mortifying and just plain moronic thought I had throughout my sophomore and junior years. And like the mob, I had the sole observer whacked. Specifically, I slipped page by page into my dad's paper shredder, leaving nothing but guilty confetti behind. (*Second* 3)

Jess's willingness to destroy diary pages reveals a desire to deny the possibility of audience beyond the unknown reader. At the same time, her documenting this impulse draws attention to a paradox: namely, that the reader has read all the pages that Jess claims to have destroyed and that, as a result, the reader has in fact been an "eyewitness" to events that Jess now claims go undocumented. This paradox, which is made possible by Jess's reliance on the logical gap between herself and reader, emphasizes Jess's struggle to discern the level of disclosure with which she is comfortable with the characters within the novels themselves.

Throughout the series, Jess reinforces her commitment to narrative intimacy through a willingness to offer detailed descriptions to the reader, a reminder that she anticipates a reader other than her future self. Indeed, the opening paragraphs of *Sloppy Firsts* focus on her birthday present from Hope, a mosaic that recreates a favorite photograph of the best friends

(3). Furthermore, the details that Jess chooses to include not only help to make her experiences more accessible to the reader but also provide clear insights into her character. At one point, for example, Jess provides detailed descriptions of each of her friends' bedrooms before describing her own:

> **My room:** Walls the color of a week-old bruise from when Hope and I tried to slap gray over the hot pink paint my parents picked when I was a baby. Dozens of dusty plaques, trophies, and ribbons unceremoniously toppling over each other on a shelf in the far corner. Several "new classics" movie posters (*Sixteen Candles, Stand by Me, Say Anything*). Mind-blowing mosaic of two smiling friends. (*Firsts* 67, bold in original)

To some degree, this level of description serves the same purpose as Mia's discussions of New York landmarks: the amount of detail Jess provides indicates not only that the reader she anticipates is not her future self—who would not need a long explanation about the color of the walls in her bedroom—but someone who has never (and likely will never) see the bedroom. At the same time, the details Jess includes here also reinforce qualities she has already begun to reveal to the reader, such as her rejection of her parents' expectations for her and the value she places on her friendship with Hope.

Jess continues to carefully set the scene for her reader even as her location changes; her time at Columbia, for example, allows her several opportunities to describe in detail the streets of New York, the coffee shops and cramped apartments she visits, and her own dorm. Like her earlier description of her bedroom, Jess's description of the latter provides as much insight into her personality as it does the location itself. She writes, "[My dorm] is one of the oldest dorms on campus and looks every minute of its age, with paint-over-paint-over-paint-over-paint jobs and industrial carpeting in that vague grayish-brownish hue designed to hide all manners of filth," and she goes on to note that all of the rooms are "depressingly cold, boxy, and utilitarian" (*Thirds* 253). While the description does allow the reader to visualize the dorm, Jess's diction also offers insight into her own emotional state while occupying this space: as she has recently gone through a breakup and has begun to question her decisions to study psychology (and take on massive debts in the process), Jess is at this point in the series experiencing a sense of isolation and despair that her descriptions of her surroundings help to convey to the reader. Although Jess never expresses the depth of her sadness and loneliness during this period to the other characters in the novel—and in fact merely skirts around the issue even in her diary entries—the by now expected physical descriptions she offers continue to make her accessible to the reader.

Jess employs the same degree of detail when discussing the people around her, providing yet another indication that she anticipates a reader who is at first unfamiliar with her friends and family. The ways in which her descriptions evolve over the course of the series, furthermore, act as a means of illustrating Jess's changing relationships with the other characters in the novel, from her flame-haired, artistic best friend Hope to her neatly dressed perfectionist mother and the high school classmates Jess can never quite escape. Just as her descriptions of the setting act as representations of Jess's personality and emotional state, in turn, her descriptions of the people around her work to illustrate her changing attitude toward intimacy, particularly in terms of her relationship with Marcus. At the beginning of the series, Jess describes Marcus as a "dreg," someone who spends more time doing drugs than doing homework. Her first detailed description of him ultimately foreshadows the evolution their relationship will undergo as they become friends, then enemies, and ultimately lovers: "He's got dusty reddish dreads that a girl could never run her fingers through. His eyes are always half-shut. His lips are usually curled into a semi-smile, like he's in on a big joke that's being played on you but you don't know it yet" (*Firsts* 23). Her consideration of his dreadlocks suggests an as yet unrecognized desire to touch his hair, while the reference to the "big joke" eventually gains greater significance when he confesses that he initially set out to seduce her, just to see if he could. When the two finally overcome their early obstacles—including his time in rehab and her doomed relationship with his best friend—Jess adds new details to her descriptions of him, including mentions of his changing hairstyles and facial hair, as well as frequent references to the fact that he smells like autumn leaves. Although their romance faces continued difficulties, including the distance that separates them when they begin college on opposite sides of the country, Jess's cheating on Marcus with a classmate, and eventually a rejected marriage proposal, Jess's attention to physical detail provides a consistent measure of her changing feelings about Marcus and their relationship.

As the novels trace Jess's journey from high school to college and early adulthood, they undergo a notable transformation of their own—the first three novels follow fairly conventional diary form, though the entries in the third diary become more sporadic and less complete; the fourth novel maintains the diary form but redirects Jess's disclosure directly to Marcus; and the fifth novel abandons diary form altogether. In the process, the narrator-reader relationship changes to reflect Jess's understanding of disclosure and discretion. In *Charmed Thirds*, as Jess faces the challenges of college life, particularly the long separations from and occasional breakups with Marcus, her dependence on the reader begins to shift. In particular, this novel calls attention to the long delays between events and writing: a year passes between the end of second and third novels, and months pass between entries as she chooses to write only while on her summer and winter breaks from college. Jess also begins to rely on flashbacks as a move away from the immediacy that has marked the first two novels, which gestures toward the possibility that she has come to rely less on the journal because she has largely learned how to deal with her secrets without it. For the first time, the reader is made aware of events in Jessica's life *after* those around her—her friends, Marcus—from whom she has likewise been withholding the information. Confessions regarding not only her cheating on Marcus but also a pregnancy scare are thus delayed for several months and presented only when Jess documents conversations in which she reveals this information to characters within the novel itself. In other words, Jess forgoes her former immediacy, instead aligning the reader with those characters who have been previously denied access to her innermost thoughts and feelings.

In *Fourth Comings*, Jess chronicles her thoughts and feelings with more immediacy than in any of the previous novels: over the course of one week, she fills a notebook with both her day-to-day activities and previously undocumented recollections of past events. However, because this notebook is constructed specifically as an attempt to respond to Marcus's marriage proposal (which she ultimately rejects) the immediacy of the narration is mitigated by the reader's being aligned not with Jess's future self (or the roles the reader has previously occupied as friend, partner in desire, and therapist) but with Marcus. Initially, in fact, Jess makes it difficult to discern the identity of her intended reader: the first use of direct address to a "you"—a parenthetical aside in which she notes that a phenomenon known as frustration-attraction "explains a lot when it comes to you and me"—could refer to the unknown reader of the first three novels (*Fourth* 39); she doesn't clarify that "you" now refers exclusively to Marcus until several pages later. Because Jess's lengthy response to Marcus's simple question primarily works to demonstrate to him how little he really knows about her, this fourth novel in the series actively creates a distance between Jess and the reader, even leading the reader to question the engagement and intimacy that mark the earlier novels.

The final novel, *Perfect Fifths*, abandons first-person voice altogether, severing the narrative intimacy that the first-person voice and diary form have worked to establish in the previous installments. Instead, McCafferty employs a variety of narrative techniques in the four sections that make up this novel: the first and last sections use omniscient third-person narration (allowing for both Jess's and, for the first time, Marcus's point of view); the second section functions as a script, offering only dialogue and stage directions; and the third section is made up entirely of a series of haikus that Jess and Marcus write back and forth to pass the time. This suggests that McCafferty herself wishes to draw attention to the role of narrative in the construction of Jess and Marcus's relationship, as well as in the implicit relationship between narrator and reader that has been evolving over the course of four novels. Jessica, who is now working as a mentor in a nonprofit program called Do Better High School Storytellers Project, further draws attention to this point when she explains to Marcus that "humans are, uh, uniquely adapted for narrative constructions. Studies indicate that we begin to see ourselves as characters in our own life stories in adolescence, with key periods serving as different chapters" (*Fifths* 130). At the end of the novel, when Marcus and Jess decide to renew their romantic relationship, they again raise the point of narrative by discussing the "story" of their relationship and how they will tell it—together—in the future.

The fact that the *Jess Darling* series ultimately moves away from diary form reflects a more general statement regarding the unique relationship between young women and diaries. Like Mia, who likewise moves from a near total dependence on her diary to her decision to stop recording her innermost thoughts and feelings, Jess experiences a progressive change in her understanding of her diary and, in turn, the reader, resulting in her abandoning her diary entirely at the age of twenty-two. That both Cabot and McCafferty use serial fiction in order to present the stories and experiences of their narrators, furthermore, indicates a more general desire on the part of both authors to trace the role of the diary in adolescence to what they suggest is its logical end.[7] Because both narrators have understood the reader as a friend, partner in desire, and therapist, the decision to distance themselves from and then cease their dependence on the reader altogether further signals a more general shift in their views of intimacy.

Cabot and McCafferty thus use the novels' progressions to intimate that each of these fictional diarists has "grown out of" her dependence on her diary because she has come to understand the role and limits of disclosure in her real-life relationships.[8]

In the *Princess Diaries* and *Jess Darling* novels, the narrators' concerns about potential readers are somewhat limited and eventually displaced by the more general construction of the reader as welcome within the private space of the diary; however, as Haddix's 1996 novel, *Don't You Dare Read This, Mrs. Dunphrey*, illustrates, not all diarists begin writing under such circumstances. By presenting narrator Tish Bonner's diary as an assignment for her high school English class, Haddix explicitly considers the problem of privacy and the complications that arise when a diarist must remain constantly aware of a possible reader. Though the titular Mrs. Dunphrey requires that the students write at least two entries a week, she offers them the option of marking entries "Do Not Read" and assures them that she will respect their privacy. Tish, who initially questions both the value of the required journal and her teacher's claims that she will not read marked entries, gradually comes to see the journal as the only space in which she can safely navigate the confusion and anger caused by her unstable home life. Over the course of the novel, furthermore, Tish's construction of the reader changes from a limited alignment with Mrs. Dunphrey to a confidante with whom she can share information she is not yet prepared to make available to anyone else. Haddix relies heavily on foreshadowing, particularly in terms of Tish's unpredictable mother and the family's financial struggles, in order to present Tish's diary as a cohesive consideration of the dangers of disclosure and the need for discretion.

When her teacher first presents the journal assignment, Tish writes only brief entries, feeling the need to firmly establish the limits of Mrs. Dunphrey's claims that she will not read marked entries before beginning to disclose truly personal information. For example, Tish includes a surprising but generally innocuous piece of information about herself—"I know how to crochet"—in an early diary entry marked "Do Not Read" (6). After testing Mrs. Dunphrey by asking her if she knows how to crochet and determining by the teacher's confused expression that she really has not read the journal entry, Tish begins to include more information about herself, though she initially remains somewhat superficial in her disclosure. Although she alludes to a problematic home life, saying, "You've probably been past my house—and if you haven't, you've seen ones just like it. Small. Poor. Falling down," she only gradually reveals the type and degree of problems she experiences at home (9). As the reader gradually learns, the return of her abusive father, who left the family years before, has begun to wreak havoc on an already dysfunctional family life; he scares Tish's little brother, hits Tish, and steals money from her mother. After he leaves the family again, Tish's already emotionally unstable mother decides to follow him, abandoning Tish and her brother with no money and no ability to contact her. As she finds the situation slipping out of her control, Tish finally records her story in its entirety in her journal and, days later, makes the decision to allow Mrs. Dunphrey to read it.

Over the course of the novel, as Tish's attitude regarding the role of the diary in her life changes, her awareness and construction of the reader shift as well. From the beginning, Tish addresses Mrs. Dunphrey directly, even in entries that are explicitly marked "Do Not Read." Frequently, her tendency to address Mrs. Dunphrey even as she refuses her access to the content of the entry allows Tish to express a thought or feeling that would otherwise go unspoken, as when she writes, "I wouldn't admit this to anyone, of course, but this journal stuff isn't too bad. . . . As long as you're not reading this, I can just put down whatever I'm thinking" (15). Such references—which explicitly assert her desire for privacy even as they signal her implicit desire for a reader—also draw attention to the complicated alignment between Mrs. Dunphrey and the reader. When the reader confronts the phrase "as long as you're not reading this," the larger significance of Tish's coming to rely on the diary signals her seeking a safe space and thus a reader who will not threaten her sense of control. Tish marks almost every entry "Do Not Read," using the more emphatic "Don't you DARE read this, Mrs. Dunphrey" for the entries she feels most anxious about. When Tish accidentally forgets to mark a real entry "Do Not Read," Mrs. Dunphrey's response—in which she praises Tish's talent as a writer and encourages her to write more—causes Tish to become even more vigilant about denying her teacher access to her most personal thoughts.[9]

At this point in the novel, Tish begins to explicitly distinguish between her possible audiences. Rather than addressing Mrs. Dunphrey, she shifts to addressing an unnamed third person, making comments such as, "So now Mrs. Dunphrey knows I'm having problems. Great" (32), and mocking the suggestion that Tish join the literary magazine, saying, "Isn't it hilarious that she thinks I should try out for *The Lodestar*? . . . Like I'd want to hang out with those snobs. Like I even care about writing anything" (33). Furthermore, having drawn a clear distinction between Mrs. Dunphrey and the unknown "you" to whom she directs such comments,

Tish becomes willing to articulate her understanding of the diary as a private yet shared space: "You don't suppose she's been reading some of this, do you? (Geez, who am I asking about that? You'd think I thought this journal was a real person" (57). In other words, by explicitly wondering about the identity of the "you" to whom she is directing her question, Tish recognizes her tendency to assume the presence of an audience and even rely upon this unknown reader as a safe recipient of her thoughts and feelings. Although Tish occasionally slips into second-person address to Mrs. Dunphrey later in the diary, the split seen here demonstrates her more general understanding that the audience is not (or is not *only*) Mrs. Dunphrey, as well as positioning the reader as a more welcome audience than the teacher has been.

From the beginning of the novel, Tish hints at and eventually reveals her unhappiness at her home life, coming increasingly to depend upon the reader as means of expressing and exploring those feelings. In particular, Tish gradually reveals her concerns about her parents and their relationship, noting her mother's "odd expression" when she makes an unexpected knock-knock joke and hinting at her distrust of her long-absent father when he returns without warning or explanation (Haddix 24, 37). She also discusses her desire to save money to buy a Nintendo for her brother's birthday by saving the money she makes working part-time at a fast food restaurant; she ultimately fails, though she notes, "Maybe I would have been able to, if Mom would give Matt and me lunch money instead of me always paying for everything" (Haddix 34). When her father once again disappears and her mother decides to follow him, leaving Tish with no explanation and almost no money, these hints from the beginning of the novel take on new significance: the concerns and frustrations that Tish has mentioned in passing become the foundations upon which she can make larger revelations to the reader and, eventually, Mrs. Dunphrey.

At the same time, Tish uses many of the techniques demonstrated by the narrators discussed in Chapter 4 in order to forestall the full revelation of her situation. For example, she attempts to distance herself from the reader by asking, "Do you know how dumb this is? What good is this journal, anyway? . . . it's not like anybody would care about my life, that they'd ever read this (or that I'd ever let anyone read this)" (67). The dismissive tone that Tish employs in addressing these questions signals her resistance to the possibility of gaining anything from the diary exercise. However, because she addresses these questions to a reader who she immediately declares does not and cannot exist, Tish does gesture toward a hesitant realization of the healing potential of disclosure. Indeed, only a few days later, she observes, "It does make me feel a little better to write, since I can't talk to anyone" (81). As Tish grows more confused, frustrated, and eventually desperate, she comes to rely more and more on the diary as the only location within which to confide her feelings. The reader, then, provides Tish with a safe space even if she is not always fully willing to depend on it.

As Tish runs out of money to pay bills or buy food, she resorts to desperate measures, even shoplifting ground beef; she also begins missing a great deal of school, often because Matt is ill but also because she is embarrassed about her clothes and lack of money. Mrs. Dunphrey notices Tish's absences and attempts to talk to her, especially after Tish fails to turn in a research paper. In response to these shows of concern, Tish writes, "I wish I could just say, 'Look, Mrs. Dunphrey, here's why that paper doesn't matter to me. You want to hear what my life's like?' It'd be such a relief to tell someone about Mom leaving" (109). That Tish specifically wants to make available to Mrs. Dunphrey the information she has already revealed to the reader reflects her understanding of the reader as a space within which to rehearse disclosure. In the case of *Don't You Dare Read This, Mrs. Dunphrey*, the distinction between disclosure to the reader and eventual disclosure to a character within the novel overlap completely; when Tish finally reaches a point of hopelessness and marks an entry "DO read this, Mrs. Dunphrey" (114), it is in order to ask her teacher to read the journal entries that the reader has already read.

In the novel's final pages, Haddix reveals that Tish and her brother have moved to Florida to live with her father's parents; their mother, embarrassed at her decision to chase their father across the country rather than care for her children, visits occasionally and sees a therapist to help her recover from the mental and physical abuse that she experienced during her marriage. While Tish admits to being annoyed by her grandparents at times, her final letter to Mrs. Dunphrey more generally reveals that she has finally begun to feel content about her life and future prospects. The novel thus figures Tish's disclosure to the diary—and her eventual willingness to let Mrs. Dunphrey read it—as a step toward healing and safety; in contrast to the experiences of Mia and Jess, who seemingly understand the diary as a space within which to gradually determine the role of discretion in their interpersonal relationships, Tish's attempts to keep secrets act as a warning about appropriate disclosure. While the diary does offer her a space within which to confront and navigate feelings that she does not feel comfortable expressing, it also forces her to realize that in some cases, disclosure is more appropriate than concealment.

In contrast to narrators who rely on diaries to document and conceal their thoughts, Anna Bloom, narrator of Julie Halpern's 2007 novel *Get Well Soon*, initially chronicles her story in the form of unsent letters to her best friend Tracy. When Anna finds herself in an institution for troubled teens—her parents having enrolled her at Lakeland Hospital in an attempt to help her overcome the depression that has plagued her for years—she must confront the feelings of loneliness, isolation, and sadness that have prevented her from making meaningful connections with those around her. Although Anna documents her day-to-day activities, thoughts, and feelings faithfully, she ultimately decides not to send the letters to Tracy. Instead, over the course of the novel, she shifts from addressing Tracy to constructing an unknown reader to whom she feels more comfortable confessing her startling realization that she has found a clearer sense of belonging in this institution than in any other place in her life. Although the form shifts from ostensible epistolary novel to more traditional diary novel, Halpern maintains a sense of coherence and continuity—qualities not typically associated with truly private diaries—by incorporating a pattern of references to writing utensils, which become symbolic of Anna's ability to create a connection not only with the reader but also, gradually, with the people around her.

In the first pages of the novel, Anna employs narrative self-consciousness as she establishes both her location and the reasons behind documenting her experiences at Lakeland. She explains, "They told me to write. Write down your feelings. It'll help you" (1). When given a pad of paper and pencil with which to carry out these instructions, she remembers a journal she once kept that was likewise intended to make her feel better and was also written in pencil:

> When I went back to read all the depressing stuff that I wrote, it was gone. Smudged away. I wrote it all down, the stories of my life, my feelings, all the crap you're supposed to write in journals so you can look back and see what a loser you used to be. But it was all gone, mushed together as if none of it mattered in the first place. Which it didn't. Because I still wound up here. (1)

While the purpose of this passage is most immediately to justify Anna's decision not to simply keep a journal, it also allows Halpern to raise the question of the purpose of a diary; because Anna has associated keeping a diary with being a loser—and has apparently believed that the diary really only offers benefits to a future self who can learn from the mistakes recorded in it—her resistance to keeping a diary now signals a more general concern on her part about the future, rather than current, implications of making disclosure to a diary. While her decision to write to Tracy allows her to subtly subvert the orders of her caretakers, then, it also demonstrates her belief that if someone else has her letters, she cannot return to them and feel worse about herself later.

Anna's initial decision to write letters rather than a diary also draws attention to the genre of the novel as a whole, particularly in terms of the construction of the narrator-reader relationship. In his discussion of epistolary and diary forms in Goethe's *The Sorrows of Young Werther*, Gerd Bayer provides this helpful distinction regarding the nature of the narrator, narratee, and reader in novels constructed as either (or both) letters or diaries:

> If the personal communication between close friends . . . provides readers with an allegedly truthful account of the story, courtesy of the text's trustworthy (and reliable) narratee more so than the reliable narrator (which Werther, for a number of reasons, is not), the complete abandonment of the dialogical nature in the adoption of a diary, which cuts out the phatic function as the central characteristic of the epistolary voice, makes such monological texts speak from a position of unquestionable integrity; or at least the readers are implicitly invited to think so. (184)

Although novels discussed elsewhere in this chapter include infrequent epistolary moments,[10] *Get Well Soon* is the only novel that initially acts exclusively as an epistolary text. Therefore, while Bayer's assertions regarding the use of epistolary features in creating a trustworthy narratee apply to varying degrees to several texts in this chapter, they are most immediately relevant to the construction of Tracy, as the reader's growing understanding of the already established friendship between Anna and the ostensible audience of her letters provides a framework within which to understand the implicit desire for trust and intimacy in the narrator-reader relationship as well. At the same time, the novel's eventual evolution from epistolary to diary form undermines this assumption by revealing that Anna has in fact withheld information from Tracy in the past.

The treatment center's strict rules—which include "No talking in the hallways" and "No touching (ever)"—initially force Anna to rely almost exclusively on her "letters" to Tracy; she has required meetings with a psychiatrist she refers to as Dr. Asshole, and she has to attend group meetings every day, but she typically refrains from speaking openly in those spaces. Despite her intentions, however, Anna soon acknowledges that she has not yet fully put her letter-writing plan into action. In one letter to Tracy, she begins, "Well, a week later and I still haven't actually mailed you a letter. I'm kind of afraid of what they'll do at the front desk if I ask for an envelope and a stamp" (48). Anna's slight paranoia regarding the conditions surrounding her letter-writing provides insight into Anna's more general struggle to fully reveal her thoughts and feelings, even to her best friend. At the same time, her earliest letters to Tracy reveal that despite their long friendship, Anna has recently withheld her most intimate feelings. In explaining her absence from school, she confesses—apparently for the first time—that "for awhile now I haven't been feeling very *normal*. Like, I can't sit through classes without getting antsy and claustrophobic and having to get up to go to the bathroom (so embarrassing). My mind starts racing and racing, and I can't concentrate on things at all" (4). That Anna has not made such a crucial piece of information available to her closest friend suggests that Anna's hesitation reflects a more general concern about the potential response she might receive from Tracy; in turn, this provides a context for her dependence on revealing her thoughts to an unknown reader who cannot respond to (or, more specifically, cannot judge or condemn) Anna's disclosure.

Because the novel begins as correspondence with someone who had been an intimate friend, Anna manages to maintain the type of immediate, engaging information that makes narrative intimacy even as the friend in question shifts. To some degree, this shift follows Anna's gradual acceptance of and growing comfort with her environment: early entries focus on the past, as she frequently begins sentences with the phrase "remember when" while providing only superficial descriptions of her surroundings and the other patients on the adolescent floor. Over time, Anna begins to reconsider the audience of her disclosure; in turn, the direct address to Tracy becomes less and less frequent while Anna offers more detailed descriptions and more complete disclosure. This shift becomes more apparent when Anna discusses a daily activity without assuming mutual knowledge of the film in question. "Today our afternoon movie was the 'classic' '80s flick *The Boy Who Could Fly*," she says before asking, "Do you know this movie?" (136). The fact that she responds to her own question with a fairly detailed description of the film reveals Anna's new expectation that the audience in question is not Tracy but an unknown reader, one who needs information to which Tracy would already have access. This change in her expectation of the reader is also signaled by her movement from direct addresses to Tracy to a more generalized "you." In other words, Tracy is eventually relegated to third person as Anna writes *about* rather than *to* her.

In addition to the shift from epistolary to diary form, *Get Well Soon* signals the expectation of an unidentified but not unwelcome reader by offering a consistent emphasis on writing and writing utensils, lending the narrative a sense of coherency that indicates a desire on Anna's part to provide accessible, engaging information to her audience. From the beginning of the novel, Anna takes note not only of the day and location of her writing but also, and eventually more importantly, her writing tool: a pencil that she dislikes because, she writes, "they smudge" (1). This concern with permanence and clarity—further expressed in the passage above in which she considers the "smudged away" contents of her last journal (1)—provides insight into Anna's more general struggles to express herself adequately to the people around her. By drawing attention to the writing process in terms of both the content and the medium, Halpern indicates the significance of pens, pencils, and other writing utensils to Anna's attempts to create connection both with the reader and, eventually, with the other patients at Lakewood.

When Anna meets her new roommate, Sandy, for example, she initially struggles to make a connection with her. Unlike Anna, who comes from a comfortable suburban home, is overweight, and has never been kissed, Sandy has been raised in a working-class home, is a tiny cheerleader, and has left behind a boyfriend. Initially, Anna worries that Sandy will think she's a dork; over time, however, she becomes more comfortable with their friendship, particularly as Sandy treats her as something of a confidante. Halpern returns to the symbol of writing utensils to illustrate this shift in their relationship: Anna receives a gift of colored pencils, which the two young women use to draw portraits of each other. Looking at Sandy's work, Anna notes, "I was pleasantly surprised at the lack of chins Sandy drew on me. . . . One could even call her drawings flattering, not *fattering*" (88). These images, as well as the colored pencils used to create them, come to symbolize their growing friendship, as they allow Anna to see herself through Sandy's eyes and recognize the potential for a connection she might not otherwise have believed possible. In turn, Anna eventually sees Sandy as a trustworthy friend, someone to whom she can reveal her secret crush and from whom she can seek advice about how to act on it (162–63).

Writing also plays a key role in Anna's relationship with Justin, the cute but shy object of Anna's secret crush. Because she has never dated and lacks self-esteem, Anna struggles to read the clues that Justin may reciprocate her feelings for him, leading her to not only report details to the reader—including a description of an elevator ride in which their hands *almost* touch (95)—but also her own insecurities about her body and the potential downsides of dating someone in (and out) of a mental institution. Eventually, however, Anna realizes that Justin shares her own concerns about expressing his feelings, a point that becomes clear when he confesses to Anna the reasons for his being institutionalized: he used to play bass in a band and dream of becoming an architect, but an accident with a saw led to his cutting off two of the fingertips on his right hand, resulting in his inability to pursue either of his future goals. Feeling that he had nothing to live for, he attempted to kill himself, but his reattached fingertips were not strong enough to pull the trigger. Even now, he is only gaining the strength to write his name, which he has been practicing prior to this disclosure. Anna gathers the courage to touch his scarred fingers, after which "he carefully gripped his pen and wrote *Anna* next to his name" (168). The pairing of their written names foreshadows the next step in their romance when they sneak a kiss while on a field trip. Writing continues to play an important role in their relationship as Anna's last day at Lakewood approaches. Justin slips her a note that says, "Write your phone number down, so I can call you if I ever get out of here" (183). In response, Anna "scribbled my phone number and tried to think of something sincere . . . to sum up all of my feelings for him over the past three weeks," though she runs out of time and "all I could get down was my name with a small, messy heart next to it" (183). This note illustrates both her willingness to pursue a continued relationship with Justin and her inability to fully disclose her feelings about him, including the doubts and fears that she presents in a series of fervent questions to the reader: "How could I ever forget about him? At the same time, would we ever really go out for coffee? . . . Do we belong together in the real world? It could never feel as special and intense as it did here in a mental hospital" (188). The distinction between what she has written to Justin and what she continues to write to the reader, then, reinforces Anna's larger efforts to navigate the limits of disclosure and discretion in her interpersonal relationships.

Indeed, the novel's conclusion allows Anna to explicitly comment on the significance of the writing process, which in turn provides Halpern an opportunity to highlight the larger importance of narrative intimacy as a means of accessing confidence and healing. When Anna is released from Lakeland three weeks after her admission, she decides not to mail the stack of letters on her desk. In explaining her decision to keep them for herself, she notes, "Pencil or not, writing everything down was pretty important. Proof I was here, that I did all this weird shit. And anyway, why would Tracy or anybody else back home want to hear about what I did in a mental hospital every day for three weeks?" (185). By simultaneously acknowledging the usefulness of the documentation process and determining that her disclosure will never be shared with anyone but the reader (as one outside the text rather than one of the people "back home"), Anna directly contradicts her earlier assertions regarding diary-keeping. At the same time, she indicates that while she has been able to grow and heal because of the writing process—an idea that Halpern emphasizes through the consistent use of pens and pencils as symbols of interpersonal connection—the narrative intimacy that exists within the pages of her diary is possible only because of the promise of secrecy inherent to the impossible narrator-reader relationship.

An explicit awareness of the narrator-reader relationship also shapes the disclosure made by Colby Cavendish, the narrator of Alyson Noel's 2009 novel *Cruel Summer*, which combines diary and epistolary forms in order to examine questions of private versus public disclosure. Seventeen-year-old Colby chronicles, in both her private diary and a public weblog, the three months she spends on Tinos, a tiny Greek island where she is sent to live with her "crazy aunt Tally" while her parents finalize their divorce. Colby's diary and blog entries, which are intertwined with letters, postcards, emails, and text messages sent to her parents and friends at home, allow Noel to draw explicit distinctions between the full disclosure that Colby eventually makes in her diary and the selective disclosure that makes up most of the content of her blog. Initially, Colby resists the impulse to write in the diary that her mother gives her just before she boards the plane to Greece; however, she quickly comes to rely on it as a safe location within which to explore her anger, doubt, and confusion regarding her parents' divorce, her tenuous new friendship with popular Amanda, and her relationship with Levi, the boy to whom she lost her virginity the night before leaving for Greece. The weblog, in turn, begins as a location for her to express her boredom and attempt to remain in touch with her friends at home; over time, however, she uses it to reveal her growing appreciation for Tinos and its occupants. By incorporating both diary entries and blog posts, Noel brings these private and public genres into conversation with one another in order to investigate Colby's complicated experiences of disclosure and discretion; furthermore, because both the diary and the blog focus extensively on Colby's experiences of isolation and loneliness, the seemingly disparate threads of the text are brought together in a cohesive way that invites the reader to not only relate to Colby but to actively interrogate her disclosure as she makes it.

The multi-strand construction of the novel, which allows for a reflection on both the theoretical and narrative implications of both diaries and blogs as locations of disclosure, is critical to Noel's project of tracing Colby's developing understanding of intimacy. In her study of blogs kept by adolescents, Lois Ann Scheidt identifies many similarities between blogs and traditional diaries; however, she notes, "two time-worn assumptions about paper diaries fall away when looking at diary weblogs. First, the view that diaries are kept only for the personal consumption of the author . . . is unsuitable when the diary is posted online. Second, the view that diary-keeping is a private and secret effort . . . is out of place when the diary is available for public access" (195). Furthermore, she presents evidence that the majority of adolescent women bloggers imagine their unknown audience as female, which she believes is a reflection of the fact that "their quest for nurturance resonates with the private domain that has been associated with women" (206). Such distinctions quickly become apparent in Colby's use of her journal and her blog. While the journal primarily acts as the only space in which she feels capable of fully articulating her thoughts and feelings, it also stands in pronounced contrast to the style and tone of her markedly less honest communications with her family and "friends." At the same time, the blog forces her to become cognizant of the possibility of an audience; when an anonymous poster begins commenting on her blog, she first struggles to identify "anonymous" as one of her friends and then realizes that, no matter who "anonymous" is, his or her presence should cause her to more carefully select the information she makes available in the blog. Colby thus uses the diary as a place to make confessions, which becomes even clearer in the face of all the lies she's telling in her other writing; her blog, in turn, emphasizes the questions of privacy and readership that she's only implicitly confronting in the diary.

When she first receives the journal, Colby associates it with boredom and desperation—indeed, many of the entries' titles begin with the phrase "Colby's Journal for Desperate Times." At least part of her reluctance to fully engage with the diary-keeping process stems from her concern that someone else will read what she has written. In the first entry, as she begins to document the night on which she lost her virginity to Levi, she stops herself:

> Okay, I was just about to write the rest of the story, but then I decided to stop because it feels really weird to be confessing in this thing. I mean, as much as I'd like to write about <u>EVERYTHING</u> that just happened (and trust me, there's <u>PLENTY</u> to write about), because I'm thinking it might really help me to get it all down on paper and maybe even clear my head and put it all back in perspective, the thing is, I can't help but think—*what if someone reads it?* (4, emphases in original)

Although Colby's concerns seem most directly related to secrecy and the possibility of her privacy being violated, this passage also implicitly gestures toward a larger concern of hers—namely, that whoever reads the diary will judge and reject her based on its contents. For example, the parenthetical aside that assures her reader that "there's <u>PLENTY</u> to write about" suggests her need to impress and titillate an unknown reader even as she professes her worries about the existence of just such a reader.

This need to impress is clearly tied to Colby's relationship with Amanda, which began to form only weeks before Colby's departure for Greece. In early diary entries, Colby freely admits that she has idolized her popular schoolmate for years; now that she has stumbled into a friendship with Amanda, Colby is determined not to lose the opportunity to climb the social ladder and has even ended her long-term friendship with a girl named Nicole in order to spend more time with Amanda. In order to ensure Amanda's continued interest in her, Colby has developed a tendency to hide her own interests and feelings; as she tells one story that includes her defensively explaining her trip to Greece, she notes, "That's how I always feel around Amanda, like I need to prove my right to exist" (22). Furthermore, by including Colby's frequent and often desperate emails to Amanda between diary entries, Noel draws attention to the degree to which Colby feels she must conceal her true thoughts and feelings from Amanda. While Colby's diary details her frustrations and sadness, her emails to Amanda (which are written in a shorthand that resembles text messages) detail fictional adventures with cute boys that Colby has made up to impress her.

Because Colby has essentially destroyed her friendship with Nicole and does not feel secure in her new friendship with Amanda, she has no real friend to whom to make the confessions she directs to her diary, especially regarding her feelings about her parents' divorce and her loss of her virginity. She relies upon the reader as a friend, then, in the absence of any characters in the novel who can fully adopt the role. Likewise, Colby comes to rely on the reader as a partner in desire as she navigates her romantic relationships with Levi at home and Yannis on the island because she believes she has no other outlets for her feelings. Her eventual descriptions of her "relationship" with Levi reveal a similar tendency to conceal her own thoughts and feelings in order to appeal to him—she recalls working hard to keep up a conversation about sports and cars and receiving only one-syllable responses. Her initial description of their physical intimacy once again reveals a desire to impress a reader, as when she writes, "Even though it was a little awkward at first . . . it wasn't long before I was totally into the zone of how he kisses, and the next thing I knew, I'd glanced at my watch and it was two hours past my curfew!" (24). At this moment, Colby reevaluates her own need to conceal her true thoughts and revises her own account, saying, "Only that's not entirely true. Because the truth is, I was kind of worried about my curfew pretty much the entire time" (24). The immediate juxtaposition of her concealing her feelings from Levi and her revealing her feelings to the reader allows Colby to gesture towards her growing understanding that Levi is not a good romantic match for her.

This moment of restatement also signals Colby's increasing willingness to document her thoughts without censoring or editing them; although she does occasionally revise her thoughts and confessions as she is writing (often by literally marking through words), she becomes more immediately honest within the context of the diary. When she first meets Yannis, for example, she writes, "I met someone ~~special~~" (61, strikethrough in original). She strikes out the last word, adding, "Okay, I just reread that and it looks totally dorky and lame. So let me just rephrase it and say I met this really cute guy, who smiled at me from across the backyard for like two full hours before he finally came over to talk to me" (61). While she once again reconsiders her words, as she does in her writing about Levi, she seems here to be driven by an impulse to clarify rather than correct. That she traces the development of her relationship with Yannis, including their increasingly intimate physical relationship, with much more honesty than she initially uses in describing her relationship with Levi further demonstrates her hope that the reader will explore her desire for Yannis with her.

Again, her sense of isolation from those characters who might otherwise act as safe locations for such disclosure drives Colby to rely on the reader almost exclusively as the recipient of her thoughts and feelings. In turn, as she becomes more open to discussing her feelings about her parents, her friendships, and her relationship with Yannis within the context of the diary, she begins to consider the possibility of trusting others with that information. This is particularly demonstrated in her spontaneous decision to confide in her aunt Tally near the end of the novel. After having an honest conversation about Tally's failed marriage, Colby decides to reciprocate her aunt's disclosure by offering her own:

> And even though I hadn't planned on sharing anything more than that, even though I really thought I'd gotten over it already, before I even realized what I was doing, I started telling her about that night with Levi, and how ashamed and stupid I felt after, and how lately I was thinking that maybe sleeping with Yannis could somehow erase it, or at the very least, correct it. (209)

Like other narrators who have depended on disclosure to the reader as a means of rehearsing similar confessions to characters within the novel, Colby uses the diary as a space within which to become increasingly comfortable with her own thoughts and feelings. In turn, she uses this new comfort and confidence to redirect her disclosure, seeking guidance from a character within the novel as a result.

In contrast to her willingness to disclose to the diary, Colby's blog demonstrates her ongoing struggle to determine an appropriate level of disclosure for another unknown readership. Unlike her insistence that the diary remain private, however, Colby acknowledges and indeed hopes for the possibility of an audience for her blog and constructs its content accordingly. For example, she tells readers not to judge her choice of favorite song and shares pictures of her surroundings "so you can get an idea of what I'm dealing with here" (31). She also ends the first blog entry with the words "Comment me! (Please!)," a semi-desperate call for attention and recognition (35). When an anonymous poster begins responding to her posts, however, Colby is forced to reconsider her desire for an audience. In her diary, she writes, "It's weird how I originally thought I wanted lots of readers and comments, but now I'm not so sure. I mean, now that I know someone is reading it, I'm no longer sure what to write." (55). As she ponders this question, she admits, "I swear, it was a whole lot easier when I was the only reader," suggesting that she struggles to discern the difference between a diary and a blog (56). This difficulty leads to Colby's often sharing information on her blog without realizing the potential repercussions of such free disclosure. When her blog gets her in trouble—Yannis reads about her plans to meet up with Levi in Mykonos and begins avoiding her—Colby realizes that she must control her disclosure in the public space of the blog more carefully. In turn, Noel implies that in the process of keeping both a diary and a blog, Colby has internalized certain cultural expectations regarding disclosure and discretion, which is highlighted by Colby's using the safe space of her diary from that point forward to practice disclosure before making amended (and usually less detailed) disclosure to those around her.

The contrast between the content of Colby's diary and her blog, then, allows Noel to emphasize questions of public and private treatments of intimacy. As Colby navigates these two potential spaces for disclosure, as well as her growing understanding of her audiences and her relationships with them, she comes to privilege her diary as the only true location of her thoughts and feelings. The reader is thus allowed access to information that is later provided to other characters only in limited or mediated forms, if at all. At the same time, Noel's novel and its treatment of narrative intimacy directly harkens to Berlant's assertions about the "corresponding publicness" of intimacy in contemporary American culture. Indeed, although Colby depends on her diary and thus the reader throughout the novel, the final pages of *Cruel Summer* are dedicated to a blog entry and comments rather than to a private diary entry. As Colby and her friends write back and forth to each other within this space, and particularly when she and Yannis implicitly express their affection for one another in their matching statements of "kalinchta!" (the Greek word for "good night"), Noel signals that Colby's new understandings about intimacy in general and narrative intimacy in specific involve a shift away from the complete disclosure that has generally defined the space of the diary in favor of discretion and appropriate public performances of intimacy.

Ultimately, it is this tension between private considerations and public performances of intimacy that renders diary novels so useful in considering the development of narrative intimacy and its relationship to larger cultural contradictions about young women's engagement with intimacy. The fictional adolescent woman diarists' explicit and implicit gestures toward the possibility of their private thoughts being made (at least somewhat) public, as well as the readers' acceptance of their violation of the diarists' private space, demonstrate both parties' active involvement in, and interaction with, cultural demands that simultaneously expect adolescent women to develop intimate interpersonal relationships and insist that those relationships comply with often contradictory expectations regarding disclosure. Much as the different types of narrative intimacy discussed in the previous chapters provide insights into the nuances of intimacy (as well as the potential violations and risks thereof), then, diary novels as a genre act as a reminder that intimacy is problematic across interpersonal relationships and throughout adolescence.

Regardless of the specific challenges and experiences faced by these fictional adolescent woman diarists, there is a shared concern about the limits of honesty and disclosure, as well as a common treatment of the diary as a safe space that allows experiments with honesty and disclosure that help the young women come to a more "mature" recognition of discretion. In other words, in novels such as those discussed here, diary-keeping is portrayed as something young women grow out of as they learn to keep their feelings *truly* to themselves. The diary as an object and as a space thus reinforces the idea appropriate disclosure is something that must be learned, practiced, and handled carefully. The tendency of these fictional diarists to abandon (and in some cases destroy) their diaries as they reach the end of adolescence, in turn, simultaneously provides a reminder that adolescent women's diaries often are not as "private" as they may seem and that young women must acquiesce to a construction of adolescent womanhood as a period during which specific, "mature" understandings about disclosure and discretion should be formed.

In addition to fictional diarists' often explicit struggles with honesty, appropriate disclosure, and the importance of discretion, diary novels such as those discussed here also provide clear insights into the degree to which adolescent women are aware of and even acknowledge the cultural contradictions they must navigate. Indeed, the paradoxes surrounding the diary form—namely, that the act of writing a private document nonetheless signals an expectation of a public readership—present clear parallels to the paradoxes of intimacy during adolescent womanhood, when young women are encouraged to form intimate relationships but discouraged from the sorts of disclosure that are understood to make intimacy possible. As fictional diarists remark upon their decisions about disclosure, from the secrets that they choose to keep from the people around them to the information they choose to make available to the anticipated readers of their diaries, they offer explicit commentary on the challenges faced by the narrators of all the novels discussed in this project. Whether they seek a reader who can be a friend, a partner in desire, a therapist, or some combination of these, then, adolescent women narrators reflect their awareness and navigation of larger, frequently complicated social expectations regarding intimacy. The construction of the adolescent woman reader, in turn, makes way for similar awareness on the part of the real reader, a point I discuss in more detail in the following chapter.

Chapter 6

"Let Me Know What You Think"
Fan Fiction and the Reimagining of Narrative Intimacy

In a discussion on Sarah-Land.ning.com, the official fan site for author Sarah Dessen, teen reader Charlene writes:

> i am really glad that you created this community . . . it gives all of us a place to come together and discuss the books . . . After reading one of the books i sought out all of the rest of them and have loved them all . . . i love how each book has a very realistic and everyday occuring [*sic*] circumstance that must be overcome . . . the books are so easy to relate to and you can find a part of yourself [in] almost every single one of the characters . . . thank you so much for this community . . . you and your books are a true inspiration. (ellipses in original)

This post, penned in response to a post by Dessen herself in which she thanks all of the members of Sarah-Land for joining the community, demonstrates the possibility of readers extending narrative intimacy beyond the narrator-reader relationship and, in the process, informing some fans' understandings of the author-narrator-reader relationship and of lived experiences of intimacy more generally. By directly addressing Dessen, Charlene suggests both a belief that Dessen herself will read this post and a more general understanding of this Internet community as a space in which to develop interpersonal connections; her claim that "you can find a part of yourself [in] almost every single one of the characters," meanwhile, explicitly identifies the importance of affinity in this teenage reader's experience of Dessen's novels. That many adolescent women fans express similar sentiments on the official websites of and discussion boards dedicated to Dessen and several of the other authors discussed in this project offers insight into the possible reconsiderations and reworkings of narrative intimacy performed by adolescent women readers.

Throughout this discussion, I have explored the development of narrative intimacy as a product of the relationship between a fictional narrator who seeks a safe space for disclosure and a reader who willingly enters that space, adopting the role constructed by the narrator. Because the real reader necessarily exists outside of the text—separated from the fictional narrator by the gap that narrative intimacy so frequently seeks to blur or destroy—narrative intimacy defines and limits the reader's role as one who receives (rather than one who makes or controls) disclosure. While, as Iser and others have argued, the reader may play an active role in the creation of a text's meaning, the reader's position outside of the text necessarily denies the possibility of the reader informing the content of the text within the fictional space of the story. In other words, novels like those discussed throughout this study construct the narrator-reader relationship, offering the reader a position (such as friend or partner in desire) to occupy but not the possibility of shaping that role. During the reading process, readers may respond to that positioning in a number of ways—enthusiastically adopting the qualities established by the text, carefully navigating the possibilities of such a relationship with the narrator, or rejecting the role as it is presented by the text—but they cannot alter the construction of the reader's role in the novel itself.[1] However, many readers seek to revisit, recreate, or reimagine their engagement with the texts and, in the process, change their understanding of the reader's role.

Using digital media such as online message boards, fan art, and especially fan fiction, some readers work to renegotiate the boundaries between the fictional world and the real; they cannot bridge the "logical gap," but they can adopt a different rhetorical position, often by conflating the roles of author and reader. Obviously, readers may also seek and find non-digital opportunities to respond to novels: book clubs, diary or journal entries, and creative responses that are not shared on the Internet may likewise allow the possibility of reconsidering narrative intimacy. However, digital media provide clear insights into the potential repositioning of the author-narrator-reader relationship and emphasize the possibility of extending narrative intimacy into the real reader's lived experiences. In particular, contemporary adolescent women readers frequently rely upon new digital media in order to extend and rework their reading experiences; in the process, as Catherine Tosenberger has argued, fan fiction and other responses distributed in Internet communities provide a unique means of quantifying the responses of the real reader.[2] In this chapter, I briefly discuss the history and current scholarly discussion of fan fiction and other new media responses to literature; establish the parallels between narrative intimacy within texts for adolescent women and the manner in which readers from this age group use online "affinity spaces"; and explore the reconfiguration of narrative intimacy by adolescent women fan fiction authors. Ultimately, I argue that many adolescent women readers employ new media in order to actively engage with, reimagine, and often subvert the implicit relationships between author, narrator, and reader that combine to develop narrative intimacy.

The central conventions that define and inform contemporary fan fiction can be traced back to oral storytelling cultures, in which listeners became authors who added their own elements to the literature they received. During the seventeenth, eighteenth, and early nineteenth centuries, fans of authors such as John Donne and Jane Austen developed communities that anticipate the contemporary "fandom," exchanging letters about and literary works inspired by their favorite authors. In the twentieth century, fan fiction began to take on its current shape; in the 1930s, the emergence of fan magazines (also known as "fanzines" or simply "zines") allowed fan fiction authors to publish and distribute their works, written in response to literature and other forms of popular entertainment. Fan fiction reached a new high point in the 1960s, when fans of the television show *Star Trek* began to write and share fiction stories based on the show. Many specific traits and types of fan fiction can be traced directly to the *Star Trek* fandom; for example, homoerotic or homosexual fan fiction, called "slash," became popular among fans who wished to explore the possibilities of a sexual relationship between Captain Kirk and Spock.[3]

As a result of its popularity among fan fiction writers, *Star Trek* was the main focus of the earliest studies of contemporary fan fiction. Henry Jenkins's seminal 1992 text, *Textual Poachers: Television, Fans, and*

Participatory Culture, focuses primarily on *Star Trek* and other "cult" shows in order to establish the basic conventions, common qualities, and possible implications of fan fiction; he argues that "fan writers do not so much reproduce the primary text as they rework and rewrite it, repairing or dismissing unsatisfying aspects, developing interests not sufficiently explored" (162). While Jenkins provides a more general overview of fan communities and responses, Camille Bacon-Smith specifically identifies fan fiction as a primarily female pursuit in *Enterprising Women: Television Fandom and the Creation of Popular Myth,* also published in 1992. Bacon-Smith argues that for many women, writing fan fiction is a subversive act that allows "housewives and librarians, schoolteachers and data input clerks, secretaries and professors of medieval literature" to flout copyright laws as they create both art and community in response to their favorite shows (3). Although Bacon-Smith focuses on the *Star Trek* fandom, scholars have more generally found that the majority of fan fiction authors are middle-aged women such as those discussed in Bacon-Smith's work. The frequency with which women become active in fan fiction communities, some scholars have argued, reflects the more general levels and types of emotional engagement that women experience while reading novels or viewing television shows.

While early studies of fan communities and fan works focus on the demographics and general conventions of fan-produced work, more recent scholarship has engaged more clearly with individual communities and texts in order to consider their cultural and literary significance. As Deborah Kaplan argues, until about 2005, "fan fiction [had] not been much studied *as fiction,* as texts that, under a literary criticism lens, can be fascinating as nonfan-produced work" (135). By expanding beyond the *Star Trek*-specific investigations undertaken by Jenkins, Bacon-Smith, and others, fan fiction scholars have thus begun to apply literary analysis to fan fiction in order to argue that fan authors frequently do more than simply replicate or expand the source material by which they are inspired. One of the most significant analytical moves undertaken by recent scholars—at least for the purposes of this conversation—is the application of narrative theory to fan fiction in order to consider the restructuring of relationships between authors, characters, and readers. Kaplan argues, for example, that "by taking advantage of the narrative games inherent to the interplay between reader knowledge and fan fiction creation, fan authors find the potential for empowering dialogue in what initially seems to be a restricted form of creation" (151).

The changing nature of fan fiction scholarship also reflects the changing nature of creation and distribution of fan works. While the writing of fictional stories that borrow characters, plot points, and settings from novels, television shows, and films is hardly a recent phenomenon, the development of Internet technology has allowed the process to become faster and more fluid. The Internet has also provided access to groups that had previously been excluded from fan communities—including adolescent fans, who have been able to participate in the creation, distribution, and reception of fan fiction in unprecedented numbers over the past decade. As Rebecca W. Black notes in *Adolescents and Online Fan Fiction*, in the advent of new technologies adolescents have become a dominant force in fan fiction, particularly in response to works of popular culture that are specifically marketed to young people. Although young people have generally become more active in fandoms, furthermore, the majority of fan fiction writers continue to be female; even in response to male-centered texts, adolescent women make up a large portion of the fan fiction authors (a fact that echoes the predominance of female fans writing about the male-centered *Star Trek* in earlier generations).

Along with the changing methods of distribution and shifting demographics of fan fiction communities, the Internet has provided a space within which to explore the possibilities of affinity and connection—not only between narrators and readers, but also between readers who share a common interest in a text, film, or television show. The prevalence of terms such as "online communities" (which usually take the form of chat rooms, message boards, and forums) particularly draws attention to an understanding that the communications that take place on the Internet are equivalent to real-life relationships. Black identifies these communities as "affinity spaces," explaining that "in affinity spaces, people interact and relate to each other because they have a shared passion, goal, or interest" (98). Because contemporary American adolescents have generally embraced the Internet as a means of communication, the importance of online affinity spaces is particularly pronounced for this group.[4] Indeed, several of the novels discussed in this study have featured such recent technologies as email, instant messaging, and text messaging as elements of the narrators' experiences with their friends and romantic partners. For example, *The Secret Rites of Social Butterflies* alludes to MySpace and Facebook, while *Charmed Thirds* refers directly to the latter. The *Princess Diaries* books include instant messaging conversations, emails, and text messages, and in addition to Colby's blog entries, *Cruel Summer* includes emails and texts.

Notably, many Internet communities explored by adolescents—both in these novels and in the real world—depend upon the concept of affinity; participants "gather" in specific forums, fan sites, and other online communities because of common interests. Because of the assumed affinity and familiarity among community members, these sites can also potentially mimic the "safe space" of narrative intimacy modeled in the novels that adolescent women read and to which they respond. This assumed safety is particularly important to fans who distribute their work, since in the process they become vulnerable to criticism and judgment from other community members. As Bronwen Thomas explains, "For many fan fiction devotees, 'writing it down' is primarily about sharing one's enthusiasms, frustrations, and creative aspirations with a community that is largely supportive, and always responsive" (153). Likewise, Black suggests that "a relatively anonymous fan fiction community might be a safer space for reticent youth to reach out for help and advice" than real-life communities (131).

The frequency with which authors of literature for adolescent women create and carefully maintain online personae suggests an awareness of the degree to which their young readers engage with the texts (and, indirectly) the authors, and more specifically suggests that narrative intimacy may purposely be extended into the "real world" relationship readers believe they can forge with the authors via the Internet. Authors such as Laurie Halse Anderson and E. Lockhart frequently update their websites and open their posts to comments from fans. Anderson and Lockhart, as well as Courtney Summers, Rachel Cohn, and Megan McCafferty, among others, also engage in other social media, including Facebook and Twitter; all of these networking sites allow readers to interact more or less immediately with their favorite authors. In addition to extending the possibility of communication, authors who use these social networking tools gesture toward an understanding of the Internet as a space in which to explore and reconsider the relationships between authors and readers. This is likewise demonstrated in the content of many authors' websites, which frequently suggest the possibility of affinity between authors and readers. For example, a feature on Lockhart's website entitled "True and Embarrassing Things About E"—which includes tidbits such as "My first kiss was at the age of sixteen"—offers (limited) disclosure about Lockhart's personal experiences as a teenager to which her young fans may presumably be able to relate.

Even as these authors make available to fans the possibility of contact and apparent connection, they also frequently explicitly address the challenges of maintaining a distinction between their personal lives and their roles as authors. Many authors articulate the limits they place on their disclosure—most will offer no details about their families, for example— as a means of delineating both their online personae and the nature of their relationships with fans. Even with such guidelines in place, however, authors frequently reveal struggles in maintaining proper levels of disclosure in their Internet relationships with their readers. For example, in a blog entry about her efforts to lose weight after a pregnancy, Dessen offers some insight into her own willingness to make available apparently very personal and often potentially embarrassing information:

> You know what's totally weird? I just spent, like, all this time writing [an entry about weight loss], and now I'm all nervous, thinking I should delete it. I mean, I'm a person who writes in this same space about how I watch *Jersey Shore* and read *US Weekly*. Clearly, I have no shame. Why is it that weight is such a (sorry) loaded topic? Entirely personal, and yet public, because when people see you, they can see if you're struggling? Oh, God, I have no idea. I'm just going to try to keep my finger off the backspace button and keep going. ("The Five!")

As Dessen indicates, her general willingness to share her thoughts and experiences with the readers of her blog (which she updates at least three times a week) occasionally poses difficulties in determining the appropriate level of disclosure to maintain in her Internet communication. Furthermore, that Dessen does post confessional moments such as this one highlights the degree to which authors—purposely or not—contribute to the possibility of understanding the author-reader relationship as a potentially intimate one, despite the likelihood that they will never meet most of their fans face to face. More generally, the levels of disclosure and possibilities of connection and affinity made possible by blogs, social networking tools, and other forms of digital media echo the construction of narrative intimacy in novels by authors such as those discussed here, suggesting the possibility that authors and readers alike may engage with the possibilities of extending narrative intimacy into the "real world."

Though authors often publicly struggle with the at times challenging evolution of author-reader relationships, fans generally seem to have little trouble projecting the narrative intimacy they experience while reading fictional texts onto their perceived relationships with the authors of those texts. One of the ways in which fans identify with their favorite authors is their shared interest in writing; indeed, so many fans contact authors with inquiries about sending drafts of their original works that Dessen, Lockhart, Cohn, and several other authors explicitly address the question in the "Frequently Asked Questions" sections of their sites.[5] At times, furthermore, these authors directly engage with questions of the writing process, particularly as it pertains to their readers and the prospect of fan fiction. Meg Cabot, for example, explicitly addresses her feelings on fan fiction inspired by her *Princess Diaries* series and other novels in a blog post on her official website. After asserting that she never reads fan fiction based on her work and admitting that she herself wrote *Star Wars* fan fiction, she offers this insight to her readers:

> Basically, the author has already created a world for the new writer to play around in, and that is a great way for new writers to learn the skills they will need in order to create their OWN universe (which I hope they will do someday, because the world needs more good stories, and it would be a shame if someone who might have some decent stories of her own to tell was depriving us of them because she was spending all her time writing, for example, *Star Wars* [*sic*] fan fics. Ahem). (Cabot "Fan Fiction")

Such comments demonstrate both authors' awareness of the fan fiction phenomenon and the possibility that the works their fans create may serve as a starting point for a potential transition from reader to author. At the same time, Cabot's encouragement to fans to create their own original works indicates a potential disconnect between the authors of original texts and authors of fan fiction: while Cabot highlights the possibility of fans becoming published authors one day, many fan authors themselves privilege the writing process—which provides a means of exploring and extending their reading experiences, their understandings of fictional characters, and their relationships to their favorite authors—over the final product and its potential publication.

In addition to seeking connections with the authors of their favorite novels, fans often use online communities to explore the potential similarities between themselves and the fictional characters to whom they feel drawn. The Sarah-Land forums include a number of discussions dedicated to such topics, indicated by thread titles such as "If you could be the main character in any Sarah Dessen book which would you choose?" and "Which character would you want as a friend?" Similarly, in a forum on Megcabot.com entitled "You know when your [*sic*] a PD [*Princess Diaries*] fan," readers offer insights into their "addictions" to the books, most of which relate to their attachment to narrator Mia. For example, user Jcrazy asserts that you know you're a *Princess Diaries* fan when "You become annoyed when trying to write in a diary at school because you're paranoid people are trying to read it over your shoulder and you wish that you were in Mia's world where apparently no one tries to do that." *Twilight* saga fans, likewise, emphasize the similarities between themselves and Bella, particularly in terms of their attraction to Edward, in ongoing conversations on discussion boards. For example, in the "Cullen Crush" forum on Fanfiction.net, a thread titled "I'm in love with a fictional vampire named Edward Cullen" features comments from adolescent women such as Won Tawn, who writes, "Half of me wants to steal him from Bella, the other half protests because they're so cute together. And I think that half knows he's fictional, otherwise I probably *would* steal him." As these comments indicate, fans often use the affinity spaces of message boards and author websites in order to further explore the possibilities of narrative intimacy, especially in their continued efforts to blur the line between fiction and reality.

Beyond their participation in discussion boards and other affinity spaces, some fans create artwork and videos that allow them to share their personal interpretations of novels. New media, again, makes possible the fluid distribution and discussion of fan works; websites such as FanPop.com offer readers the opportunity to post their sketches, paintings, and digital art. *Twilight* saga fans, for example, have created everything from highly stylized imaginings of Bella and Edward to watercolor images of Robert Pattinson, who portrays Edward in the film adaptations of Meyer's novels. Fans have also used photo and video editing software to create visual representations of their favorite characters and stories. On YouTube.com, fans post videos in response to their favorite texts; some take the form of "book trailers" (which, like movie trailers, present general plot synopses), some offer dramatic interpretations of novels, and others are presented as music videos set to their creators' favorite songs. For example, eighteen-year-old user emruking's video "Dreamland Trailer (Based on the Book)," inspired by Dessen's novel, incorporates scenes from music videos by Miley Cyrus and Taylor Swift interspersed with title cards that offer some insight into the novel's plot and characters. In another video, teenage user imanorrange11 (along with her obliging parents) acts out crucial scenes from Lockhart's *Ruby Oliver* series in the video "The Boyfriend List." Like fan fiction, then, fan art and videos allow readers both to demonstrate their understanding and analysis of a given text and its characters and to engage with their emotional responses to the reading experience. More importantly, fan art allows readers to exercise a degree of creative control and interpretation, effectively redefining their relationships with the text, as well as its author and narrator.

While readers may engage in a variety of new media tools in order to respond to and prolong their reading experiences, the most useful for this conversation is fan fiction, which allows for the clearest consideration of the shifting relationships between authors, narrators, and readers. In particular, the possible implications of fan fiction as vicarious experience—as expressed by Walsh, Iser, and Scholes and Kellogg, among others—depend upon the model of narrative intimacy, as fictional characters provide "experiences" that readers and fan fiction writers may be able to revisit for their own learning purposes. For example, a reader drawn to the cautionary tale of *Story of a Girl* might create a fan fiction story in order to further explore Deanna's regrets and come to a clearer understanding of the potential dangers of sex without actually experiencing the alienation and isolation that Deanna describes. Likewise, novels such as *Speak* that invite the reader to act as a therapist could inspire readers to construct fan fiction as their own means of rehearsing disclosure, exploring their feelings through the fictional space of a story in order to, as characters such as Melinda do, gain the confidence to seek the healing possibilities of disclosure in their own lives. However, as it complicates the relationships and distinctions between authors and readers, fan fiction also makes possible the intersection of fictional and real experiences. As Jenkins asserts, in fan fiction "the reader's activity is no longer seen simply as the task of recovering the author's meanings but also as reworking borrowed materials to fit them into the context of the lived experience" (51). The concept of the reading process as a vicarious experience is thus potentially subverted when fan fiction writers bring their own reading and life experiences to bear on the fictional stories they craft in response to literature.

Several of the novels included in this study have inspired fan fiction, most of which has been written by the adolescent women to whom such texts are marketed. Both the popularity of these novels and the influence of narrative intimacy on fan response can be seen in the number of fan fiction stories posted in response to works about and for adolescent women on sites such as FanFiction.net. For example, Anderson's *Speak* has inspired about 100 stories on FanFiction.net, Dessen's novels (all told) have inspired about 200 stories, and Cabot's *Princess Diaries* books have inspired around 800. Remarkably, Meyer's *Twilight* saga has inspired more than 198,000 stories, a total that is second only to J. K. Rowling's *Harry Potter* series (which has inspired almost 600,000). Notably, several of the novels and series that have generated larger numbers of fan responses—including series such as the *Gemma Doyle* trilogy (more than 700 stories), the *Gossip Girl* series (more than 9,000 stories), and the *Hunger Games* trilogy (almost 18,000 stories)—are likewise written for and about adolescent women, which suggests the growing prevalence of adolescent women in the fan fiction community more generally. In contrast, the majority of the more than 1,200 novels and series listed on FanFiction. net have inspired fewer than 50 stories; only about 130 have inspired more than 100 stories, and of those only a few dozen have inspired more than 1,000 stories.[6]

Although fans' specific reasons for composing and distributing fan fiction may vary widely, certain patterns in the stories themselves highlight the manner in which fan authors such as those discussed here draw on the model of narrative intimacy in order to reconsider their narrative positioning. Specifically, fan fiction authors frequently model the style of their works after the original texts, which suggests that many authors seek to reconstruct the original reading experience even as they make changes and additions that privilege their own desires. For many authors, the continuation of assumed affinity with the narrator is also a crucial factor, particularly as some authors assert views of those characters that challenge or even contradict those in the original texts. In contrast, some authors respond to favorite texts by implicitly or explicitly inserting fictional versions of themselves into the plots and settings of their favorite texts; these new characters frequently act as a means of both extending affinity and enacting wish fulfillment on the authors' part. A substantial number of fan fiction authors also create notable divergences from the original texts in terms of style, setting, plot points, or relationships between major characters, often as a means of privileging the reader's desires over the intentions of the original texts. That many fan fiction authors seem to privilege their own interpretations of and hopes for the narrators of their favorite novels over those offered by the original authors signals a larger implication of narrative intimacy—namely, that readers do feel a degree of possessiveness over and insight into those characters as a result of the affinity emphasized in the construction of the intimate relationship between narrator and reader.

The fan fiction stories I discuss here, which act as a sample of the larger body of work written in response to authors such as Dessen, Cabot, and Meyer, demonstrate both these general fan fiction trends and the manner in which adolescent women authors engage with the model of narrative intimacy established in their reading in order to construct their own works of fiction. All of the stories discussed here have been posted by their authors on the website FanFiction.net, though it is important to note that fan fiction can also be found on author websites and fan sites dedicated to specific authors or texts. Using user profiles and self-reported information (both in these profiles and in the frequently detailed/telling authors' notes that precede and follow many stories), I have narrowed my discussion to fan fiction written by adolescent women in response to novels discussed earlier in this project. I have also limited my discussion to relatively short works of fan fiction, though it is important to note that many fan authors create novel-length works of fiction that rival the word counts of the texts that inspired them.

For many readers, writing fan fiction allows them the opportunity to more thoughtfully approach a text, particularly in terms of characters' actions and possible motivations. As Bauble, a young woman who writes fan fiction for a variety of book and television series, explains, "Writing fanfic is a way to understand characters that were created in someone else's mind that I might never have come up with myself. . . . It allows me to dig deeper into people that I might not necessarily have ever thought about or tried to understand before." Jenkins echoes the importance of analysis and interpretation in the world of fan fiction, explaining, "Fandom celebrates not exceptional texts but rather exceptional readings" (284). Indeed, this approach to writing as a form of literary analysis is a major reason that so much current research on fan fiction and adolescence relates to literacy studies and education.[7] Even as authors engage with close, critical readings of texts, however, most incorporate details or distinctions that demonstrate their own attempts to correct perceived mistakes in or satisfy personal desires evoked by the original works.

In her story "My Version: Forever Mia," a *Princess Diaries* fanfic, author Pisces28—who identifies herself in her profile as a "typical teenage girl who has an obsession with dreams and believes in (endless) love"—likewise models her story after the narrative form used in Cabot's original texts, maintaining both the general diary format and the specific date, time, and location recording method that Mia uses throughout the ten novels that make up the *Princess Diaries* series. As she chronicles Mia's current set of stressful circumstances—including the fact that she is dating J. P. but still has feelings for her ex-boyfriend, as well as a request from the Genovian government to present a speech—Pisces28 follows Cabot's style closely, demonstrating an awareness of the specific tics that define Mia's narrative style. For example, she ends the second chapter with a series of short sentences, a style Cabot frequently employs in the novels:

> Ugh. This always happen[s] to me.
> Too bad Lilly's not here to write a speech for me.
> Too bad I kissed J. P.
> Darn his good looks.

By borrowing stylistic markers and plot points from the original texts, Pisces28 clearly works within the characterization of Mia established in Cabot's novels; furthermore, her version allows her to explore possibilities for the character that, while not present in the novels, fit neatly with their scope and content. In the process, Pisces28 demonstrates the possibility that narrative intimacy—specifically, the implicit, intimate relationship between Mia and the reader cultivated throughout the series—has equipped her to engage critically with and perform close readings of the *Princess Diaries* novels.

Although this and many other stories attempt to remain true to the style of the source materials, some authors rely almost too heavily on the language of the original texts while incorporating plot points that depart dramatically from the novels. For example, "*New Life*," a *Twilight* saga story by volturiprincess949, duplicates chapters 15 and 16 of Meyer's *New Moon* almost exactly—until it abandons the original plot at the pivotal moment when Bella decides to dive off a cliff, which determines all of the following events in the novel and the series as a whole. By modeling the style and language so closely on Meyer's work that it in some moments approaches plagiarism even as her plot effectively denies the majority of the content in the saga, volturiprincess949 reflects contradictory impulses demonstrated by many fan fiction writers as they navigate their engagement with the texts and their desire to create original work.[8] Overall, these stories and others that attempt to maintain the style, form, and tone that mark the original texts demonstrate an effort on the part of the authors not only to explore a possible affinity with the original authors—in other words, by modeling their work on another author's style, these reader-authors imagine the original text as a space shared with the original author—but also to further develop the textual elements they admire and wish to develop in their own writing.

While many authors make a concerted effort to maintain the style of the original works that inspire their fan fiction, others focus more explicitly on their desire to explore their emotional reactions to plots or characters. In this way, some fan fiction stories act more clearly as continuations of the perceived affinity and understanding between narrator and reader than as attempts on some readers' parts to explore possible artistic affinity with an author. Because many authors construct an understanding of a reader who can identify with the thoughts, feelings, and experiences the narrators describe, many fan fiction writers use their stories as a means of further exploring similarities they see between themselves and the narrators, often focusing on qualities that they most wish to emulate or develop. In her study of fan artists who work with graphic arts, Marjorie Cohee Manifold found that such affinity and desire to reconsider the possibility of sharing space with a character in fact inspires fan works of all types:

> Over 70 percent of the subjects described being drawn as fans to specific characters in narratives of popular culture because they saw desirable traits in the characters that they wished to possess, or emulate. This connection to character was frequently described in passionate language as, for example, a desire to "get inside the skin" or "experience the soul" of the fictive. (10)

In her consideration of two adolescent women's engagement with the process of co-writing fan fiction, Angela Thomas identifies a similar impulse among fan fiction authors; she quotes one of the young women as saying, "You let the characters become a part of you, let yourself be able to think like they would, and it works the other way around" ("Blurring" 160). The young fan fiction writer's expression of "letting the characters become a part of you" signals a larger desire made possible by narrative intimacy— namely, that readers may seek to prolong the experience of affinity with a fictional character by recreating a shared space in which narrator and reader may be able to metaphorically become one person.

For adolescent fan fiction writers in particular, the "experience" of revisiting a story from this perspective may allow for the specific exploration of the narrator-reader relationship as a means of understanding intimacy and interpersonal relationships. In "Windows," a story based on Dessen's *Someone Like You*, fifteen-year-old author Harvard Baby follows and alters the final pages of Dessen's novel in order to provide a different version of closure for narrator Halley. Unlike Dessen's original work, which actively rejects the possibility of a romantic reunion between Halley and her bad boy ex-boyfriend Macon, Harvard Baby constructs a new scenario in which the two can overcome their past differences. Walking home in the rain after the birth of her best friend Scarlett's baby—a setting that mirrors a scene in the novel, in which Halley and Scarlett find Macon walking home from a funeral in the rain—Halley finds herself pondering her feelings for Macon: "Maybe I hadn't taken the easy way out this time, because being separated from Macon this way was unlike anything I had ever felt. And I knew he was bad for me, like an intense craving for chocolate while on a diet." When he pulls up beside her in his truck and offers her a ride, she accepts and finds herself forgiving him and taking comfort in the warmth of his arms. Harvard Baby ends the story with a platitude that echoes many of those found in Dessen's works, though she alters the message to fit her version of Halley's happy ending: "the most important things are always found after taking a chance." Therefore, while Harvard Baby does make some efforts to reflect Dessen's original work, she favors her own reading of Halley and Macon's relationship over that presented in the original text.

As these stories demonstrate, many fan fiction authors do compose their stories as a means of asserting an interpretation of characters and motivations that they find as useful, if not more so, than those found in the original texts. Some authors, however, seek not to revise the original character but to replace that narrator with a fictionalized version of themselves; as Angela Thomas notes, "It is common for fan fiction writers to insert versions of themselves into their characters" (158). In other words, when readers undertake the writing process, they borrow from the models of affinity-seeking narrators by constructing an understanding of the narrator as sharing similar qualities and feelings. For some authors, however, the feelings and desires they project upon their narrators transform them from extensions of the original text into idealized versions of the authors themselves; some authors, in fact, replace the original character with a new character of their own creation. Typically, these characters— which have come to be known among fan fiction authors and readers as "Mary Sues"—are virtually perfect, universally appealing to the male characters in the stories, and marked by a single "flaw" such as clumsiness.

These so-called Mary Sues provide the possibility of wish fulfillment and the most explicit exploration of fans' personal engagement with texts.[9]

Although Mary Sue stories can be found in many fan fiction communities, they are particularly common in stories inspired by Cabot's *Princess Diaries* books; adolescent readers, attracted to Mia's glamorous princess life, her funny outlook on life, her hot boyfriend Michael, or all of the above, frequently insert versions of themselves into the plot of the original novels. For example, high school student lovelessfighter007, whose real name is Symmone, replaces Mia with a thinly veiled version of herself. This character, also named Symmone, seems in many ways to be occupying the original space of the novels: she, like Mia, is tall, thin, and afraid of public speaking; she, like Mia, is owner of a fat cat and best friend to a strong-willed political activist. Unlike Cabot's narrator, however, Symmone has a twin sister, and she uses British slang and spellings (a surprising attribute, considering that her profile information places lovelessfighter007 in North Carolina). Also notable is lovelessfighter007's abandonment of the diary form and incorporation of a variety of narrative perspectives. That lovelessfighter007 borrows the basic plot of the books—focusing primarily on the main character's transformation from plain and unpopular to gorgeous and royal—suggests that her engagement with the original texts allows her to explore possibilities of self-improvement and self-esteem within the safe space of the story; that she erases Mia and replaces her with a version of herself, furthermore, indicates the degree to which she wishes to prolong the exploration of the desires evoked by Cabot's tales.

The explicit replacement of the narrator with a new character demonstrates the most common type of Mary Sue, but it is important to note that a character may be rewritten by fan authors in such a way that she more closely resembles the fan than the text. For example, in "Spoke, the Aftermath of Speak," teenager Marie Poe illustrates the manner in which Mary Sue characters can act as wish fulfillment on the author's part. In this story, Melinda suffers from none of the problems that plague her during Anderson's novel: she suddenly has all of her old friends back, enjoys a happy, healthy relationship with her parents, and dates David Petrarkis, who in this author's imagining drives a Mercedes and surprises Melinda with picnics on the beach. Aside from the fact that she speaks to a therapist about recovering from her rape, Melinda's life is presented as ideal. Though Marie Poe does not change Melinda's name, she does make such substantial changes to Melinda's personality—replacing her trademark sarcastic humor with uncharacteristic sentimentality, for example—as to suggest that the character more clearly reflects Marie Poe's own hopes and desires than those assigned to the character by Anderson.

Although I have focused on stories that remain at least somewhat loyal to the novels, it is important to note that many fan fiction authors venture far from the original texts, particularly in terms of plot, characterization, and setting—at times maintaining little more than the characters' names. Such divergent treatments of texts are particularly common in the *Twilight* saga fan fiction community. Many authors signal their departure by framing their stories as responses to hypothetical situations; summaries of these stories often begin with the words "What if . . ." For example, CullenGirl09 begins the summary of her story "Shape of My Heart" by asking, "What would happen if Bella had a twin sister?" Margo Vizzini-Montoya's story "Forever, Everlasting," meanwhile, addresses the following questions: "What if Bella wasn't unique? What if Bella and Edward's story could occur again to another hopelessly mis-matched [*sic*] pair?" Other *Twilight* fan fiction authors abandon the supernatural elements at the center of Meyer's novels by creating what they call "All Human" ("AH") stories, in which the vampire and werewolf characters are human, and "Alternative Universe" ("AU") stories, which are set in a variety of times and places and which frequently change the most basic characters and their relationships.[10] More generally, when fan fiction authors diverge from the source material, they often do so in order to address what they perceive to be "gaps" in the original texts; this impulse indicates a fairly widespread desire of fan fiction authors to explore possibilities suggested by but not pursued in the original texts themselves.

While some "gap-filling" stories provide backstory for minor characters or explore possible activities that take place outside of the narrator's observation, it is worth noting that one of the "gaps" that *Twilight* fan fiction writers most frequently seek to fill relates to Bella and Edward's sex life. For example, "Breaking Dawn: The Deleted Scenes," by high school student skyofdreams, provides a clear example of the gap between the reader's expectations and Meyer's novels. Maintaining Bella's first-person narration, skyofdreams describes the moments before the consummation of Edwards and Bella's marriage in diction that closely resembles Meyer's own: "A voice in the back of me [*sic*] head told me that this probably wasn't a good idea, but I trusted Edward with my life, and the sensation his kisses were causing in my body made it very difficult to think properly. If Edward was willing to do it, then so was I." Echoing assertions Bella repeatedly makes in the novels about her overwhelming response to Edward's kisses and touches—demonstrated best in *Twilight* when, forgetting to breathe during a kiss, she literally swoons—skyofdreams also clearly borrows Meyer's emphasis on Bella's unqualified trust in Edward.

Unlike Meyer's novels, however, skyofdreams explores how these elements function in the context of a more explicitly erotic tale. "Breaking Dawn: The Deleted Scenes" thus offers fairly graphic scenes of manual and oral stimulation, maintaining the tone and romantic context of the original novels but allowing readers access to the moments Meyer omits. She writes,

> We both groaned in perfect harmony and he entered me, the joining more amazing than I had ever imagined it would be. He fit perfectly inside me, and the little pain I felt at being completely penetrated was so far out of my mind that I could barely feel it.
>
> This was what I had waited for my entire life. This bliss, this perfection.

Again, skyofdreams works within the original characterizations in Meyer's texts; for example, Bella's ability to ignore pain (established repeatedly as clumsy Bella ends up with at least one substantial injury in each of the novels) allows her to remain fully immersed in the passion of the moment. This emphasis on passion, furthermore, is explicitly acknowledged by the adolescent author herself, who identifies the story as a "porno." The high incidence of stories featuring graphic descriptions of sex indicates that *Twilight* readers consider Meyer's shift away from voyeuristic inclusion in Bella and Edward's interludes—which I discuss in Chapter 3 as evidence that Bella abandons narrative intimacy at the end of the saga—to be a "loose end" that they wish to address. This suggests the possibility that readers who have accepted the role of partner in Bella's desire seek to continue the exploration of desire made possible by narrative intimacy, even when the books themselves explicitly depart from this version of the narrator-reader relationship.

Perhaps for this reason, many fan fiction writers create stories around "non-canon" pairings that allow them to explore their own desires for characters by redirecting Bella's romantic and sexual interests to characters with whom she has only platonic relationships in the novels. While some pairings maintain Bella's heterosexuality—for example, many writers explore the possibilities of a romantic relationship between Bella and Jasper—fans have also embraced "slash" and "femslash" fiction, reworking the canon relationships of Bella and Edward, Jasper and Alice, and Rosalie and Emmett into a complex network of possible pairings, most of which reject the assumption of heterosexuality. The femslash pairing of Alice and Bella, for example, has become one of the most popular non-canon pairings in adolescent women's *Twilight* fan fiction. Many Bella/Alice stories, such as Jocelyn Torrent's "Those Little Things," build upon the original texts, using "canon" material as a foundation. In "Those Little Things," Bella considers the small gestures that let her know that Alice cares, such as "the delicate way in which she holds me, cradled gently in her surrounding arms" (Alice frequently hugs Bella, and on at least two occasions in *New Moon* holds her at length); in contrast, Bella thinks, the "big things" that Edward does—"The way he instigates the lust, kissing me slowly and passionately only to pull away"—are less important.

In terms of narrative intimacy and the subversion of the narrator-reader relationships, these divergences from the source material suggest that, for many authors, composing fan fiction has more to do with the personal feelings elicited and fantasies inspired by the texts than loyal recreations or extensions of the texts themselves; the reading experience is thus understood as not only creating meaning within but also fundamentally altering the novels themselves in favor of reimaginings that privilege the reader's thoughts and feelings over those presented by the narrator in the text itself. Although the construction of narrative intimacy within young adult novels in general (and in Meyer's works in particular) tends to reinforce compulsory heterosexuality, young women's reconsiderations and manipulations of the characters, plots, and relationships indicate a desire to extend the boundaries beyond this limit.[11]

Just as the examples discussed here demonstrate fans' negotiation and alteration of original texts, the authors' notes and comments that surround stories offer insight into the ways that fan fiction writers more generally seek to change their understanding of the relationships between authors, narrators, and readers, an impulse to which many of them gesture in the author's notes that accompany most stories. Many authors include explicit requests for reviews and comments, imploring their readers with such requests as, "Let me know what you think" or "Tell me if you liked it!" Authors also offer insights into their inspirations and motivations, inviting readers to engage not only with the story itself but also with the larger process of reading and writing. For example, in the note to her story "Passing Notes," high school student Strawberry Shortcake123 explains that "I love the *Ruby Oliver* series. I saw there was only one story in this section, so I decided I wanted to write the second! . . . I adore Roo and Noel. :) Let me know if you liked!" These authors' notes (and similar comments made in forums and review sections) illustrate the degree to which fan authors blur the boundaries between author and reader, both by referencing their own experiences as a reader and by integrating their readers more immediately into the writing process.

Such a reconsideration of the author-reader relationship is demonstrated by teen fanfic writer mitty in the author's note to her story "Wasteland," which reconsiders Dessen's novel *Dreamland* from the point of view of the abusive Rogerson. Seventeen-year-old mitty explains her motivation:

> Anyway the reason why I started writing this story was because a lot of the Rogerson POV's were either too sentimental for him (at least I think) or too . . . plain I guess. NOT TO BASH! I like them its [*sic*] just not really what im [*sic*] looking for, plus they never update XD
>
> So I decided hey if I cant [*sic*] find what im [*sic*] looking for then fine ill write it. But im [*sic*] just warning you guys that im [*sic*] totally changing the ending whether you like it or not!

In her desire to explain her inspiration, mitty not only explicitly identifies her own engagement with the characters in the text—particularly her reading of Rogerson—but also invites her own readers to provide their responses to her work. At the same time, by articulating her motivation for writing this story, she highlights her experiences as a reader of both the original novel and other fan fiction. In other words, mitty's author's note acts as an example of the potential repositioning of the fan fiction writer as simultaneously occupying the roles of reader and author; her own responses to one text, then, may also act as a model for her own reader's engagement with the story she has written.

The immediacy of reader response made possible by Internet sites and forums also highlights the mutability of the author-reader relationship. In addition to the authors' notes and reviews that writers and readers can post to each other, furthermore, young fans have also taken advantage of Internet affinity spaces to become collaborators who can simultaneously act as writers and readers of shared stories. For example, the discussion boards on Sarah-Land.ning.com feature several threads dedicated to collaborative story-building exercise. In one thread, teen author Caroline W posts, "I had a great beginning for a story in my head and I can't think of what should happen next" before inviting her fellow Dessen fans to add their own content to her work. Over the course of more than thirty replies, Caroline W and her collaborators follow the story of a narrator— whom they collectively dub "Holly"—who is struggling to enjoy herself at a party full of her drunken high school classmates. Though the story is not a direct response to any of Dessen's novels, the protagonist, setting, and prevailing themes indicate that Caroline W and her co-writers are clearly influenced by Dessen's style. Furthermore, the authors' contributions are frequently marked with either requests for feedback or other expressions of desire for affirmation. As the collaborative nature of this work magnifies the way in which fan responses to literature actively blur the author-narra-tor-reader relationships, it also provides insights into the intersections of narrative intimacy constructed by novels and the types of intimacy read-ers enact in their own writing processes.

Indeed, the writing of fan fiction is clearly a community-driven activity that depends on interpersonal relationships, even though said relation-ships tend to exist exclusively in online spaces. Fan fiction authors fre-quently communicate with their readers throughout the writing process by relying upon "beta readers" (an online version of peer reviewers who offer suggestions and corrections before the author posts the story online for a more general audience) as well as through reviews and discussion forums.[12] In many cases, beta readers become friends as well as editors, a trend indicated by the sheer number of authors' notes that make refer-ence not only to betas but also to inside jokes and terms of endearment exchanged by author and beta. More generally, the request to "let me know what you think" that frequently appears in authors' notes demon-strates the degree to which fan fiction writers welcome the interaction with readers that the online medium makes available. That adolescent women create communities of readers and writers around the rewriting of other people's works suggests the possibility that the shared experi-ence of the story expands beyond the original narrator-reader relation-ship; as these adolescent women fan fiction writers create their own texts, they also develop a community of readers who all understand the story as shared experience.

The more general use of new media and the Internet at large as a space within which to explore intimacy inspired by impossible relation-ships with fictional characters provides a useful lens for considering the ongoing prevalence of cultural messages to and about adolescent women. More than any other group in contemporary American society, adolescent women are understood as vulnerable to the potential abuses of intimacy made possible by the Internet, particularly in terms of chat rooms and real-life meetings with people first encountered in affinity spaces like online forums.[13] At the same time, the constantly reinforced understanding that young women should constantly seek connection and interpersonal relationships is certainly reflected in the number of sites aimed almost exclusively at this group that emphasize the importance of community, including those associated with publications such as *Seventeen* and *Teen* magazines, as well as the fan sites discussed in this chapter. Like more general expectations of adolescent women's engagement with intimacy, then, the Internet offers contradictory messages regarding the benefits and threats of interpersonal relationships, particularly because the relationships made possible by the Internet generally exist *only* in the affinity spaces that suggest the possibility of safe disclosure.

Narrative intimacy in fan fiction and other fan works thus provides a representation of what narrator-reader relationships model and evoke in terms of readers' reading experiences and post-reading desires. The fact that young fan fiction writers have reimagined so many contemporary American novels for adolescent women signals the frequency with which adolescent women readers seek to explore narrative intimacy beyond the limits established by the texts they read. While I have only considered a small number of stories in this chapter, these works indicate the possibility that young women actively seek to prolong narrative intimacy in a manner that grants them the freedom and control to explore their own responses to literature may be a potentially fruitful point of departure for future studies of narrative intimacy, particularly as it pertains to adolescent women in contemporary American culture. The fan fiction discussed briefly here demonstrates some of the implications of my larger argument regarding the construction and application of narrative intimacy in contemporary American literature for adolescent women, particularly in terms of the ability of narrative intimacy to reflect and reinforce cultural expectations regarding interpersonal relationships and disclosure.

The complicated and often contradictory messages about intimacy that are propagated by contemporary culture shape representations and experiences of interpersonal relationships across genres, as well as across age, gender, race and class. However, as this project has illustrated, adolescent women—who are generally presented as white, heterosexual, and middle-class—have become one of the groups most immediately influenced by the understanding that intimacy simultaneously depends upon disclosure and represents a threat *because of* disclosure. Furthermore, that the novels I have discussed represent only a small number of the works of contemporary young adult fiction (and popular culture more generally) that employ narrative intimacy suggests the larger prevalence of this construction as a model with which adolescent women readers are invited to engage. Ultimately, because the content of these novels so frequently presents warnings about disclosure within interpersonal relationships even as they construct narrator-reader relationships based upon the assumption that the narrator can confide all of her thoughts, feelings, and experiences to the reader, narrative intimacy particularly acts as an embodiment of contradictory expectations regarding disclosure and discretion in young women's relationships. Whether or not young women accept the constructed roles of the reader as friend, partner in desire, or therapist made available to them by the texts they read, the expectation that they will not only recognize but willingly engage with the possibilities of narrative intimacy inevitably reflects and perpetuates those cultural contradictions.

Appendix: Awards and Prizes

Anderson, Laurie Halse. *Speak*. Named a National Book Award finalist, an *SLJ* Best Book of the Year, and a Printz Honor Book.

Cabot, Meg. *The Princess Diaries*. Named an ALA Best Book for Young Adults.

Caletti, Deb. *Honey, Baby, Sweetheart*. Named a National Book Award finalist, an *SLJ* Best Book of the Year, a New York Public Library Book for the Teen Age, and an International Reading Association Children's Book Award Notable Book.

Cohn, Rachel. *Gingerbread*. Named an ALA Best Book for Young Adults, an ALA Quick Pick for Young Adults, and an *SLJ* Best Book of 2002.

Cohn, Rachel. *Shrimp*. Named a *Kirkus* Editor's Choice.

Dessen, Sarah. *Dreamland*. Named an ALA Best Book for Young Adults, a New York Public Library Best Book for the Teen Age, and a YALSA Best Book for Young Adults.

———. *Keeping the Moon*. Named an ALA Best Book for Young Adults, an *SJL* Best Book of the Year, and an IRA Young Adult Choice.

———. *Someone Like You*. Named an ALA Best Book for Young Adults, an ALA Quick Pick for Young Adults, and an *SLJ* Best Book of the Year, 1998.

Friend, Natasha. *Perfect*. Winner of the Milkweed Prize for Children's Literature.

Haddix, Margaret Peterson. *Don't You Dare Read This, Mrs. Dunphrey!* Winner of the International Reading Association Award; named an ALA Best Book for Young Adults.

Halpern, Julie. *Get Well Soon*. Named a Kirkus Reviews Best YA Book of 2007 and an IRA Young Adult Choice of 2009.

Hemphill, Stephanie. *Things Left Unsaid*. Winner of the Myra Cohn Livingston Award, presented by the Southern California Council on Literature for Children and Young People for an outstanding work of poetry.

Lockhart, E. *The Boyfriend List*. Named an ALA Best Book for Young Adults.

McCafferty, Megan. *Sloppy Firsts*. Named a YALSA Best Book for Young Adults and a New York Public Library Book for the Teen Age.

Meyer, Stephenie. *Twilight*. Named an *SLJ* Best Book of 2005, one of ALA's Top Ten Best Books for Young Adults, a *New York Times* Editor's Choice, and *Publishers Weekly* Best Book of the Year.

Zarr, Sara. *Story of a Girl*. Named a 2007 National Book Award finalist, an ALA Best Book for Young Adults, and a New York Public Library Best Book for the Teen Age.

Notes

Chapter 1

1. As many critics have noted, familiar, relatable first-person narration has become something of a hallmark of contemporary adolescent literature; indeed, that this narrative construction has become so common means that it has almost been taken for granted rather than serving as a focus for the type of analysis I perform. In "Shift out of First: Third-Person Narration Has Advantages," first published in 1983, Elizabeth Schummann refers to first-person narration as the "preferred technique" in young adult literature (314). This trend and critical assessments of it have become even more pointed in the last two decades. Emma Heyde claims, "If a single feature could be said to characterize writing for young adults in the late 1990s, it would be first-person narrative" (65). For a detailed discussion of the uses and potential authenticity of the adolescent voice in young adult novels, see Mike Cadden's "The Irony of Narration in the Young Adult Novel."

2. Psychological studies have repeatedly found that intimacy generally has a positive impact on people's feelings of happiness and self-worth. Brenda Schaeffer describes intimacy as "a profound expression of our identities that leaves us in a euphoric state" (57–58), while Karen J. Prager has asserted that intimacy is imbued with *"affect,* which is positive and reflects feelings of warmth, acceptance, caring, love, pride, and appreciation" (242). Carin Rubenstein and Phillip Shaver, furthermore, emphatically encourage readers to *"realize that intimacy and friendship are sources of health; they prolong life"* (202, emphasis in original).

3. Derlega and Chaikan cite an example of a man on a train who tells his seatmate, a stranger, about problems at home and work; in the midst of this disclosure, the man indicates that he has not been able to tell his wife or friends this information. Another example that has become a staple in popular culture involves strangers becoming

trapped in an elevator or other confined space and quickly divulging their hopes, fears, and deepest secrets to one another. Indeed, this trend has become so prevalent that Jessica Darling, narrator of a series of books to be discussed in the fifth chapter, comments, "I know . . . that people are inclined to reveal intimate details to people they barely know because it somehow feels more anonymous, and therefore safer, than talking to a friend or family member. It's the same principle that keeps psychotherapists in business" (McCafferty, *Thirds* 256).

4. In his article "Faux Friendship," William Deresiewicz asserts that these sites "have falsified our understanding of intimacy itself, and with it, our understanding of ourselves. The absurd idea . . . that a MySpace profile or '25 Random Things About Me' can tell us more about someone than even a good friend might be aware of is based on desiccated notions about what knowing another person means." I more closely consider the role of the Internet and new media in the conclusion, which discusses the ways in which social networking, online communities, and the digital distribution of fan created responses to literature influence and reshape relationships between authors, characters, and readers.

5. As Marnina Gonick notes, "In the current period, it has been teenage girls, rather than youth in general, who are the focus of social concern" (17).

6. In the introduction to this work, Shandler expresses her admiration of and gratitude to Pipher's work but explains that she compiled the writing of adolescent women such as herself in order to "take the adult intermediary out from between us [adolescent women]. I wanted us to see one another's intelligence and experience, pain and power directly, free from adult interpretation" (xiii). This move signals a desire on Shandler's part for an intimate relationship with her adolescent women contributors and readers.

7. For the purposes of this discussion, particularly the defining and describing of the concept of narrative intimacy, several aspects of narrative theory may be addressed only briefly or not at all. For example, traditionally, discussions of the relationship between narrator and narratee have been concerned with questions of reliability, as narrative theorists have grappled with the degree to which the narrator presents truth (and Truth), as well as the degree to which the narratee and implied reader are meant to understand the narrator as a truth- (and Truth-)teller. However, for the purposes of this discussion, questions of reliability must be limited in favor of a larger discussion of relatability. In other words, the development of narrative intimacy (both as a concept and as an experience) depends more on the degree to which the narrator appears familiar and relatable than on the degree to which the narrator appears trustworthy. More generally, in keeping with recent efforts to streamline the vocabulary of narrative theory, I will be limiting my use of specific narratological terms such as diegesis, locutionary and illocutionary acts, mimesis, and paralaxis; while these concepts have helpfully contributed to the field of narrative theory, I will rely primarily on more common, familiar terminology regarding narrators, readers, and the relationships between them.

8. Models of narrative as a formal system have primarily involved the work of Russian Formalists and, more recently, the French Structuralists and are primarily concerned with the difference between story ("the what") and discourse ("the how"). In turn, approaches to narrative that treat it as an ideological act privilege the political and the dialogic aspects of narrative.

9. It is important to note that not all first-person narration strives for or achieves narrative intimacy; indeed, many first-person narrators actively work to conceal information about themselves, misrepresent themselves, or distract from their own thoughts and feelings by focusing on those of another character. Examples of such narrators include *Villette*'s Lucy Snowe, *The Great Gatsby*'s Nick Carraway, and *The Catcher in the Rye*'s Holden Caulfield. For the purposes of this discussion, I examine narrators whose goal in telling their stories is generally, if not always exclusively, to make themselves known to another.

10. Lanser notes, "Because the narratee does not necessarily undertake speech acts on his or her own behalf, it is likely that his or her identity will be conveyed through deep structural levels of the text" (180), most often through the narrator's choices in anticipation of the narratee's responses. In some cases, the narratee is so carefully and fully developed that the apparent differences between that character and the implied reader are so great as to make identification with the narratee difficult or impossible; in others, the narratee is so loosely defined that the distinction between narratee and ideal reader is indiscernible. In the cases of the novels discussed here, the narratee is most commonly of this second type; however, three novels discussed in Chapter 5—Megan McCafferty's *Fourth Comings*, Margaret Peterson Haddix's *Don't You Dare Read This, Mrs. Dunphrey*, and Julie Halpern's *Get Well Soon*—address narratees who are explicitly named and identified as characters within the texts.

11. The distinctions between these two selves are particularly evident in works such as *David Copperfield* and *To Kill a Mockingbird*, which feature adult narrating selves and child experiencing selves.

12. Indeed, reception theory that is specifically concerned with adolescent women readers emphasizes the points raised by Flanagan. Holly Virginia Blackford's study of girl readers, *Out of This World: Why Literature Matters to Girls*, provides evidence for Flanagan's point, as well as many of the assertions made by Walsh, McCallum, and others. After interviewing several young women and girls regarding their reading habits and their feelings about literature, Blackford found that escapism is often a motivating factor; girls read, she says, because "in their view, literature is an invitation to move beyond the self, beyond the politics of identity, within which we live our everyday lives" (2). In accordance with Walsh's relevance model, the young readers whose comments inform Blackford's argument assume fictionality and are able to negotiate the roles made available to them by the novels they read.

13. Most of the novels discussed in this project have been critically well received; I have included an appendix that identifies works that have been awarded prizes and/or included on "best of" lists.

Chapter 2

1. Screenwriter Tina Fey adapted the screenplay for this film from *Queen Bees and Wannabes*.

2. The other trend in popular culture is to avoid the question of friendships altogether, as Clea Hantman notes: "All those magazines we read, they cover makeup and hair, hot sexy boys and quizzes, but they don't talk about friendship—it's as if it's assumed that all is perfect in friend-land" (1).

3. One in a series, *Love You Like a Sister* is credited to Camy Baker; the publishing information lists no other authors or editors. However, as many reviewers have noted, the voice and style of the book suggests that it was written by an adult. An email to the publisher seeking clarification received no response.

4. As the authors of this study point out, much of the research that has been performed regarding adolescent women's friendships has focused primarily or exclusively on white, middle-class subjects. For the purposes of this discussion, which mainly explores fictional works for and about white, middle-class adolescent women, these findings remain applicable. However, recent psychological studies about this subject—such as Niobe Way and Lisa Chen's "Close and General Friendships Among African American, Latino, and Asian American Adolescents from Low-Income Families" and Jesse Rude and Daniel Herda's "Best Friends Forever? Race and the Stability of Adolescent Friendships"—have helpfully explored the ways in which race, class, and other socioeconomic factors influence young women's friendships.

5. Notably, a study by Noel A. Card, et al., found that despite widespread belief among teachers, parents, and even adolescents themselves that young women are more likely to rely on indirect aggression in their dealings with friends than their male counterparts, "the general pattern is of *similarities* rather than differences among boys' and girls' use of indirect aggression" (1204).

6. Throughout the novel, Caroline Dawes acts as the embodiment of the "queen bee" concept outlined by Wiseman. By relying on what has become a pop culture trope, Dessen again signals the construction of a susceptible reader who will recognize and potentially embody the expected responses to such a character.

7. The emphasis that Friend places on the role group therapy plays in Isabelle's recovery reflects the points about the "corresponding publicness" of intimacy that I discuss in the introduction.

8. The dangerous possibilities that might accompany a reader's identification with a character who offers insight into how to develop or maintain an eating disorder provide a particularly useful demonstration of Nikolajeva's "identification fallacy." In other words, identification with Isabelle here may result in some uncritical readers' failure to carefully consider the potential consequences of her actions, even as the novel as a whole provides clear warnings against anorexia and bulimia.

9. As Isabelle explains, because her mother is Christian and her father was Jewish, her family has always celebrated both Christmas and Hanukkah; following the death of

Isabelle's father, her mother has not wished to acknowledge the Jewish holidays that the family used to observe.

10. At her therapist's recommendations, Ruby reconsiders her relationships with her friends and with the boys that she has dated, kissed, flirted with, or secretly liked (the "boyfriend list" of the title); revisits "The Boy Book," a notebook she had kept with her friends; and creates a "treasure map" of her friendships that ends up comprising entirely of boys.

11. The possibility of shared attraction to Noel is explored further in the final novel of the series, *Real Live Boyfriends*; while this text does consider the role of friendship in Ruby's life, its more general interest in her romantic life sets it outside of the discussion of the first three novels, all of which treat romance as peripheral rather than central to Ruby's narrative.

Chapter 3

1. Korobov and Thorne's article also raises the crucial point that adolescent women's friendships and the discourse about romance that such relationships engender help to perpetuate heteronormative expectations of romantic and sexual relationships. As the authors note, "In western cultures, compulsory heterosexuality typically prescribes compulsory romance as the *sine qua non* romantic orientation, especially for white middle-class adolescent women" (50). The novels discussed in this chapter focus on white, middle-class adolescent women and privilege representations of heterosexual romance and sex; in this regard, Korobov and Thorne's work provides helpful insights into my discussion while acting as a useful reminder of the ways in which assumptions of heteronormativity exclude a number of people and experiences, both in general and specifically in novels for and about adolescent women. Although this chapter will not be exploring novels about non-white, non-heterosexual adolescent relationships, it is important to note that works such as Julie Anne Peters's 2003 novel *Keeping You a Secret* (which follows narrator Holland as she begins a relationship with a new girl at school) may simultaneously feature narrative intimacy and in some ways challenge the paradigm I establish in this discussion.

2. For example, in *Teen Love: On Relationships*, from the *Chicken Soup for the Soul* series, author Kimberly Kirberger offers this attempt to define or describe love: "When we are in love, life has an extra sparkle to it. Things seem more real, and all of our experiences are enhanced by it" (90).

3. For example, the television series *One Tree Hill* (which premiered in 2003) features a couple who married at the age of sixteen and, despite obstacles such as their parents' objections, temptations to commit adultery, and eventually an unplanned pregnancy, remain married throughout the series. Indeed, after their first simple wedding on the beach, the couple renews their vows in a formal wedding two seasons later.

4. The contrast between these two sets of expectations is clearly demonstrated in attitudes toward the loss of one's virginity: young women are generally directed to consider their virginity a "gift" to be protected while young men often face pressure from peers to lose their virginity as quickly as possible. This understanding of young women's virginity is perhaps best illustrated by the True Love Waits (TLW) movement. Introduced by LifeWay Christian Resources, TLW encourages teenagers to remain celibate until marriage and, according to their website, "utilizes positive peer pressure by encouraging teenagers who make a commitment to refrain from premarital sex to challenge their peers to do the same" ("TLW Overview"). Participants are encouraged to sign "covenant cards" declaring their intentions to abstain from sex and to take part in national celebrations, the first of which took place in 1994. Variations include purity rings and "commitment ceremonies" in which young girls pledge to their fathers that they will remain virgins until marriage. While young men do take part in such rituals/activities, young women are the prime target of lessons about abstinence and make up the majority of participants in such programs. Peter S. Bearman and Hannah Brückner offer a helpful discussion of programs such as TLW in their article "Promising the Future: Virginity Pledges and First Intercourse."

5. Although some of these books—such as Maureen Lyon and Christina Breda Antoniades's *My Teen Has Had Sex: Now What Do I Do?*—suggest that parents of boys and girls all need guidance in this area, many adopt "she" as the primary generic pronoun; others, such as Buddenberg and McGee's *There Are No Simple Rules for Dating My Daughter!*, focus on young women because "of the unique external pressures and internal desires that girls grapple with" and because "parents, especially dads, seem more concerned about their daughters" (3).

6. Many novels, such as Maureen Daly's *Seventeenth Summer* (1942) and Beverly Cleary's *Jean and Johnny* (1965), feature the development of adolescent romance, following the teen protagonists through the first nervous phone calls, dates, and kisses, while ignoring the possibility of a sexual relationship; meanwhile, novels such as Ann Head's *Mr. and Mrs. Bo Jo Jones* (1968) implicitly discourage sexuality by presenting the dangers of engaging in sex outside of marriage.

7. As many critics have noted, however, the secondary characters in *Forever* . . . are not so lucky. Sybil, who is described as being somewhat promiscuous, faces an unplanned pregnancy, while closeted teenager Art attempts suicide as a result of his failed heterosexual relationship.

8. Warhol adopts this term from Gerald Prince's term "unnarratable," which he generally employs as a means of describing an act that is not worthy of inclusion in a narration, generally because of its insignificance or lack of impact on the narrator or narrative; Warhol's use of the term in *Having a Good Cry* more accurately describes that which is not expressible in the language available to the narrator, particularly in terms of depth of emotion.

9. See Catherine S. Chilman's "The Development of Adolescent Sexuality," which notes that young women in particular learn about sexuality and sex from books,

television, and films; these sources allow for a sort of mediated voyeurism that provides access to information and potentially titillation at something of a safe remove.

10. Michael, Scarlett's boyfriend and the father of her child, dies in a motorcycle accident the day after they have sex, a fate that notably echoes the didactic messages of many mid-twentieth century adolescent novels about sex, in which teens who engaged in sexual activity met unfortunate ends.

11. In the paperback edition of *Lost It*, these warnings are echoed by the two pages of advertisements following the text—one for Bronwen Pardes's book *Doing It Right: Making Smart, Safe, and Satisfying Choices About Sex,* the other for an organization called Know HIV/AIDS, including its website and hotline information.

12. Although *Breaking Dawn* is the official final volume of the saga, Meyer published a *Twilight*-related novella—*The Short Second Life of Bree Tanner,* which follows the story of a minor character in *Eclipse*—in May 2010. Meyer also began a fifth *Twilight* saga novel entitled *Midnight Sun,* which retells the events of *Twilight* from Edward's perspective; after several chapters were leaked on the Internet without her permission in August 2008, Meyer released an unfinished manuscript on her official website. She currently has no plans to complete this novel. Although the reframing of Bella and Edward's story from Edward's perspective certainly does have interesting implications, because Edward is not an adolescent woman, a consideration of his role as narrator in *Midnight Sun* lies beyond the scope of this discussion.

13. Meyer offers a context for Bella's view of love as permanent and unchanging in the relationships of the vampires and werewolves around her. All of the other members of Edward's family are married, and, as Edward explains to Jacob, the love he and his fellow vampires experience is, for all intents and purposes, eternal: "We are set the way we are, and it is very rare for us to experience a real change. When that happens, as when Bella entered my life, it is a permanent change" (*Eclipse* 500). Meyer underscores this construction of love with a subplot about the Quileute werewolves' tendency to "imprint" upon the objects of their affection, a process Jacob describes as "more absolute" than finding a soul mate (*Eclipse* 123). Although Jacob initially presents imprinting as "the rare exception, not the rule" (*Eclipse* 122), by the end of the saga, the majority of the wolves in his pack have imprinted—including Jacob, who eventually imprints on Bella's infant daughter.

Chapter 4

1. Although it is difficult to determine whether the actual rates of abuse and assault against adolescent women have increased in the past fifteen years, the number of sociological, anthropological, and especially psychological studies devoted to the victimization of adolescent women has increased dramatically: a sample search of articles and books on the subject shows that the number of studies published since 1994

(the year of *Reviving Ophelia*'s publication) has increased by almost two-thirds over studies published prior to that year.

2. In "Gender and Contextual Factors in Adolescent Dating Violence," Christian Molidor and Richard M. Tolman discuss incidences of physical abuse perpetrated against adolescent men and women in heterosexual dating relationships. While their study found that "31.3 percent of girls and 32.6 percent of boys experienced some physical violence in a dating relationship," a closer interrogation of the data reveals that adolescent women were far more likely than adolescent men to experience severe violence, to suffer physically or emotionally from that violence, and to perceive the violence as a serious assault (185). Furthermore, they argue that "much of girls' violence towards boys may be the result of self-defense, either to fend off physical attacks or coercive sexual behavior" (190).

3. In the case of *Saving Beauty from the Beast*, for example, Crompton begins with the story of her fifteen-year-old daughter Jenny's victimization and eventual murder at the hands of an abusive boyfriend.

4. Although I am primarily interested in the impact abuse and assault have on concepts of intimacy, it should be noted that victims also struggle with their understandings of safety and justice. Judith Herman, in *Trauma and Recovery: The Aftermath of Violence—from Domestic Abuse to Political Terror*, argues that "sharing the traumatic event with others is a precondition for the restitution of a sense of a meaningful world. . . . These two responses—recognition and restitution—are necessary to rebuild the survivor's sense of order and justice" (70).

5. It is important to note that this chapter focuses on situations in which the perpetrator of the abuse is a peer rather than an adult or family member. Because I am primarily concerned with relationships between adolescents, works such as Laura Wiess's *Such a Pretty Girl*, Sapphire's *Push*, and Elizabeth Scott's *Living Dead Girl*, in all of which the perpetrator of the abuse or assault is an adult do not directly relate to this discussion of narrative intimacy.

6. Unlike physical and sexual abuse, rates of emotional abuse do not decrease during adolescence; researchers hypothesize that this results from the fact that the "perceived negative consequences of that type of abuse on relationships is not as apparent" as in cases of physical or sexual abuse (Foshee et al. 394).

7. In his article "Why Won't Melinda Just Talk about What Happened? *Speak* and the Confessional Voice," Chris McGee asserts that while there is "great power in Melinda's silence, her questioning and resistance to power, and her willingness to work through her own traumas in her own way," Anderson's novel ultimately sends the message that "it is okay not to speak for a little while . . . but in the end you should never hide anything from adults" (185). However, because Melinda has relied so heavily on the reader rather than any adult audience, and because the content of her disclosure to Mr. Freeman will, we can assume, repeat much of the information she has already made available to the reader, I disagree with the emphasis that McGee places on revealing secrets to adults.

8. In her 2002 novel *Catalyst*, Anderson briefly revisits Melinda a year after the events chronicled in *Speak*. *Catalyst*'s narrator Katie Malone, a senior at the same school that Melinda attends, speaks to Melinda in passing; to the reader, Katie notes that Melinda pressed charges against rapist Andy, "which is cool" (134). Melinda herself appears confident and upbeat, even inviting Katie to take part in an art project.

Chapter 5

1. In "Privat (Sic) Keep Out: The Diary as Secret Space," Joan W. Blos fondly recalls a diary she had as a girl, particularly "the charm of its tiny lock, with its matching, miniscule key. Looking back, I think it was the lock that intrigued me most of all—the lock whose presence signaled the expectation that one might write in the diary what no one else would read" (236).

2. Notably, Anne herself doubted that anyone would be interested in the content of the diary: "It's an odd idea for someone like me to keep a diary; not only because I have never done so before, but because it seems to me that neither I—nor for that matter anyone else—will be interested in the unbosomings of a thirteen-year-old schoolgirl. . . . As I don't intend to show this cardboard-covered notebook, bearing the proud name of 'diary,' to anyone, unless I find a real friend, boy or girl, probably nobody cares" (2).

3. Although *Go Ask Alice*, *Treacherous Love*, and *Annie's Baby*, among others, all purport to be true diaries written by anonymous teenage girls, readers and critics have expressed doubts regarding the true authorship of the works. Sparks, a former therapist, has publicly claimed that *Go Ask Alice* combines real entries from a former patient's diary and fictionalized entries written by Sparks herself, but the veracity of this assertion remains in question. The Library of Congress tellingly categorizes these works as fiction.

4. In her consideration of the diaries of famous authors such as Virginia Woolf and Anaïs Nin, Alexandra Johnson remarks on this possibility: "How many writers, casting a nervous side glance at fame, secretly contemplate their diaries being published? If over the centuries the diary has helped writers discover the *author* in *authority*, confronting the *public* in *publication* still remains an issue for many" (16, emphasis in original).

5. As Field notes, "The diary is a one-way channel of communication, for all that it may be an attempt to increase self-knowledge or to explain one's self for the benefit of others" (9).

6. There are ten official volumes in the series, as well as three "in-between" volumes, such as *The Princess Present: A Princess Diaries Book (Volume VI and a Half)*.

7. Other authors have likewise combined diary fiction and series fiction; Melody Carlson, for example, has written fifteen volumes in the popular Christian *Diary of a Teen Girl* series, while British author Louise Rennison has followed narrator Georgia Nicolson through ten diary novels, beginning with *Angus, Thongs, and Full-Frontal Snogging*.

8. It is interesting to note that McCafferty published excerpts of the diary that she herself kept as an adolescent on Twitter and her personal blog. In an interview with Stephen Levy, McCafferty explains that the practice began as a response to fans' requests for more information about her; because "she wasn't comfortable sharing details of her current home life, and wanted to save her observations about pop culture for her novels," Levy says, "she typed out her journals and used them as postings" (18). This process, which she refers to as "retro-blogging," has also been undertaken by other bloggers. For example, in August 2009, a blogger named Damiella (whose blog can be found at metadiary.blogspot.com) began posting and commenting on diaries she kept from 1985 into the early 1990s.

9. In both her resistance to sharing her thoughts with her teacher and in her mistakenly making those thoughts accessible to Mrs. Dunphrey, Tish echoes the experiences of Mia and Jess, both of whom also confront the writing of a journal as an English assignment. That these three narrators, among many others in young adult literature, are required to keep a diary as homework suggests a larger cultural expectation that the journal may provide students with an opportunity to expand their writing skills and interests; as all three of these narrators' reactions suggest, however, many students respond by limiting rather than expanding their disclosure.

10. Mia includes emails she sends and receives, while Jess's diary entries are occasionally interrupted by the inclusion of a letter she has written to Hope; Colby, who will be discussed in the next section of this chapter, likewise includes emails, letters, and blog entries between passages from her diary.

Chapter 6

1. As Kimberley Reynolds has noted, fan fiction challenges Roland Barthes's assertion that "when reading, pleasure is bound up with knowing from the first page that a book will end" because it "exists to extend indefinitely the textual experience" (183).

2. In "Homosexuality at Online Hogwarts," Tosenberger notes, "For anyone who wishes to observe the cultural impact of J. K. Rowling's Harry Potter series, the online fandom is an excellent place to start. Readers who participate in the Potter fandom do not simply passively absorb the texts but actively respond to them" (200).

3. The term "slash" comes from the shorthand fan fiction authors use to mark the central relationships in their stories, which lists the two characters names with a slash between them. Stories about Kirk and Spock, then, were often labeled "Kirk/Spock." In addition to slash fiction, fan fiction authors also explore the possibilities of lesbian relationships in stories that are often labeled "femslash" or "femmeslash."

4. A 2010 Pew study found that 93 percent of all American teenagers use the Internet, and 73 percent of those teenagers use social networking sites and other online communities on a regular basis (Lenhart et al). Furthermore, according to Kaveri Subrahmanyam and Patricia Greenfield, studies have suggested that "for today's youth,

media technologies are an important social variable and that physical and virtual worlds are psychologically connected; consequently, the virtual world serves as a playing ground for developmental issues from the physical world, such as identity and sexuality" (124).

5. All of these authors apologize for their inability to read all the drafts that readers want to send and offer suggestions to aspiring writers.

6. FanFiction.net is by far the largest fan fiction repository on the Internet, featuring stories about books, movies, and television shows. While many fans post their fan fiction elsewhere—on sites such as LiveJournal.com, personal blogs, and author websites, for example—I focus exclusively on FanFiction.net because it allows for the clearest discussion of adolescent women's fan fiction in the larger context of fan communities and response. All figures from FanFiction.net are as of May 2012.

7. For example, articles such as Donna E. Alvermann's "Why Bother Theorizing Adolescents' Online Literacies for Classroom Practice and Research?" and Dana J. Wilber's "Understanding and Connecting to the Digital Literacies of Adolescence" consider how fan fiction may be used as a diagnostic tool or other device in contemporary classroom settings. Other scholars have offered insight into the potential uses of fan fiction as a tool for young people learning English as a second language.

8. To some degree, such changes reflect Bronwen Thomas's assertion that "fan fiction here is about wrestling control away from the makers of the source text, especially where the fans disapprove of the direction taken in characterization, plotting, and so on" (146).

9. Fan fiction author Merlin Missy discusses the problematic nature of Mary Sues in her online article "Mary Sue, Who Are You?" She includes among these characters' primary characteristics "names that are a takeoff on the author's name, or his/her middle name," "a twin, clone, or close sibling of the same gender (especially if the author writes more tales about the twin)," and "a certain 'charming' klutziness that results in minor or major disasters but is rectified by the end of the piece."

10. Interestingly, one popular AU plot involves real readers finding themselves transported into the original text or characters from the text being transported into the "real world" (the latter is often complicated by the character encountering fan fiction written about him- or herself); these metafictional constructions draw further attention to the blurring of the fiction-reality gap that fan fiction often attempts.

11. See Catherine Tosenberger's "Homosexuality at the Online Hogwarts: Harry Potter Slash Fan Fiction" for a detailed discussion of adolescent fan fiction authors' engagement with slash. In particular, Tosenberger notes, while published literature for adolescents continues to reflect an anxiety to "contain adolescent sexuality within parameters acceptable to adult sensibilities," fan fiction is not restricted by the concerns of traditional publishing and thus allows young writers space to explore treatments of sexuality that are not typically portrayed in novels for this audience.

12. In "The Audience as Editor: The Role of Beta Readers in Online Fan Fiction Communities," Angelina I. Karpovich identifies the beta reading process as unique to

Internet-based fan fiction. She also links the use of beta readers to the more general understanding of fan fiction as facilitating relationships within fandoms, explaining that "there is an aspect of community maintenance to this convention, as the continuing dialogues between the fan writers and their betas help to maintain personal links to the community" (174).

13. While both adolescent men and women face multiple potential risks by engaging in online conversations and communities, popular culture focuses on young women as potential victims; shows such as *Dateline*'s *To Catch a Predator* focus almost exclusively on young women as vulnerable to Internet-related crime. In "High Tech or High Risk: Moral Panics about Girls Online," Justine Cassell and Meg Cramer argue the panic over young girls at risk from communication technologies "is not new rhetoric in America. There has been a recurring moral panic throughout history, not just over real threats of technological danger, but also over the compromised virtue of young girls, parental loss of control in the face of a seductive machine, and the debate over whether women can ever be high-tech without being in jeopardy" (54).

References

Works Cited

Abbott, H. Porter. *Diary Fiction: Writing as Action*. Ithaca: Cornell University Press, 1984.

Ahrens, Courtney E. "Being Silenced: The Impact of Negative Social Reactions on the Disclosure of Rape." *American Journal of Psychology* 38 (2006): 263–74.

Alsup, Janet. "Politicizing Young Adult Literature: Reading Anderson's *Speak* as a Critical Text." *Journal of Adolescent and Adult Literacy* 47.2 (2003): 158–68.

Altmann, Anna. "Desire and Punishment: Adolescent Female Sexuality in Three Novels." *Canadian Children's Literature* 21.4 (1995): 20–33.

Anderson, Laurie Halse. *Catalyst*. New York: Speak, 2003.

———. *Speak*. New York: Penguin, 1999.

Appleyard, J. A. *Becoming a Reader: The Experience of Fiction from Childhood to Adulthood*. New York: Cambridge University Press, 1990.

Ashcraft, Catherine. "Ready or Not . . . ?: Teen Sexuality and the Troubling Discourse of Readiness." *Anthropology and Education Quarterly* 37.4 (2006): 328–46.

Ashton. "Me and Her Are Practically Related." Review of *Sloppy Firsts* by Megan McCafferty. Amazon.com, 29 February 2004. Web, 13 September 2008.

Bacon-Smith, Camille. *Enterprising Women: Television Fandom and the Creation of Popular Myth*. Philadelphia: University of Pennsylvania Press, 1992.

Baker, Camy. *Love You Like a Sister: 30 Cool Rules for Making and Being a Better Best Friend*. New York: Skylark, 1998.

Bakhtin, Mikhail. *Problems of Dostoyevsky's Poetics*. Trans. and ed. Caryl Emerson. Minneapolis: University of Minnesota Press, 1984.

Bauble. "There Is Eccentric and then There Is Nutterbutter." *My Atelier*. Livejournal.com, 3 March 2010. Web, 10 March 2010.

Bayer, Gerd. "Deceptive Narratives: On Truth and the Epistolary Voice." *Literaturwissenschaft und Linguistik* 39.154 (2009): 173–87.

Berlant, Lauren. "Introduction to Special Issue." In *Intimacy*. EdIted by Lauren Berlant. Chicago: University of Chicago Press, 2000, 1–8.

Black, Rebecca W. *Adolescents and Online Fan Fiction*. New Literacies. New York: Peter Lang, 2008.

Blackford, Holly Virginia. *Out of This World: Why Literature Matters to Girls*. New York: Teachers College Press, 2004.

Bloom, Lynn. "'I Write for Myself and Strangers': Private Diaries as Public Documents." In *Inscribing the Daily: Critical Essays on Women's Diaries*. Amherst: University of Massachusetts Press, 1996, 23–37.

Blos, Joan W. "Privat (Sic) Keep Out: The Diary as Secret Space." In *Secret Spaces of Childhood*, edited by Elizabeth Goodenough. Ann Arbor: University of Michigan Press, 2003, 236–44.

Booth, Wayne C. *The Rhetoric of Fiction*. 2nd ed. Chicago: University of Chicago Press, 1983.

Brown, Lyn Mikel, Niobe Way, and Julia L. Duff. "The Others in My I: Adolescent Girls' Friendships and Peer Relations." In *Beyond Appearances: A New Look at Adolescent Girls*, edited by Norine G. Johnson, Michael C. Roberts, and Judith P. Worrell. Washington, D.C.: APA, 2001, 181–204.

Buddenberg, Laura J., and Kathleen M. McGee. *There Are No Simple Rules for Dating My Daughter! Surviving the Pitfalls and Pratfalls of Teen Relationships*. Boys Town, NE: Boys Town Press, 2006.

Burks, Bobbie K. "Emotional Abuse of Women." In *"Intimate" Violence Against Women: When Spouses, Partners, or Lovers Attack*, edited by Paula K. Lundberg-Love and Shelly L. Marmion. Westport, CT: Praeger, 2006, 15–30.

Burnham, Niki. *Sticky Fingers*. New York: Simon and Schuster, 2005.

Cabot, Meg. "Fan Fiction." MegCabot.com. 8 March 2006. Web, 10 May 2010.

———. *Forever Princess*. New York: HarperCollins, 2009.

———. *Party Princess*. New York: HarperCollins, 2006.

———. *The Princess Diaries*. New York: HarperCollins, 2000.

———. *Princess in Love*. New York: HarperCollins, 2002.

———. *Princess in Pink*. New York: HarperCollins, 2004.

———. *Princess in the Spotlight*. New York: HarperCollins, 2001.

———. *Princess in Training*. New York: HarperCollins, 2005.

———. *Princess in Waiting*. New York: HarperCollins, 2003.

———. *Princess Mia*. New York: HarperCollins, 2008.

———. *Princess on the Brink*. New York: HarperCollins, 2007.

Cadden, Mike. "The Irony of Narration in the Young Adult Novel." *Children's Literature Association Quarterly* 25.3 (2000): 146–54.

Caletti, Deb. *Honey, Baby, Sweetheart*. New York: Simon and Schuster, 2004.

Card, Noel A., et al. "Direct and Indirect Aggression During Childhood and Adolescence: A Meta-Analytical Review of Gender Differences, Intercorrelations, and Relations to Maladjustment." *Child Development* 79.5 (2008): 1185–1229.

Caroline W. "A Story." *Sarah-Land.* Penguin Group, 3 January 2010. Web, 20 May 2012.

Cassell, Justine, and Meg Cramer. "High Tech or High Risk: Moral Panic about Girls Online." In *Digital Youth, Innovation, and the Unexpected.* The John D. and Catherine T. MacArthur Foundation Series on Digital Media and Learning. Cambridge, MA: MIT Press, 2008, 53–76.

Charlene. Reply to "Thanks for Joining!" *Sarah-Land.* Penguin Group, 31 May 2009. Web, 7 July 2010.

Charles, John, Shelley Mosley, and Ann Bouricius. "Romancing the YA Reader." *Voice of Youth Advocates* 21.6 (1999): 414–16.

Chatman, Seymour. *Story and Discourse: Narrative Structure in Fiction and Film.* Ithaca: Cornell University Press, 1978.

Chilman, Catherine S. "The Development of Adolescent Sexuality." *Journal of Research and Development in Education* 16.2 (1983): 16–26.

Christian-Smith, Linda K. "Young Women and Their Dream Lovers: Sexuality in Adolescent Fiction." In *The Politics of Women's Bodies: Sexuality, Appearance, and Behavior*, edited by Rose Weitz. New York: Oxford University Press, 1998, 100–111.

Claire. "No Fairy Tale, but Lots of Magic." Review of *The Princess Diaries* by Meg Cabot. Amazon.com, 15 August 2004. Web, 13 September 2008.

Cohn, Dorrit. *Transparent Minds: Narrative Modes for Presenting Consciousness in Fiction.* Princeton, NJ: Princeton University Press, 1978.

Cohn, Rachel. *Cupcake.* New York: Simon and Schuster, 2007.

———. *Gingerbread.* New York: Simon and Schuster, 2002.

———. *Shrimp.* New York: Simon and Schuster, 2005.

Crompton, Vicki, and Ellen Zelda Kessner. *Saving Beauty from the Beast: How to Protect Your Daughter from an Unhealthy Relationship.* Boston: Little, Brown, 2003.

Deresiewicz, William. "Faux Friendships." *The Chronicle of Higher Education*, 6 December 2009. Web, 3 March 2010.

Derlega, Valerian J., and Alan L. Chaikan. *Sharing Intimacy: What We Reveal to Others and Why.* Englewood Cliffs, NJ: Prentice-Hall, 1975.

Dessen, Sarah. *Dreamland.* New York: Viking, 2000.

———. "The Five!" *Writergrl.* Livejournal.com, 1 April 2010. Web, 10 May 2010.

———. *Keeping the Moon.* New York: Speak, 1999. Print.

———. *Someone Like You.* New York: Speak, 1998.

emruking. "Dreamland Trailer (Based on the Book)." YouTube.com, 27 February 2009. Web, 7 July 2010.

Feldhahn, Shaunti, and Lisa A. Rice. *For Young Women Only.* Atlanta: Multnomah, 2006.

Field, Trevor. *Form and Function in the Diary Novel.* Totowa, NJ: Barnes and Noble, 1989.

Fischer, Judith L., Joyce Munsch, and Shannon M. Greene. "Adolescence and Intimacy." *Psychosocial Development During Adolescence*, edited by Gerald R. Adams, Raymond Montemayor, and Thomas P. Gullotta. Advances in Adolescent Development. Vol. 8. Thousand Oaks, CA: Sage, 1996, 95–129.

Flanagan, Caitlin. "What Girls Want." *Atlantic Monthly Online,* December 2008. Web, 3 March 2009.

Foshee, Vangie A., et al. "The Development of Four Types of Adolescent Dating Abuse and Selected Demographic Correlates." *Journal of Research on Adolescence* 19.3 (2009): 380–400.

Foucault, Michel. *The History of Sexuality.* Translated by Robert Hurley. Vol. 1. New York: Pantheon, 1978.

Frank, Anne. *Diary of a Young Girl.* 1952. New York: Sanval Books, 1993.

Friend, Natasha. *Perfect.* Minneapolis: Milkweed, 2004.

Genevieve Lee. "Promises." *FanFiction.net,* 13 November 2007. Web, 2 March 2010.

Gilligan, Carol. "Exit-Voice Dilemmas in Adolescent Development." In *Adolescent Identities: A Collection of Readings,* edited by Deborah L. Browning. New York: Taylor and Francis, 2008. 141–56.

Gonick, Marnina. "Between 'Girl Power' and 'Reviving Ophelia': Constructing the Neoliberal Girl Subject." *NWSA Journal* 18.2 (2006): 1–23.

Haddix, Margaret Peterson. *Don't You Dare Read This, Mrs. Dunphrey.* New York: Simon and Schuster, 1996.

Halpern, Julie. *Get Well Soon.* New York: Square Fish, 2007.

Hantman, Clea. *30 Days to Finding and Keeping Sassy Sidekicks and BFFs: A Friendship Field Guide.* New York: Delacorte, 2009.

Harvard Baby. "Windows." *FanFiction.net,* 20 July 2009. Web, 3 July 2010.

Hemphill, Stephanie. *Things Left Unsaid.* New York: Hyperion, 2005.

Herman, Judith. *Trauma and Recovery: The Aftermath of Violence—from Domestic Abuse to Political Terror.* New York: BasicBooks, 1992.

Heyde, Emma. "Inviting Spaces: First Person Narrative in Young Adult Fiction." *English in Australia* 126 (December—January 1999–2000): 65–68.

Hogan, Rebecca. "Engendered Autobiographies: The Diary as Feminine Form." *Prose Studies* 14.2 (1991): 95–107.

imanorrange11. "The Boyfriend List." YouTube.com, 25 March 2009. Web, 7 July 2010.

Iser, Wolfgang. *The Implied Reader: Patterns of Communication from Bunyan to Beckett.* Baltimore: Johns Hopkins University Press, 1978.

Jcrazy. Reply to "You know when your a PD fan." MegCabot.com, 22 January 2010. Web, 8 September 2010.

Jenkins, Henry. *Textual Poachers: Television, Fans, and Participatory Culture.* New York: Routledge, 1992.

Jocelyn Torrent. "Those Little Things." *FanFiction.net,* 6 July 2011. Web, 20 May 2012.

Johnson, Alexandra. *The Hidden Writer: Diaries and the Creative Life.* New York: Doubleday, 1997.

Joyner, Kara, and J. Richard Udry. "You Don't Bring Me Anything but Down: Adolescent Romance and Depression." *Journal of Health and Social Behavior* 41.4 (2000): 369–91.

Kaplan, Deborah. "Construction of Fan Fiction Character Through Narrative." In *Fan Fiction and Fan Communities in the Age of the Internet*, edited by Karen Hellekson and Kristina Busse. Jefferson, NC: McFarland, 2006, 134–53.

Karpovich, Angelina I. "The Audience as Editor: The Role of Beta Readers in Online Fan Fiction Communities." In *Fan Fiction and Fan Communities in the Age of the Internet*, edited by Karen Hellekson and Kristina Busse. Jefferson, NC: McFarland, 2006, 171–88.

Kaywell, Joan. *Using Literature to Help Troubled Teenagers Cope with Abuse Issues.* New York: Greenwood Press, 2004.

Khy. "Ruby Oliver Is Back and Better than Ever." Review of *The Boyfriend List* by E. Lockhart. Amazon.com, 28 July 2009. Web, 1 February 2010.

Kirberger, Kimberly. *Teen Love: On Relationships, A Book for Teens.* Deerfield Beach, FL: Health Communications, Inc., 1999.

Korobov, Neil, and Avril Thorne. "The Negotiation of Compulsory Romance in Young Women's Friends' Stories about Romantic Heterosexual Experiences." *Feminism and Psychology* 19.1 (2009): 49–70.

Kuhn, Annette. *The Power of the Image: Essays on Representation and Sexuality.* Boston: Routlege and Kegan Paul, 1985.

Lamarque, Peter. *Fictional Points of View.* Ithaca: Cornell University Press, 1996.

Lanser, Susan Sniader. *The Narrative Act: Point of View in Prose Fiction.* Princeton: Princeton University Press, 1981.

Lejeune, Philippe. "How Do Diaries End?" *Biography* 24.1 (2001). Web, 3 February 2010.

Lenhart, Amanda, et al. "Social Media and Mobile Internet Use Among Teens and Young Adults." *Pew Internet and American Life Project.* Pew Research Center, 3 February 2010. Web, 18 March 2010.

Levy, Barrie. *In Love and in Danger: A Teen's Guide to Breaking Free of Abusive Relationships.* Seattle: Seal Press, 1997.

Levy, Stephen. "Dear Diary—And Everyone Else, Too." *Newsweek* 147.20 (15 May 2006): 18.

Lockhart, E. *The Boy Book.* New York: Delacorte, 2006.

———. *The Boyfriend List.* New York, Delacorte, 2005.

———. *Real Live Boyfriends.* New York: Delacorte, 2010.

———. *The Treasure Map of Boys.* New York :Delacorte, 2009.

———. "True and Embarrassing Things About E." ELockhart.com, 2010. Web, 10 May 2010.

lovelessfighter007. "The Princess Diaries: A Romance." *FanFiction.net*, 6 November 2008. Web, 3 July 2010.

Manifold, Marjorie Cohee. "Fanart as Craft and the Creation of Culture." *International Journal of Education through Art* 5.1 (2009): 7–21.

Marie Poe. "Spoke, the Aftermath of Speak." *FanFiction.net*, 6 May 2010. Web, 3 July 2010.

Martens, Lorna. *The Diary Novel*. Cambridge: Cambridge Univeristy Press, 1985.

Martinson, Deborah. *In the Presence of Audience: The Self in Diaries and Fiction*. Columbus: Ohio State University Press, 2003.

McAdams, Don P. *Intimacy: The Need to Be Close*. New York: Doubleday, 1989.

McCafferty, Megan. *Charmed Thirds*. New York: Three Rivers Press, 2006.

———. *Fourth Comings*. New York: Three Rivers Press, 2007.

———. *Perfect Fifths*. New York: Three Rivers Press, 2009.

———. *Second Helpings*. New York: Three Rivers Press, 2003.

———. *Sloppy Firsts*. New York: Three Rivers Press, 2001.

McCallum, Robyn. *Ideologies of Identity in Adolescent Fiction: The Dialogic Construction of Subjectivity*. New York: Garland, 1999.

McGee, Christopher. "Why Won't Melinda Just Talk About What Happened? *Speak* and the Confessional Voice." *Children's Literature Association Quarterly* 34.2 (2009): 172–87.

McNelles, Laurie R., and Jennifer A. Connolly. "Intimacy Between Adolescent Friends: Age and Gender Differences in Intimate Affect and Intimate Behaviors." *Journal of Research on Adolescence* 9.2 (1999): 143–59.

Merlin Missy. "Mary Sue, Who Are You?" *FirefoxNews.com*, 7 January 2007. Web, 10 May 2010.

Merten, Don E. "Enculturation into Secrecy Among Junior High School Girls." *Journal of Contemporary Ethnography* 28.2 (1999): 107–37.

Meyer, Stephenie. *Breaking Dawn*. New York: Little, Brown, 2008.

———. *Eclipse*. New York: Little, Brown, 2007.

———. *New Moon*. New York: Little, Brown, 2006.

———. *Twilight*. New York: Little, Brown, 2005.

mitty. "Wasteland." *FanFiction.net*, 4 March 2008. Web, 3 July 2010.

Molidor, Christian, and Richard M. Tolman. "Gender and Contextual Factors in Adolescent Dating Violence." *Violence Against Women* 4.2 (1998): 180–94.

Murray, Jill. *But He Never Hit Me: The Devastating Cost of Non-Physical Abuse to Girls and Women*. New York: iUniverse, Inc., 2007.

———. *But I Love Him: Protecting Your Teen Daughter from Controlling, Abusive Dating Relationships*. New York: HarperCollins, 2000.

Neubauer, Joan R. *Dear Diary: The Art and Craft of Writing a Creative Journal*. Salt Lake City: Ancestry, 1995.

Nikolajeva, Maria. *Power, Voice and Subjectivity in Literature for Young Readers*. New York: Routledge, 2009.

Noel, Alyson. *Cruel Summer*. New York: St. Martin's, 2008.

Noonan, Rita K., and Dyanna Charles. "Developing Teen Dating Violence Prevention Strategies: Formative Research with Middle School Youth." *Violence Against Women* 15.9 (2009): 1087–1105.

Paul, Elizabeth L., Amy Wenzel, and John Harvey. "Hookups: A Facilitator or a Barrier to Relationship Initiation and Intimacy Development?" In *Handbook of Relationship Initiation*, edited by Susan Sprecher, Amy Wenzel, and John Harvey. New York: Psychology Press, 2008, 375–90.

Phelan, James. "Narrative Theory, 1966–2006: A Narrative." In *The Nature of Narrative*. Fortieth anniversary. Edited by Robert Scholes and Robert Kellogg. New York: Oxford University Press, 2006, 283–336.

Pipher, Mary. *Reviving Ophelia: Saving the Selves of Adolescent Girls*. New York: Putnam, 1994.

Pisces28. "My Version: Forever Mia." *FanFiction.net*, 26 November 2008. Web, 3 July 2010.

Prager, Karen J. "Intimacy in Interpersonal Relationships." *Close Relationships: A Sourcebook*, Edited by Clyde Hendrick and Susan S. Hendrick. Thousand Oaks, CA: Sage, 2000, 229–42.

Prince, Gerald. "Introduction of the Study of the Narratee." In *Essentials of the Theory of Fiction*, edited by Michael J. Hoffman and Patrick D. Murphy. Durham, NC: Duke University Press, 1996, 213–33.

Raghavan, Ramesh, et al. "Sexual Victimization Among a National Probability Sample of Adolescent Women." *Perspectives on Sexual and Reproductive Health* 36.6 (2004): 225–32.

Raitt, Fiona E., and M. Suzanne Zeedyk. "Rape Trauma Syndrome: Its Corroborative and Educational Roles." *Journal of Law and Society* 24.4 (1997): 552–68.

Reynolds, Kimberley. *Radical Children's Literature: Future Visions and Aesthetic Transformations in Juvenile Fiction*. New York: Palgrave, 2007.

Rickert, Vaughn I., Roger D. Vaughan, and Constance M. Wiemann. "Adolescent Dating Violence and Date Rape." *Current Opinion in Obstetrics and Gynecology* 14 (2002): 495–500.

Rubenstein, Carin, and Phillip Shaver. *In Search of Intimacy*. New York: Delacorte, 1974.

Saxton, Ruth O. *The Girl: Constructions of the Girl in Contemporary Fiction by Women*. New York: St. Martin's, 1998.

Schaeffer, Brenda. *Is It Love or Addiction?* Center City, MN: Hazelden, 1997.

Scheidt, Lois Ann. "Adolescent Diary Weblogs and the Unseen Audience." In *Digital Generations: Children, Young People, and New Media*, edited by David Buckingham and Rebeckah Willett. New York: Routledge, 2006, 193–210.

Scholes, Robert, and Robert Kellogg. *The Nature of Narrative*. Fortieth anniversary ed. New York: Oxford University Press, 2006.

Schuhmann, Elizabeth C. "Shift out of First: Third-Person Narration Has Advantages." *Two Decades of the ALAN Review*. Edited by Patricia P. Kelly and Robert C. Small, Jr. Urbana, IL: NCTE, 1999, 314–319.

Schwenke Wyile, Andrea. "The Value of Singularity in First- and Restricted Third-Person Engaging Narration." *Children's Literature* 31 (2003): 116–41.

Shandler, Sara. *Ophelia Speaks: Adolescent Girls Write About Their Search for Self*. New York: HarperCollins, 1999.

Shaw, Victoria F. *Best Buds: A Girl's Guide to Friendship*. Girls' Guides. New York: Rosen, 2000.

Silverstein, Herma. *Date Abuse*. Issues in Focus. Springfield, NJ: Enslow Press, 1994.

Simons, Judy. "Invented Lives: Textuality and Power in Early Women's Diaries." In *Inscribing the Daily: Critical Essays on Women's Diaries*, edited by Suzanne L. Bunkers and Cynthia A. Huff. Amherst: University of Massachusetts Press, 1996, 252–63.

Sinor, Jennifer. *The Extraordinary Work of Ordinary Writing: Annie Ray's Diary*. Iowa City: University of Iowa Press, 2002.

Skorczewski, Dawn. "From Confession to Testimony: Refiguring Trauma in the Classroom." In *Compelling Confessions: The Politics of Personal Discourse*, edited by Suzanne Diamond. Madison: Farleigh Dickinson University Press, 2011, 162–79.

skyofdreams. "Breaking Dawn: The Deleted Scenes." *FanFiction.net*, 19 December 2008. Web, 14 August 2010.

Smith, Erica. *Write It Down! A Girl's Guide to Keeping a Journal*. New York: Rosen, 1999.

Stahl, Sandra Dolby. *Literary Folkloristics and Personal Narrative*. Bloomington: Indiana University Press, 1989.

Strawberry Shortcake123. "Passing Notes." *FanFiction.net*, 10 September 2010. Web, 1 October 2010.

Suarez, Kathryn E. "Teenage Dating Violence: The Need for Expanded Awareness and Legislation." *California Law Review* 82.2 (1994): 423–71.

Subrahmanyam, Kaveri, and Patricia Greenfield. "Online Communication and Adolescent Relationships." *Future of Children* 18.1 (2008): 119–46.

Summers, Courtney. *Cracked Up to Be*. New York: St. Martin's, 2009.

Taylor, Julie. *The Girls' Guide to Friends: Straight Talk on Making Close Pals, Creating Lasting Ties, and Being an All-Around Good Friend*. New York: Three Rivers, 2002.

Thomas, Angela. "Blurring and Breaking Through the Boundaries of Narrative, Literacy, and Identity in Adolescent Fan Fiction." In *A New Literacies Sampler*, edited by Michael Knobel and Colin Lankshear. New York: Peter Lang, 2007, 137–65.

Thomas, Bronwen. "Gains and Losses? Writing It All Down: Fanfiction and Multimodality." In *New Perspectives on Narrative and Multimodality*, edited by Ruth Page. Routledge Studies in Multimodality. New York: Routledge, 2010, 142–54.

Thompson, Sharon. *Going All the Way: Teenage Girls' Talk of Sex, Romance, and Pregnancy*. New York: Hill and Wang, 1995.

"TLW: Overview." *Lifeway: True Love Waits*. Lifeway, 2007. Web, 27 July 2009.

Tolman, Deborah L. *Dilemmas of Desire: Teenage Girls Talk About Sexuality*. Cambridge: Harvard University Press, 2002.

———. "Female Adolescent Sexuality in Relational Context: Beyond Sexual Decision Making." In *Beyond Appearance: A New Look at Adolescent Girls*, edited by Norine G. Johnson, Michael C. Roberts, and Judith Worell. Washington, D.C.: APA, 2001, 227–46.

Tosenberger, Catherine. "Homosexuality at the Online Hogwarts: Harry Potter Slash Fan Fiction." *Children's Literature* 36 (2008): 185–207.

———. "'Oh My God, the Fanfiction!' Dumbledore's Outing and the Online Harry Potter Fandom." *Children's Literature Quarterly* 33.2 (2008): 200–206.

Tracy, Kristen. *Lost It.* New York: Simon and Schuster, 2007.

Travis, Molly Abel. *Reading Cultures: The Construction of the Reader in the Twentieth Century.* Carbondale: Southern Illinois University Press, 1998.

Vivian, Siobhan. *A Little Friendly Advice.* New York: Push, 2008.

volturiprincess949. "*New Life*." *TwilightArchives.Com*, 31 July 2009. Web, 16 March 2010.

Walsh, Richard. *The Rhetoric of Fictionality: Narrative Theory and the Idea of Fiction.* Columbus: Ohio State University Press, 2007.

Warhol, Robyn R. *Having a Good Cry: Effeminate Feelings and Pop-Culture Forms.* Theory and Interpretation of Narrative Series. Columbus: Ohio State University Press, 2003.

———. "Toward a Theory of the Engaging Narrator: Earnest Interventions in Gaskell, Stowe, and Elliot." *PMLA* 101.5 (1986): 811–18.

Weston, Carol. *Girltalk: All the Stuff Your Sister Never Told You.* 3rd ed. New York: HarperCollins, 1997.

White, Emily. *Fast Girls: Teenage Tribes and the Myth of the Slut.* New York: Scribner, 2002.

Wilber, Jessica. *Totally Private and Personal: Journaling Ideas for Girls and Young Women.* Edited by Elizabeth Verdick. Minneapolis: Free Spirit Press, 1996.

Wilde, Oscar. *The Importance of Being Earnest.* 1899. Clayton, DE: Prestwick House, 2005.

Wiseman, Rosalind. *Queen Bees and Wannabes: Helping Your Daughter Survive Cliques, Gossip, Boyfriends, and Other Realities of Adolescence.* New York: Crown, 2002.

Won Tawn. "I'm in Love with a Fictional Vampire Named Edward Cullen." *Cullen Crush.* *FanFiction.net*, 17 July 2008. Web, 3 March 2010.

Zarr, Sara. *Story of a Girl.* New York: Little, Brown, 2007.

Zindel, Lizabeth. *The Secret Rites of Social Butterflies.* New York: Viking, 2008.

Works Referenced

Baskin, Julia, et al. *The Notebook Girls: Four Friends, One Diary.* New York: Grand Central Press, 2006.

Bearman, Peter S., and Hannah Brückner. "Promising the Future: Virginity Pledges and First Intercourse." *American Journal of Sociology* 106.4 (2001): 859–912.

Begos, Jane DuPree. "The Diaries of Adolescent Girls." *Women's Studies International Forum* 10.1 (1987): 69–74.

Blume, Judy. *Forever . . .* 1975. New York: Simon and Schuster, 2007.

Brontë, Charlotte. *Villette.* 1853. New York: Penguin Classics, 2004.

Cleary, Beverly. *Jean and Johnny.* 1959. New York: HarperCollins, 1996.

Cowan, Gloria. "Beliefs About the Causes of Four Types of Rape." *Sex Roles* 42.9/10 (2000): 807–23.

Daly, Maureen. *Seventeenth Summer.* 1942. New York: Simon and Schuster, 1985.

Dellasega, Cheryl. *Surviving Ophelia: Mothers Share Their Wisdom in Navigating the Tumultuous Teenage Years.* New York: Ballantine, 2002.

Devillers, Julia. *GirlWise: How to Be Confident, Capable, Cool, and in Control.* New York: Three Rivers Press, 2002.

Drill, Esther, Heather McDonald, and Rebecca Odes. *Deal with It!: A Whole New Approach to Your Body, Brain and Life as a Gurl.* New York: Pocket, 1999.

Elman, Natalie Madorsky. *The Unwritten Rules of Friendship: Simple Strategies to Help Your Child Make Friends.* Boston: Little, Brown, 2003.

Filipovic, Zlata. *Zlata's Diary: A Child's Life in Wartime Sarajevo.* New York: Puffin, 1994.

Fitzgerald, F. Scott. *The Great Gatsby.* 1925. New York: Scribner, 1999.

Giannetti, Charlene C., and Margaret Sagarese. *Cliques: Eight Steps to Help Your Child Survive the Social Jungle.* New York: Broadway, 2001.

Hatchell, Deborah. *What Smart Teens Know . . . About Dating, Relationships, and Sex.* Oxford: Piper Books, 2003.

Head, Ann. *Mr. and Mrs. Bo Jo Jones.* New York: Signet, 1968.

Levy, Barrie, and Patricia Occhiuzzo Giggano. *What Parents Need to Know About Dating Violence.* Seattle, Seal Press, 2005.

Lyon, Maureen, and Christina Breda Antoniades. *My Teen Has Had Sex—Now What Do I Do? How to Help Teens Make Safe, Sensible, Self-Reliant Choices when They've Already Said Yes.* Beverly, MA: Fair Winds, 2009.

Mackoff, Barbara. *Growing a Girl: Seven Strategies for Raising a Strong, Spirited Daughter.* New York: Dell, 1996.

Meyer, Stephenie. *Midnight Sun. StephenieMeyer.com.* The Official Website of Stephenie Meyer, 28 August 2008. Web, 26 March 2010.

——. *The Short Second Life of Bree Tanner.* New York: Little, Brown, 2010.

Owens, L. L. *Frenemies: Dealing with Friend Drama.* Edina, MN: Abdo Press, 2009.

Pardes, Bronwen. *Doing It Right: Making Smart, Safe, and Satisfying Choices About Sex.* New York: Simon and Schuster, 2007.

Peters, Julie Anne. *Keeping You a Secret.* Boston: Little, Brown, 2005.

Rennison, Louise. *Angus, Thongs, and Full-Frontal Snogging.* New York: HarperCollins, 2001.

Rosenberg, J. "One-Third of Teenagers Experience Abuse Within Heterosexual Relationships." *Perspectives on Sexual and Reproductive Health* 34.2 (2002): 108.

Rude, Jesse, and Daniel Herda. "Best Friends Forever? Race and the Stability of Adolescent Friendships." *Social Forces* 89.2 (2010): 585–607.

Rutledge, Jill Zimmerman. *Dealing with the Stuff that Makes Life Tough: The 10 Things that Stress Girls Out and How to Cope with Them*. Columbus, OH: McGraw-Hill, 2003.

Salinger, J. D. *The Catcher in the Rye*. 1951. Eastsound, WA: Turtleback, 1991.

Sapphire. *Push*. 1996. Movie tie-in ed. New York: Vintage, 2009.

Scott, Elizabeth. *Living Dead Girl*. New York: Simon and Schuster, 2009.

Simmons, Rachel. *Odd Girl Out: The Hidden Culture of Aggression in Girls*. New York: Harcourt, 2002.

Sparks, Beatrice, ed. *Annie's Baby: The Diary of Anonymous, a Pregnant Teenager*. New York: HarperCollins, 2004.

———. *Go Ask Alice*. 1971. New York: SimonPulse, 2005.

———. *Treacherous Love: The Diary of an Anonymous Teenager*. New York: HarperCollins, 2000.

Walker, Lenore E. *The Battered Woman*. New York: HarperCollins, 1979.

Way, Niobe, and Lisa Chen. "Close and General Friendships Among African American, Latino, and Asian American Adolescents from Low-Income Families." *Journal of Adolescent Research* 15.2 (2000): 274–301.

Wiess, Laura. *Such a Pretty Girl*. New York: MTV, 2007.

Index